CORA SHEIBANI

JEWELS

BY WILLIAM GRANT

ACC ART BOOKS

I FOREWORD 11

II HEIMAT 13

III BIRTH OF A PASSION 23

IV FINDING A VOICE 31

V COLLECTIONS 47

VI DESIGN PHILOSOPHY 193

VII APPENDICES 217

Cora Sheibani, 2021

I

FOREWORD

Cora behind her *Copper Mould Collection Cookbook*

I first became aware of Cora Sheibani's jewelry in 2008, when she launched her 'Copper Mould' collection in New York, at the downtown loft of a friend. I was immediately taken by her *Cupcake*, *Linzer Torte* and *Pudding* rings and pins fashioned in hard stones, such as malachite, lapis lazuli, blue chalcedony and red jasper, set in yellow, white or rose gold. Having worked with Andy Warhol, a jewelry aficionado, not to say addict, as editor of *Interview* in the 1970s and early 1980s, I had seen quite a lot of everything from classic Van Cleef & Arpels and Cartier to exotic Moghul and Mexican to flashy Verdura, Seaman Schepps and David Webb (not to mention 1930s Bakelite bracelets), all of which he collected. But I had never seen anything quite like Cora's creations, which were clearly made with a sense of play as well as great invention and craft.

By 2008, Cora had been designing jewelry for several years and had held several wellreceived pop-up exhibitions in London – the first in 2002. That was the year she founded her own business, under her own name by marriage to Kaveh Sheibani rather than that of her prominent parents, Bruno and Yoyo Bischofberger, the Swiss contemporary art dealer and his chic American-born wife. One could see it as a declaration of independence, but also as an act of modesty, and a refusal of what might have been an easier path to success when she launched her career.

Of course, growing up with Warhol, Julian Schnabel, Francesco Clemente, Kenny Scharf and Jean-Michel Basquiat, all of whom were represented by Bruno's gallery, as frequent visitors and house guests at the family homes in Zurich and St Moritz had its effect. From the beginning, Cora's creative instincts and business model have always gravitated toward the aesthetic and one-of-a-kind pieces offered exclusively to private clients, rather the commercial and multiple editions distributed wholesale to retailers. Although she has clearly stated that she does not consider her work 'art', there are many who would disagree, including this writer.

In 2006, for the launch of her first thematic collection, 'Valence', she published the first in a series of exquisite pocket-sized books, designed by her sister Lea, with photographs of the jewelry by Iranian artist Ashkan Sahihi and text by Ettore Sottsass, the founder of the Italian design collective Memphis, and the architect of the Bischofberger's house outside Zurich. I have saved every one.

And now, another half-dozen collections later – 'Clouds with a Silver Lining', 'Cactaceae', 'Colour & Contradiction', 'Eyes', 'Glow', 'Pottering Around' – Cora has produced a large, but not *too* large, comprehensive and beautiful volume simply titled *Cora Sheibani – Jewels*. She chose William Grant, the biographer of Andrew Grima, the great English modern jewelry designer of the 1960s and '70s, to write the text. She modelled her creations throughout, as she always has, because in the early days she couldn't afford a professional model. 'This project is in part a way to make sure I am in control of my own narrative,' she told me.

She is. Magnificently so.

II

HEIMAT

Cattle Drive, 1854
Bischofberger Collection, Männedorf – Zurich
painting by Bartholomäus Lämmler (1809–1865)

Heimat is a German word that does not translate directly into many European languages (including English). The word refers to a place towards which one has a strong sense of belonging, a place of origin which is therefore not necessarily the same as one's place of birth.

Cora Elisabeth Anna Victoria Bischofberger was born in Zurich, Switzerland on 9 March 1980 to an American mother, Christina, and Swiss father, the art dealer Bruno Bischofberger.

Cora's passport lists her place of birth as Zurich, but her 'Heimatsort' or place of origin as Appenzell Innerrhoden. This tiny Catholic enclave is home to Cora's paternal ancestors and the family name Bischofberger or 'bishop's mountain dweller' refers to the fact that they inhabited land in the canton owned by the bishop of nearby St Gallen.

Therefore, although she spent her childhood alternating between family homes in Zurich and St Moritz, Appenzell is nevertheless a familiar and comforting place where some of her relatives still live and where her father used to take her as a child on day trips, together with her brother Magnus. It's a tranquil place she returns to every year to discuss her latest designs with the local goldsmith, a family friend whom she has known her whole life.

Cora's paternal antecedents were soldiers, doctors, dentists, politicians and artists – a healthy genetic admixture of science and creativity.

Her great-grandfather and great-great-grandfather (both called William Bischofberger) were apprenticed as sculptors working with wood and as cabinet makers. The latter changed his profession to open the first pharmacy in Appenzell, which in turn produced a generation of doctors in the family.

Cora's mother, Christina (known by everyone as Yoyo), was born in California but moved to Zurich at three months old when her father Mark Clifton, a pilot, was hired by the newly founded Swissair. Mark, whose grandfather Colonel Charles Clifton was an early pioneer in the American automobile industry, had met and married Cora's grandmother Ella, not long before the move.

Grandmother Ella went on to become a house model for Christian Dior in Paris, and for one winter

Portrait in Silhouette of Bruno Bischofberger,
1995/1996
painting by David McDermott & Peter McGough

Christina Clifton (Yoyo) and her mother Ella Clifton (née Miller), circa 1958

modelled for the Swiss jewellery house Gübelin. Cora's mother met her father at a gallery opening in Zurich in 1969. They married in 1971 and a year later had their first child, Lea. Sister Nina was born in 1975, followed by Cora in 1980 and a son, Magnus, in 1981.

Her parents have been hugely influential in the formation of Cora's artistic and aesthetic identity. Her father studied art history and archaeology at the University of Zurich, and her mother had intended to go to art school before she got married. From an early age, Cora was taught to look at everything with the critical eye of an art historian. A shoe, a sink, a painting or a jewel were all worthy of the same attention and each could be considered a work of art.

She recalls the kitchen table being stacked with the latest auction catalogues covering every possible subject and object from primitive to modern. It was here, over breakfast, that her father would teach her to distinguish between different types of French 18th-century furniture or else demonstrate the finer points of Pre-Columbian art.

Other vivid recollections include his habit of quizzing his children about the various plants and flowers encountered on family walks in the countryside and describing the different styles of classical music playing on the car stereo. Family holidays and outings always had a cultural focus and invariably were tailored around excursions to museum exhibitions, old churches, archaeological sites, or else visiting artists' studios. The sharing of knowledge, concerning art, music or nature was a constant in the Bischofberger household.

Bedtime was another formative experience. 'Instead of a bedtime story, my father and I sang Swiss children's songs together...it was our ritual before going to sleep. The one my father liked best (which we each sang in a different octave) was a winter song that drove everyone crazy when we sang it out of season, so he changed the words to make a summer version and we stuck with it for ever...to this day it is our go-to song.'

Then, in 1988, Cora and her brother Magnus (aged eight and seven, respectively) finally got

HEIMAT

their own bedrooms and were encouraged to furnish them with items chosen from their parents' Memphis group collection.

All the IKEA furniture was duly replaced by colourful, post-modern pieces – in Cora's case, a chair by Michele De Lucchi, and the rest by Ettore Sottsass.

'I remember doing my homework sitting on a crazy-looking chair, dwarfed by a giant, two-metre-long desk with a leopard pattern on top. The sideboard had a red lightbulb attached to a metal bar, and when I turned it on at night, the yellow painting above my bed glowed pink.'

Cora's father is mainly associated with contemporary art, but he and Yoyo are passionate collectors with an encyclopaedic knowledge of art and eclectic tastes.

Together, over many decades, they have accumulated a broad and very deep range of collections beginning with folk art from Appenzell, which Bruno started buying as a teenager, and subsequently expanding into the applied arts and design.

Rome, summer 1984
self-timer photograph by Yoyo Bischofberger

FROM LEFT TO RIGHT
Roberta di Giambattista, Claudio di Giambattista, Valerio di Giambattista, Alba Clemente, Jean-Michel Basquiat, Bruno Bischofberger, Magnus Bischofberger, Nina Bischofberger, Francesco Clemente, Chiara Clemente, Lea Bischofberger, Nina Clemente, Mabe Tosi, Yoyo (Christina) Bischofberger, Cora Bischofberger

Collaboration, winter 1983/1984
painting by Cora and Jean-Michel Basquiat
© Estate of Jean-Michel Basquiat. Licensed by Artestar, New York

HEIMAT

'My parents are constantly in awe of old things that look modern because of their minimal simplicity. The stone axe and object collection is a good example of this. Naturally, growing up surrounded by these "Wunderkammern" has influenced my taste and my artistic eye.'

As her father had a gallery, which he opened in 1963, the artists he represented would visit the family homes in Zurich and St Moritz, and many spent Christmas with the Bischofbergers at one time or another. 'The smell of oil paint always brings back strong memories of my childhood, walking to the studio my parents built in their back garden at home.'

Like most young children, Cora enjoyed making art, especially when grown-ups joined in the fun. She was not at all shy about approaching the artists who came to visit her parents and welcomed any opportunity to spend time drawing or painting with them.

In 1984, Jean-Michel Basquiat asked her to make a painting with him in their garage at St Moritz. Nearly four at the time, she remembers thinking, 'This guy can draw much better than me' … 'which was kind of funny because his aim was trying to draw more like a four-year old child.'

Inspired by this event, her father soon after commissioned a series of 'collaboration paintings' between Andy Warhol, Jean-Michel Basquiat and Francesco Clemente.

The following year, in 1985, Cora's father hosted a show designed specifically for children. The idea came about because he got tired of always having to lift his children up in museums so they could see the works of art. He decided to ask his artists to make a children's painting for an exhibition to be hung at a low height in his gallery in Zurich 'so the adults had to bend down for a change.' He approached Andy Warhol first, because if he said yes, he knew the others would join in.

In the event, Warhol liked the idea so much that he did the whole show himself. He designed wallpaper for the exhibition, and this was hung with his own 'children's' paintings to suit the heights of Cora (aged five) and her brother Magnus (aged four).

First chair, Memphis, 1983
by Michele De Lucchi
lacquered wood chair, coated metal frame

Magnus and Cora Bischofberger at the 'Paintings for Children' exhibition by Andy Warhol at Galerie Bruno Bischofberger, Zurich, 1983
photograph by Andy Warhol
© 2022 The Andy Warhol Foundation for the Visual Arts, Inc./Licensed by DACS, London

In 1993, Cora followed her older sisters to Aiglon College, a boarding school in the Swiss Alps. Prior to this she had attended an English-speaking international school in Zurich.

In 1997, Cora, by then determined to pursue some sort of artistic career, completed a life drawing course at the Slade School of Fine Art in London during the summer holidays. Whilst there, she occasionally met up with her future husband and family friend Kaveh Sheibani. She has fond memories of being taken to Quo Vadis, a restaurant in Dean Street, Soho, which featured many paintings and artworks by the artist (and co-owner) Damien Hirst.

She also recalls being struck by Kaveh's knowledge of art and enthusiasm for collecting.

On completing her A levels and wanting to fill the gaps in her general knowledge, Cora decided against accepting a place at Rhode Island School of Design, and instead went to New York University (NYU). She spent her first year at NYU's campus in Florence where she learned to speak Italian and more importantly to absorb the art and culture of the city. She graduated with a degree in the history of art three years later.

At weekends she met up with Kaveh, visiting different cities and the art that filled them.

In 2001, Cora and Kaveh were married in Zurich and set up home in London were Kaveh was based. They have three children: Aryana (b.2003), Nouri (b.2005) and Dara (b.2014); two dogs (Snowy and Billie), a goldfish (Filbert) and a pet snake (Frey).

HEIMAT

Portrait of Cora and Her Mother Yoyo, Zurich, 1985
photograph by Jeannette Montgomery Barron

III

BIRTH OF A PASSION

Portrait of Christina Bischofberger, 2002
wearing an ancient bronze bracelet, emerald bead necklace
and Jean Després ring
painting by Francesco Clemente

Cora was always creative, but it took a while for her to decide how to turn that trait into a career. Being dyslexic, she naturally became a highly visual person and learner. As a child she filled a sketchbook with designs for Barbie doll clothes, but trying to make the tiny garments on her mother's sewing machine proved too much of a fiddle for a ten-year-old and she abandoned the project. Although fashion did not fully satisfy the creative urge, it did establish the notion that she had an aptitude for and enjoyed the process of designing.

Her interest in making jewellery began at a young age. 'Like all young girls I used to string beads together.' Unlike all young girls she was determined to go deeper into the subject and frequented markets, where she would pester the people on the stalls to disclose their trade secrets, such as how to make complex knotted silk bracelets.

Cora's mother, Yoyo, was very influential in how she perceives fashion and jewellery. 'She had style and knew how to wear jewellery, wear a brooch, wear old stuff and new stuff…cheap stuff and expensive stuff and put it all together. If you have style, you can do that.'

In Switzerland, Yoyo liked to commission small pieces of jewellery, which she helped to devise, so the notion of designing your own jewellery was familiar to Cora.

Andy Warhol, who collected jewellery, also had a formative, albeit vicarious influence. 'He had a serious collection of Jean Després and one of those rings when he died, my father bought from the estate auction for my mum. Ten years earlier my parents had met Després in person. He was an old man at the time, living in the countryside and because they had a big design collection, they convinced him to sell them two of his pieces which were a ring and brooch from the Art Deco period. He was the first jewellery designer I became aware of.'

The first piece of precious jewellery Cora had a hand in designing, aged ten, was a gift from her mother: 'There was this mineral shop in Zurich called Siber & Siber which we passed by every Wednesday after my violin lesson on our way to Café Schober. My mother said I could choose a stone there and she would set it in gold for me as a ring. I chose a small lentil-shaped carnelian. I loved the orange colour, which is still one of my favourites to wear.'

It was not long before Cora's taste in jewellery evolved, and she began to covet more exotic specimens: 'One day my parents came home with some large bronze antique Greek or Roman rings and gave one each to my older sisters. They were completely rusted and green all over. I thought they looked so cool. Even though my fingers were still too small to wear such rings, my mother realised I felt left out and so pulled me aside and whispered to me that one day I could have this ring on her finger. It was a small gold Bulgari ring with an antique peach intaglio. She thought I would be happy with this prospect of an antique ring of my own one day. I don't remember how much I voiced my discontent, but I was distraught. I wanted a bronze ring that was green, rusted and bold.'

So, taking matters into her own hands, Cora saved up some money, went to an antique dealer in Zurich she knew through her parents and chose a tiny bronze ring. 'It fitted my pinkie finger when I was aged eleven or twelve and was so cheap that she gave it to me for nothing. I wore it every day but shortly after it broke in two at a school fair.'

A few years later, aged fifteen, Cora earned some money over the summer working as a receptionist at her father's gallery. 'So, I went back to the antique dealer and bought myself a Greek and a Roman ring with a bit over half my earnings. The Greek ring had a winged figure holding a bird and the Roman one was a very interesting shape with a round disc on top which had turned completely green. I ended up wearing the Roman ring throughout my teenage years and right up until I got married.'

Another time, her parents came home from a business trip to Paris with a bracelet from an African art dealer. The dealer's daughter had assembled the bracelet using bright yellow African trading beads strung together with elastic and safety pins. 'I thought it was so great and went off to a bead store in Zurich called "Schmuck-it-yourself" and made two more just like it.

Cora's personal antique bronze rings. Roman (left) and Greek (right) with winged figure holding a bird. She bought these rings with the first money she ever earned as a teenager in 1996

BIRTH OF A PASSION

Amazingly enough I still own all three bracelets which now need the elastic replacing so I can wear them again.'

Thinking back, Cora now recognises the true extent to which her parents influenced her fascination with jewellery. They gave her the confidence to develop her own 'eye' and taught her to be unafraid to combine contrasting influences. Moreover, she acknowledges that the immersive upbringing she was exposed to – the daily discourses over auction catalogues, the visits to galleries and museums, being surrounded by art and artefacts – proved invaluable in expanding and developing her aesthetic awareness and sense of good taste. 'Of course, complete kitsch was always appreciated for its own sake also!'

Before leaving school, Cora became interested in graphics, corporate identity, and packaging design and completed a brief internship at Sottsass Associati's graphic design department in Milan. She had planned to follow this up by attending The Pasadena School of Design to study packaging after NYU but eventually realised she didn't want a career that involved sitting in front of a computer all day or being told how to be creative by a corporate client.

Cora's personal bracelets. The one on the left is made from African trading beads, a gift from her parents, held together by safety pins and elasticated thread. The two on the right are versions Cora made as a teenager in the 1990s using modern glass beads

'Corrida' brooch, Pablo Picasso, 1959 © Succession Picasso 2022 gold, engraving

Following her marriage and move to London in 2001, Cora continued to pursue her interest in jewellery and absorb new influences as she plotted the next steps towards her future career as a designer. She made research trips to the jewellery department at the V&A, which at the time was only open by appointment, and began to compile an extensive library covering the development of jewellery from pre-history to the modern era. She also began to collect images in a scrapbook of pieces that interested her not so much because of who designed them but rather because they piqued her curiosity, more especially so if at the same time they looked modern for the period in which they were made.

Early on in their marriage Cora and her husband began to collect different genres of jewellery, starting with Berlin ironwork – wonderfully graphic cast iron jewellery from the early 1800s and a technological wonder of the time. This shared enthusiasm, together with Cora's admiration for other, somewhat esoteric genres such as Greek and Roman bronze rings, ancient Hallstatt jewellery, volcanic lava cameos and memento mori pieces made from hair (Cora has even kept plaits of her own hair intending to make them into jewellery one day), illustrates her passion for jewellery, its history and most of all for designs that exhibit unconventional shapes and materials.

Some of Yoyo Bischofberger's personal jewellery

FROM LEFT TO RIGHT

'Sputnik' ear clips, Cartier, 1960

Biwa pearl necklace, Japan, 1970

Amethyst and diamonds brooch, Christina Bischofberger, circa 1980

Ring (formerly owned by Andy Warhol), Jean Després, 1932

IV

FINDING A VOICE

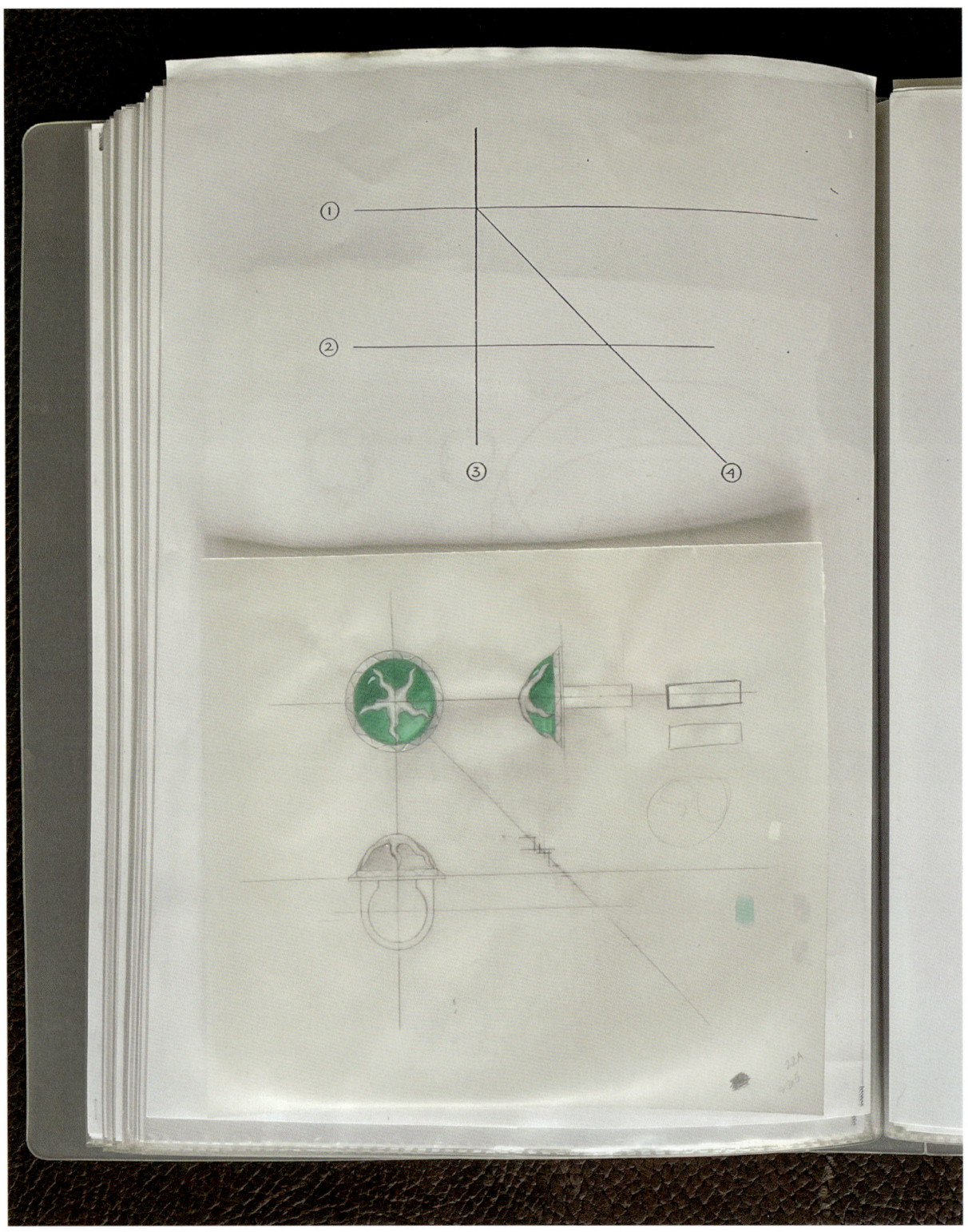
GIA technical drawing exercise showing a ring in three elevations, summer 2002

By the time Cora arrived in London following her marriage, she had already decided to embark on a career in jewellery design. As a first step she enrolled on the full-time, one-year Graduate Gemmologist programme at the London campus of the GIA (Gemological Institute of America). Here she studied the identification and grading of diamonds and coloured stones, how to use gemmological equipment, and how gems are mined, fashioned, valued and brought to market. Having attained her Graduate Gemmologist certificate, Cora then completed a jewellery drawing course. The GIA programme enabled Cora to acquire a professional level of knowledge, including the technical expertise and practical skills necessary to evaluate gemstones. She also gained an appreciation of the way the cut of a stone can greatly influence its life, its colour and thus its beauty, as well as an understanding of the vast range of gemstones that exist in nature and how they might be used in jewellery.

The jewellery drawing course, meanwhile, helped her to transpose her design ideas formally onto paper and to create technical drawings to scale and from different elevations, which enable a goldsmith to make accurate prototypes. It is one thing to design a ring; it is quite another to design a ring around a specific stone that is in proportion, matches a specific ring size, is comfortable to wear and sits well on the finger.

Not every aspect of the drawing course was positive, however. Some of the designs she made were criticised for being impossible to make. There was a well-held nostrum amongst the teachers that you should not design anything that you could not explain how to make yourself. As someone who likes to push boundaries and question convention, Cora felt this attitude was both restrictive and wrong, and that technical complexity was not a valid reason to tone down or simplify a design. One just needed to collaborate with a goldsmith with sufficient skill, patience and problem-solving ability to realise the design in the way it was intended.

The GIA course provided Cora with an excellent grounding, but her childhood fascination with jewellery supplemented and complemented this recently acquired knowledge. She recalled stones and minerals from her youth such as lapis lazuli, carnelian and porphyry which the GIA only briefly touched on or, in the case of imperial porphyry – a deep-purple, crystal-infused rock, forged in volcanos and carved into monuments and all kinds of precious objects in antiquity – not at all. It was from this material that she made her first two pieces: a *Frame Brooch* and the *Heart-Spade-Arrow Ring*.

Cora began her life as a jewellery designer working part-time from home. Coming from an entrepreneurial background it felt natural to start her own business and as a young mother she needed to balance work with the demands of family life. Learning by doing is valuable but when it's just you it can take a lot longer, with many mistakes along the way. Had she known then what she knows now, she admits she would never have dared to start up on her own without working for someone else in the jewellery business beforehand. 'Thank God for naïveté and a supportive husband!'

In the early stages of her career, Cora was undecided about whether to make unique pieces or produce jewellery in Asia to sell in multiple editions. Although the latter might have made more commercial sense, she realised that designing individual pieces was where her true passion resided.

'I was determined to support European goldsmiths and to make things to the highest standards of quality and craftsmanship. This notion was something I really treasured from the get-go and set me apart from those contemporaries who operated in my price range.'

Having put aside the idea of making multiple editions for wholesale distribution, Cora continued to collaborate with her goldsmith, Sebastian Fässler in Appenzell. Sebastian's father, Emil, was an old family friend and passionate collector, as Cora's father was, of Appenzell folk art. A saddler by trade, Emil Fässler crafted the leather and brass objects worn by the most beautiful cows in the canton, and the farmers who owned them when wearing their Sunday best. He was the most accomplished saddler in the region.

Sebastian Fässler's workshop, Appenzell, Switzerland, 2017

Sebastian Fässler,
London, 2022

Sebastian was not apprenticed to his father, but as a child had already learned how to hammer out figures and patterns directly from brass plates to be riveted onto leather. He has inherited his father's passion for the craft (and eventually his old tools and workshop as well) and still occasionally produces the same traditional leatherwork, cow bells with decorative brass pieces, and belts with silver buckles that his father used to make. He is widely recognised in the region as being the best maker of his generation. At the age of sixteen, Sebastian built on these inherited skills to become an accomplished goldsmith, undertaking two apprenticeships, firstly in St Gallen and then to a goldsmith outside Geneva who made jewels for Bulgari. Unlike most goldsmiths, he often favours brass as a material to make into models rather than wax or silver. He is also a self-taught stone setter and an accomplished engraver, painter and illustrator. He's the guy in the village who does

Cora's Appenzeller belt handmade by Emil Fässler (Sebastian's father), circa 1995

leather, silver

everything artistic, but his talents would shine anywhere; Cora's main stone supplier refers to him as '*ein Genie*'.

Sebastian Fässler's relationship with Cora is based on trust, mutual understanding and the instinctive collaboration that has evolved out of the many projects they have worked on together over two decades. Cora has come to realise that she needs to work with a person who shares her aesthetic vision, and Sebastian can do that. He understands what Cora is striving to achieve with her designs and has developed a natural facility for taking her drawings and turning them into perfect prototypes. It has taken many years for Cora to find others who can work in this way.

Frame Brooch, 2001
yellow gold, imperial porphyry

The first piece of jewellery Cora collaborated on with Sebastian was the *Frame Brooch* (shaped like a picture frame) which was cast in New York from a wax model she had made herself. 'In 2001 I did a wax carving course whilst in my last year at NYU and started to make a frame brooch.' The piece was finished off in Switzerland by Sebastian who used a slice of imperial porphyry that Cora had sourced in Rome to fill the frame. To her it looks like a miniature abstract painting but conceptually it pays tribute to her mother's Picasso etching brooch (see page 29) or perhaps to one of the framed marble panels on the interior walls below the dome of the Pantheon.

The first piece made entirely by Sebastian was her *Heart-Spade-Arrow Ring*. 'The claws that held the stone looked like a heart-shaped spade or arrow.' The ring was made with green porphyry mounted in rose gold. A second *Heart-Spade-Arrow Ring* was made in imperial porphyry. In both rings the cabochon stone is inverted so the flat side is on top. Cora later made a blue chalcedony version (still in her possession) mounted in yellow gold with an inclusion that looks like a mountain relief when viewed from the side.

Cora's first exhibition was held on 2 December 2002 – a one-night 'pop-up' in Albemarle Street, London. Here she showed a comprehensive range of her early work including several *Heart-Spade-Arrow* rings, *Circle* rings, *Frame* brooches

Heart-Spade-Arrow Ring, 2002
yellow gold, blue chalcedony

and rings, the *Medusa Ring*, *Flower* rings and earrings, the *Aryana Ring* (named retrospectively for her daughter) the *Eagle Eye Ring* and the *Temple Ring*.

Her sister Nina, an architect, was working as a civil engineer in London at the time and designed the show. She transformed the rather mundane display cases into miniature hanging gardens by wrapping them in evergreen foliage and placing the jewels on mossy mounds.

Following the show, in 2003, to round out her stock of jewellery beyond rings and brooches, Cora made her first mini-collection of reversible *Lentil* bracelets and necklaces in two different shades of gold. These and other recently finished pieces were exhibited in 2004 at a first-floor gallery space in Savile Row, London. Once again, Cora's sister Nina, together with her husband Florian Baier, helped to curate the show which featured two of the gallery walls covered with specially designed jewel-patterned wallpaper and display cases containing stacks of A3 paper, capped with black-and-white photocopies of body parts, and precision-cut for the jewels to fit into.

Throughout much of 2005, Cora occupied herself with preparing for another show, trying to find a suitable studio space, and discovering she was pregnant, finally giving birth to her second child, Nouri. 2005 also proved to be a transitional year in her career as she naturally progressed from designing ad hoc pieces and mini-collections towards the creation of larger, themed collections.

FINDING A VOICE

Circle rings (each an edition of twenty), 2002
rose gold, yellow gold, white gold

FROM LEFT TO RIGHT

Temple Ring, 2003
yellow gold, rhodolite garnet

Flower Ring, 2002
white gold, cultured pearl,
mother-of-pearl

Frame Ring, 2002
yellow gold, rubellite tourmaline

Heart-Spade-Arrow Ring, 2002
yellow gold, blue chalcedony

Circle Ring with stones on the
side, 2002
yellow gold, pink sapphires

Large Oval Ring, 2003
yellow gold, green beryl, onyx

Reversible Lentil Necklace, 2003
yellow gold, ebony, antique ivory

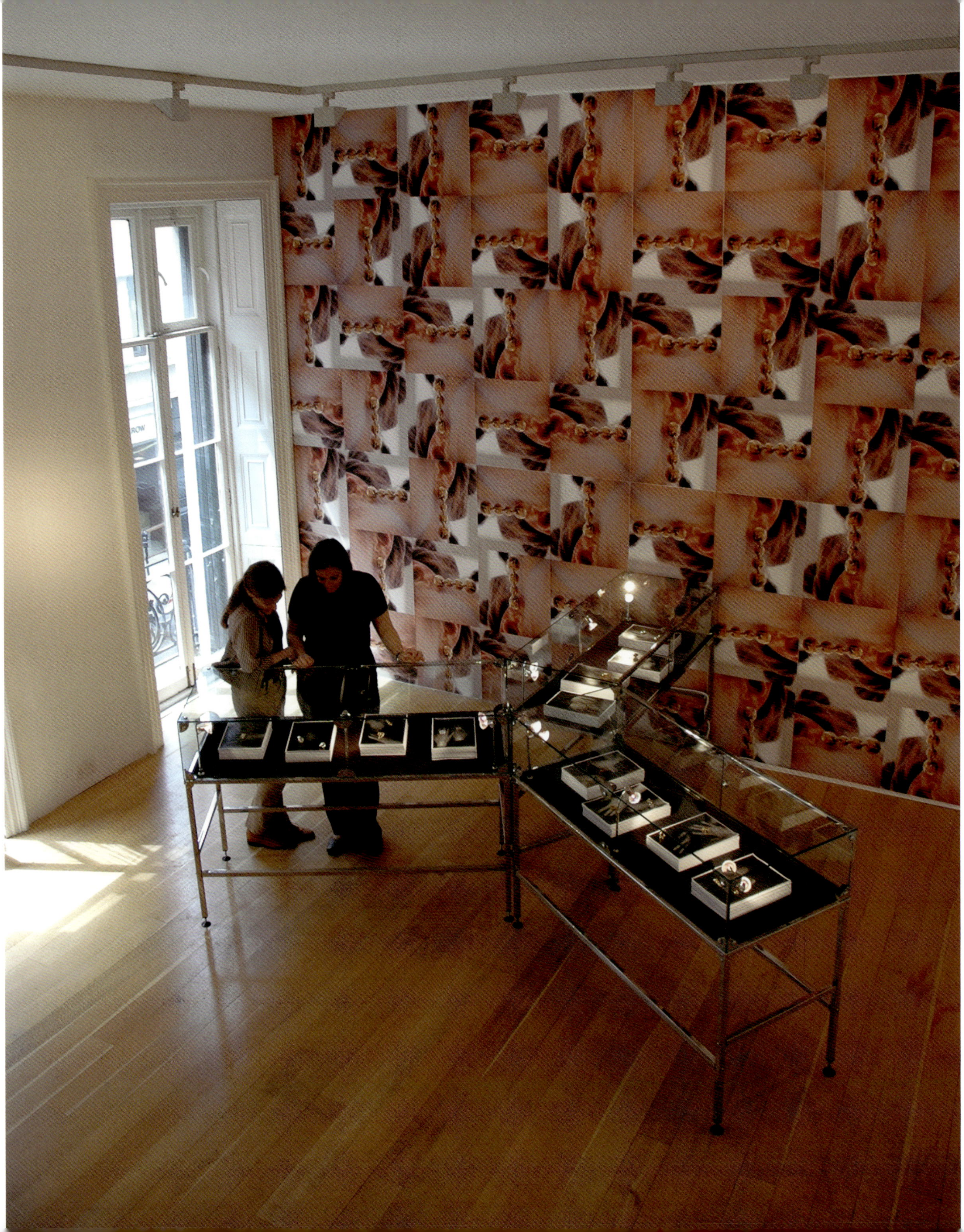

Savile Row exhibition, London,
June 2004
designed by Nina Baier-
Bischofberger and Florian Baier

Photocopy displays

FROM TOP LEFT CLOCKWISE

Circle Ring, 2002 & *Lentil Bracelet*, 2003
yellow gold

Circle rings with stones on top, 2002
yellow gold, rubies & yellow gold, tsavorite garnets

Heart-Spade-Arrow rings, 2001 & 2002
white gold, lapis lazuli & rose gold, green porphyry

Confetti Earrings, 2003
white gold, peridot, amethyst, fire opal

Temple Ring, 2003
rose gold, green tourmaline

Flower Ring & Earring, 2002
white and red gold

43

44

FROM LEFT TO RIGHT

20 Ltd Valence Plus Pendant, 2005
rose gold, aquamarine

Medusa Earring, 2004
white gold, rubellite tourmaline,
pink sapphires, amethyst

Flat Circle Brooch, 2006
yellow gold, quartz

Reversible Lentil Necklace, 2003
white and yellow gold, diamonds

Aryana Ring, 2003
yellow gold, rubellite tourmaline,
tsavorite garnets

Renaissance Frame Brooch, 2002
yellow gold, gold in quartz

V

COLLECTIONS

Five years into her career as a jeweller, Cora Sheibani began working on the first of a series of eight themed collections which were launched between 2006 and 2021. Prior to this her output had been restricted to individual pieces of jewellery and two mini-collections. Cora's jewellery collections feature a strong element of storytelling; they reflect a personal journey drawing inspiration from experiences that have evoked an emotional and creative response. These can range from childhood memories to objects she has admired, to interactions with people and places, to the rituals of everyday life. Her collections are open ended meaning that they have a starting point but then continually evolve as new stones are discovered, new pieces commissioned, and as original pieces are sold to be replaced by new designs. There are no repeats, so everything sold is unique in its combination of gold, colour and type of stone.

From 2006 onwards, virtually the only exceptions to designing and making themed collections are when Cora undertakes customer commissions.

VALENCE (+PLUS) 50

COPPER MOULD 68

CLOUDS WITH A SILVER LINING 86

CACTACEAE 104

COLOUR & CONTRADICTION 120

EYES 138

GLOW 154

POTTERING AROUND 170

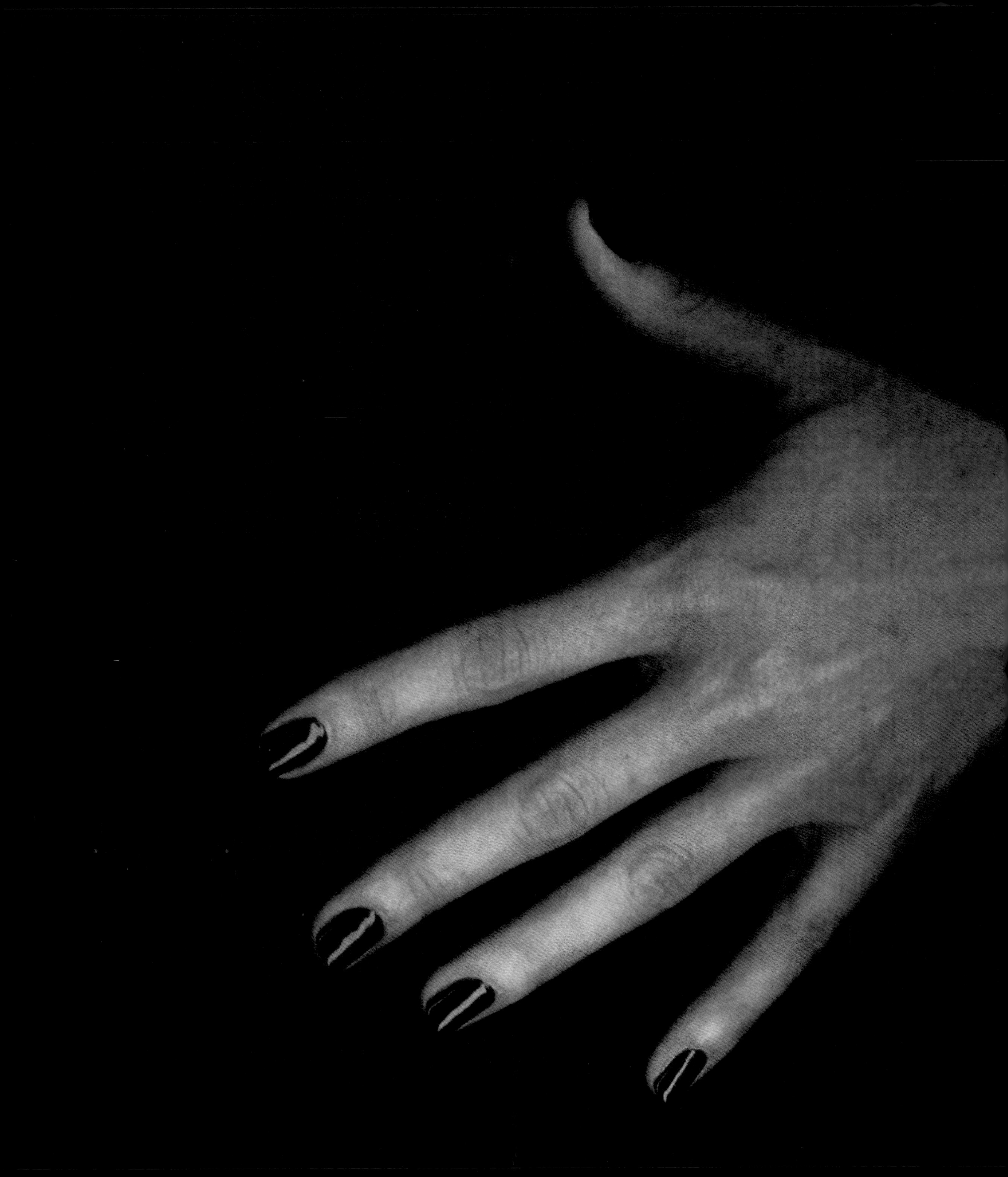

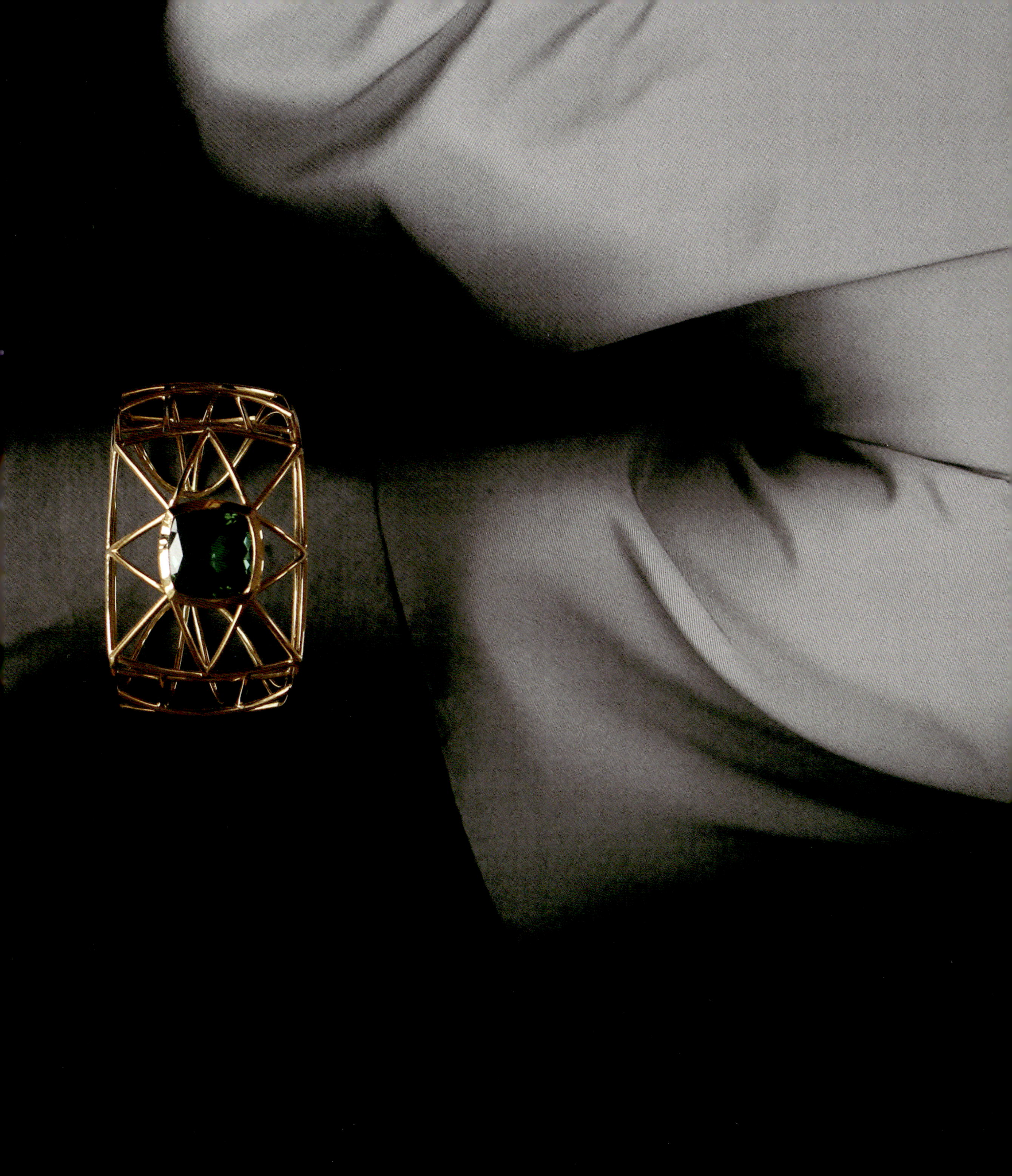

'Valence' is one of Cora Sheibani's more abstracted collections, comprising geometric shapes and lines as opposed to the largely graphic elements which characterise much of her later work.

As is usually the case, Cora begins with a need or desire to design something for herself. In this instance the need for a simple gold brooch to close a knitted top by Azzedine Alaïa. Then, having made the piece, she felt that a single brooch was not enough on its own, and so decided to make a set of three 'a bit like old brooches when people used to wear them in sets'. Pleased with the results, she took the design and turned it into a ring (by putting the brooch design back-to-back) and soon after added pendants, earrings and a cuff bracelet. Before she knew it, Cora had designed her first fully formed collection.

The name 'Valence' came later when Cora, who enjoyed science as much as art at school, thought the finished pieces somewhat resembled diagrams of atomic structures she remembered from her chemistry textbooks.

'I realised that a lot of the spheres in the design were in fact "empty space" in the same way that the atom is largely empty space. Protons and neutrons form the centre of an atom and then there is a big empty space then the electrons. The 'valency' is the relationship with and the power of the electrons. The whole structure and the size of the piece is defined by the empty space.'

The early pieces were designed as prototypes for an intended wholesale collection. A dealer friend had advised that the only way to make a commercial success of her business was to add a wholesale line manufactured in Turkey or the Far East and offered to help. There followed some confusion about who would spend time abroad managing production – something that Cora (who had two small children to look after) would find difficult to do. It also transpired that there were complicated technical issues that made translating the prototypes faithfully into multiple editions extremely difficult. It proved to be the ultimate test of Sebastian Fässler's craftsmanship and skill as a goldsmith. In the end, the prototypes he made were presented as a collection to sell directly to customers. As this was Cora's first major collection, she knew that she needed an impactful marketing tool to assist with the launch.

Target Valence Brooch (part of a set of three), 2006
rose gold
Photograph by Ashkan Sahihi for the *Valence Collection Book*

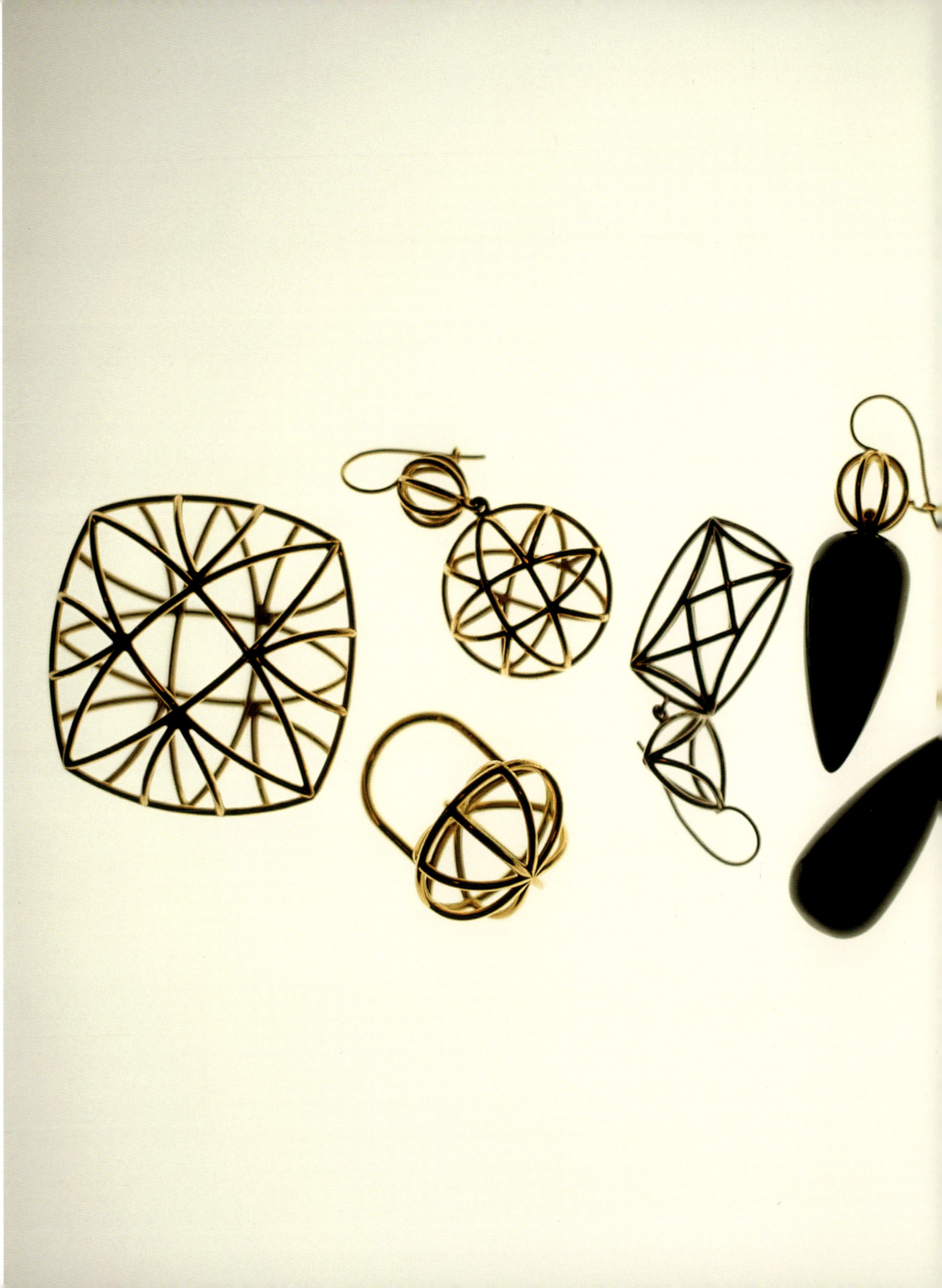

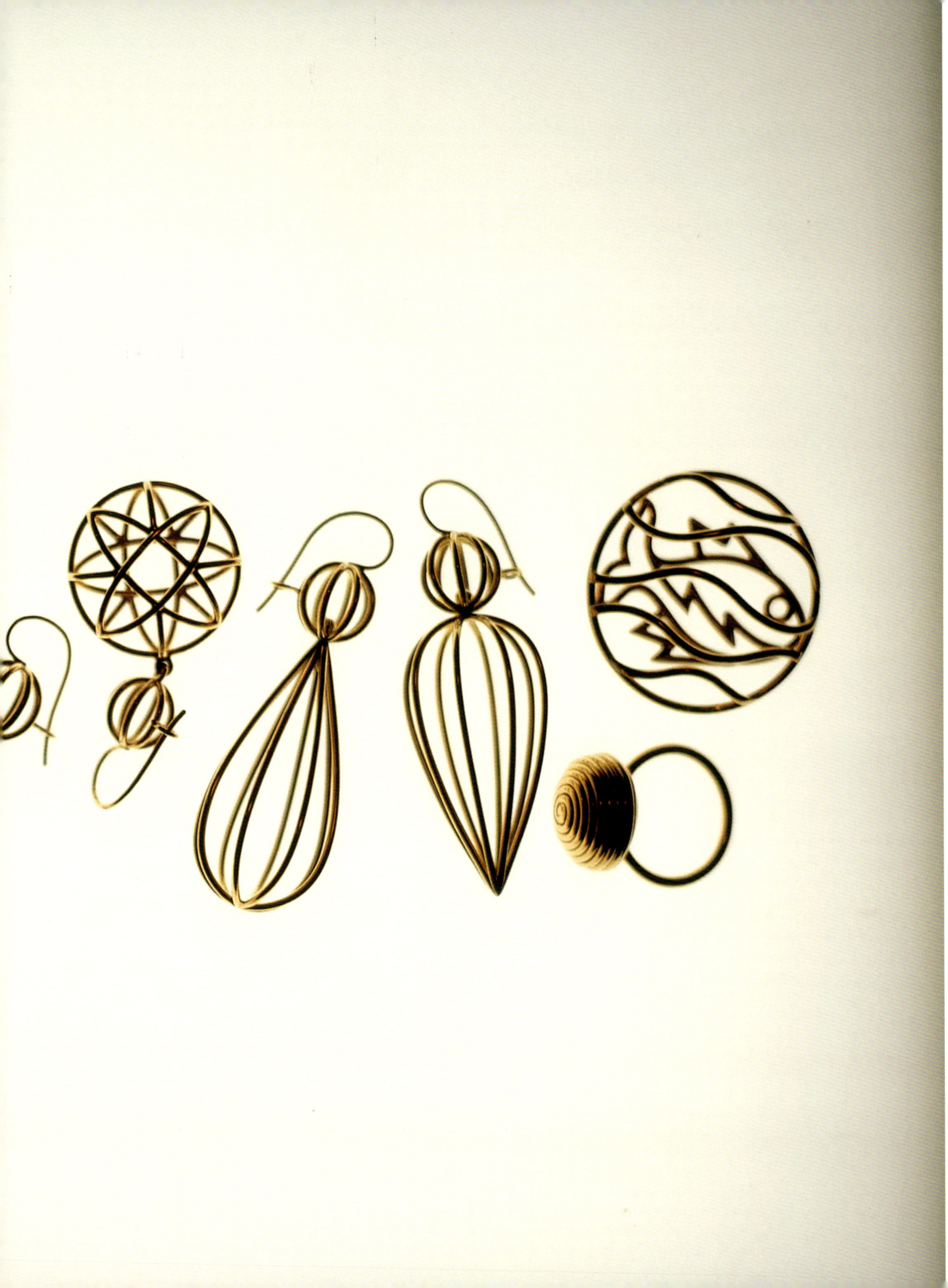

PP.54-55
A group of 'Valence' pendants, rings and earrings, 2006
yellow gold, rose gold, white gold, jet

LEFT
Valence Plus Pendant, 2013
yellow gold, brownish-orange tourmaline, leather cord

Floral Valence Cuff, 2012
yellow gold

Sketch for *Floral Valence Cuff* with tourmaline

The idea she came up with was to produce a high-quality pocket-sized book to promote 'Valence'. She approached family friend and father figure of the Memphis group of architects and designers, Ettore Sottsass, asking him to write the words. He was ninety-two at the time but liked her jewellery and agreed. The 'Valence' book was designed by Cora's sister Lea, with images by the photographer and artist Ashkan Sahihi. It was not conceived as a catalogue, but rather as an introduction to Cora Sheibani the jeweller – accompanied by a set of beautiful, ethereal images designed to give an impression of the collection and entice the reader into discovering more. It was the first in a series of small square books she produced to showcase her collections.

'As everybody knows what gold looks like I asked Ashkan to take the photographs in black and white and we printed them in neon pink.'

The gold-wire pieces photographed for the book have energy

VALENCE (+PLUS)

and movement; by delineating rather than occupying space they suggest volume without heaviness. In form they are intricate and complex but at the same time give a sense of symmetry and order.

Following on from the original 'Valence' collection, Cora incorporated gemstones to create 'Valence Plus' (as in 'Valence' plus stones). Here, large faceted gemstones such as bi-coloured ametrines, tourmalines, tanzanites, amethysts, beryls and spinels were deployed as the centrepiece of the design to add interest and opulence without sacrificing the original intent of creating simple, voluminous structures.

'I realised you could set quite big gemstones in a pendant or earrings that are easy to wear and it's actually quite magical that you can create volume and interest without adding much weight.'

The 'Valence' collection was launched in October 2006 at a gallery in Mayfair, London. Ben Brown, an art dealer and close friend of Cora's husband Kaveh, kindly lent her his space for the night.

Valence Plus Pendant, 2011
white gold, mauve tourmaline, leather cord

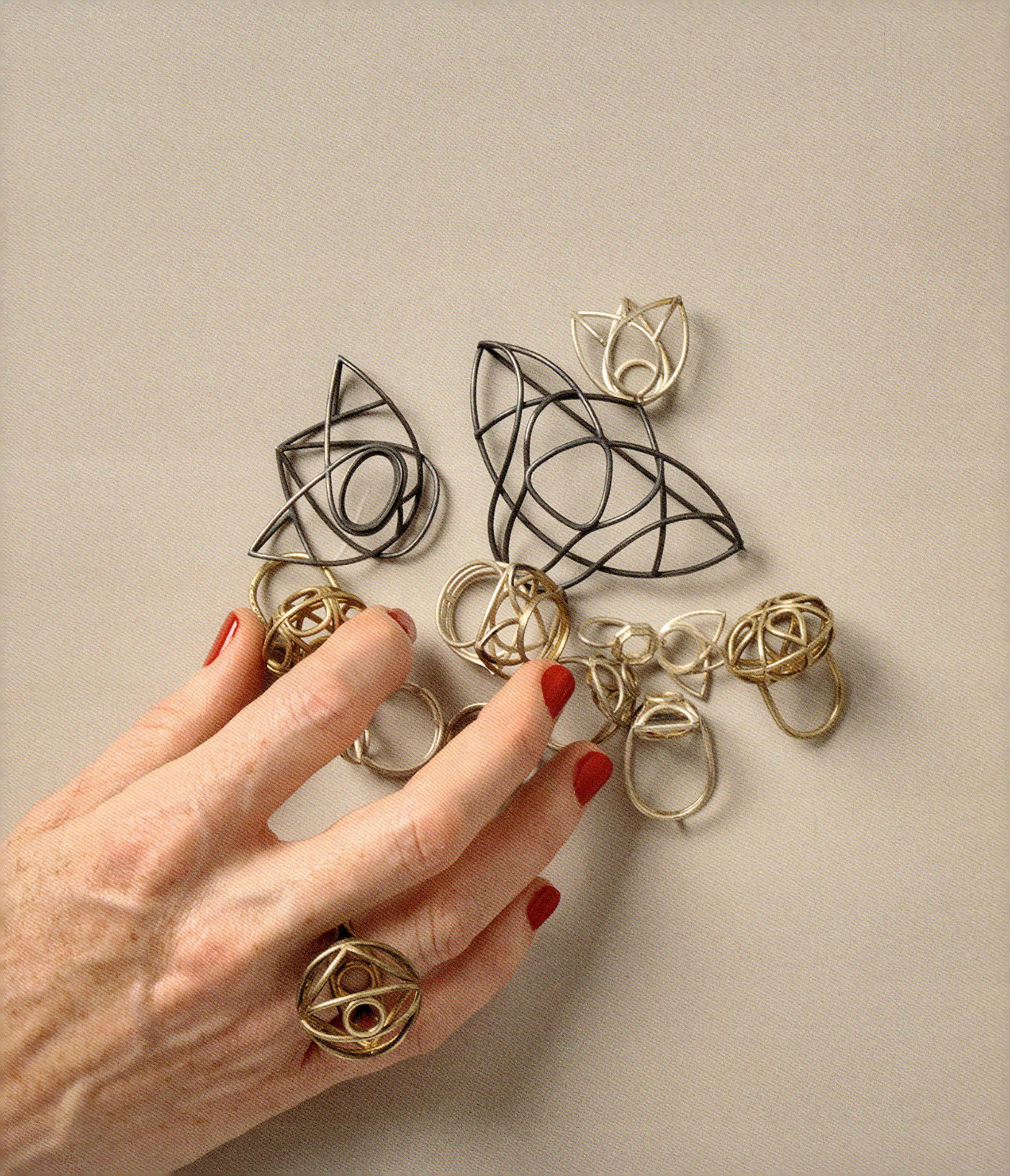

LEFT
Prototypes of 'Valence' and
'Valence Plus' pieces, 2006-2019
gold-plated matt silver, silver,
blackened silver

RIGHT
Sketches for 'Valence' pieces
including final sketch for
Reverse Orchid Earrings in the
centre, 2015

BELOW
Reverse Orchid Earring, 2016
white gold, tanzanite

Valence Plus Earring, 2015
yellow gold, orange tourmaline

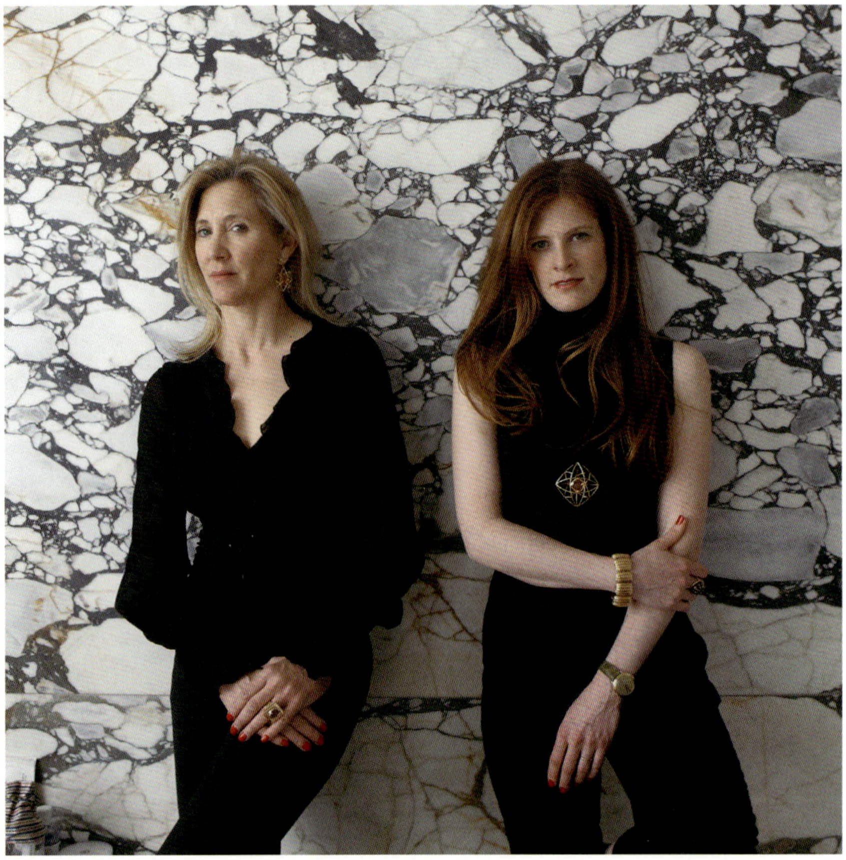

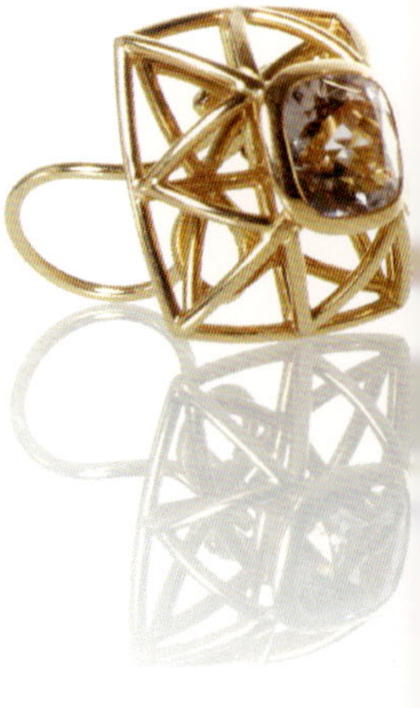

Carol Gardey and Cora,
London, 2015

Carol wears
Valence Plus Earrings, 2012
yellow gold, orange tourmaline

Temple Ring, 2010
rose gold, burgundy red spinel

Cora wears
Valence Plus Pendant, 2013
yellow gold, brownish-orange tourmaline

Texan Cactus Bracelet, 2012
rose gold

Decorated Gugelhupf Ring, 2015
yellow gold, ebony, rubies

FROM LEFT TO RIGHT
Valence Plus Earring, 2016
rose gold, pinkish-grey tourmaline

Cobweb Ring, 2008
white gold, colourless sapphire

Angular Valence Plus Pendant, 2012
yellow gold, ametrine

Angular Valence Plus Cuff, 2012
yellow gold, rubellite tourmalines

Valence Plus Earring, 2010
yellow gold, greenish-blue tourmaline

Simple Valence Plus Ring, 2012
yellow gold, green tourmaline

BELOW
Fire Opal Valence Plus Brooch, 2015
yellow gold, fire opal

RIGHT
Cobweb Ring, 2008
white gold, colourless sapphire

Valence Plus Eye Cuff, 2017
white gold, greyish-pink tourmaline

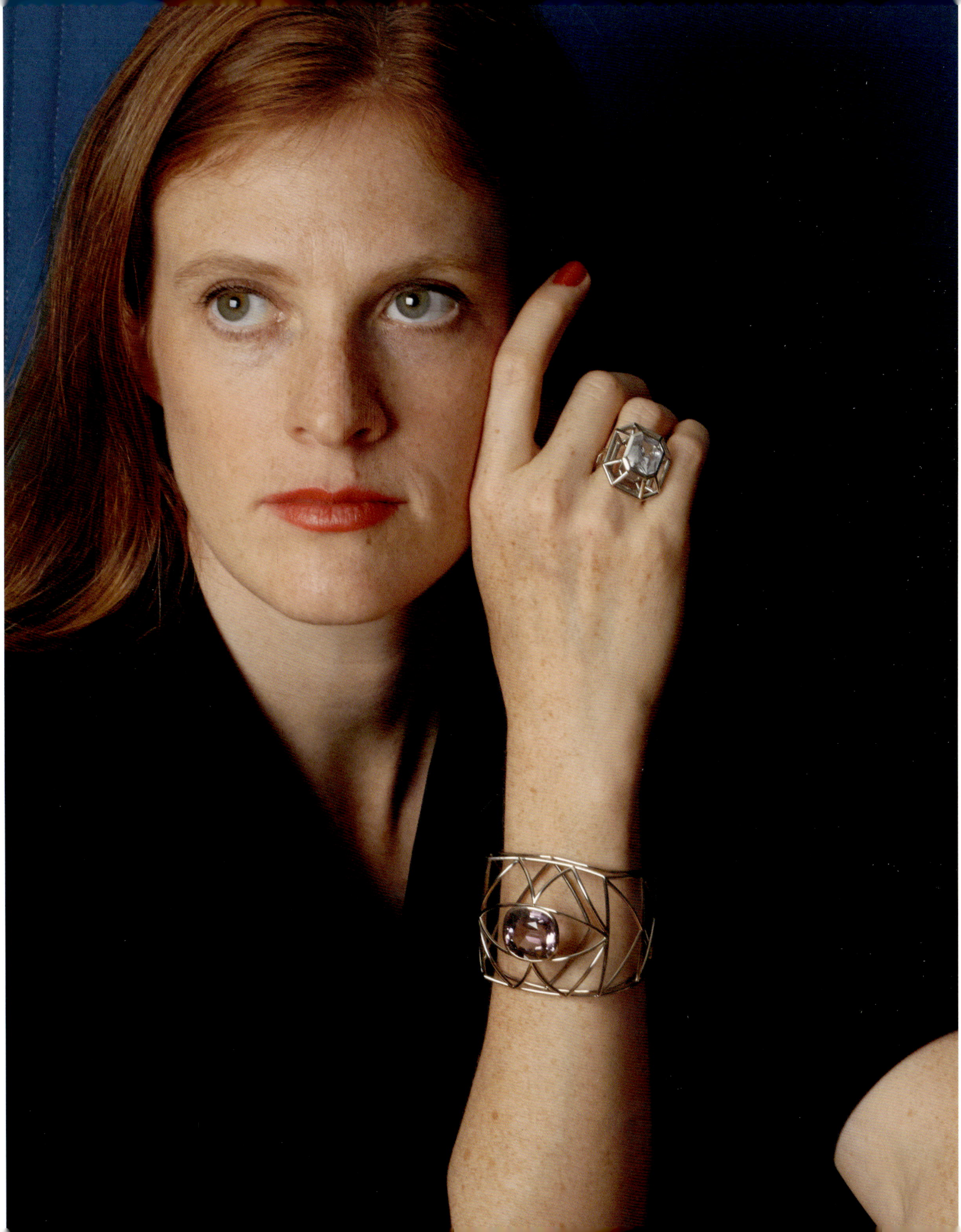

Moth Valence Plus Brooch, 2018
yellow gold, light green tourmaline

Double Insect Valence Plus Pendant, 2020
yellow gold, orangey-brown tourmalines

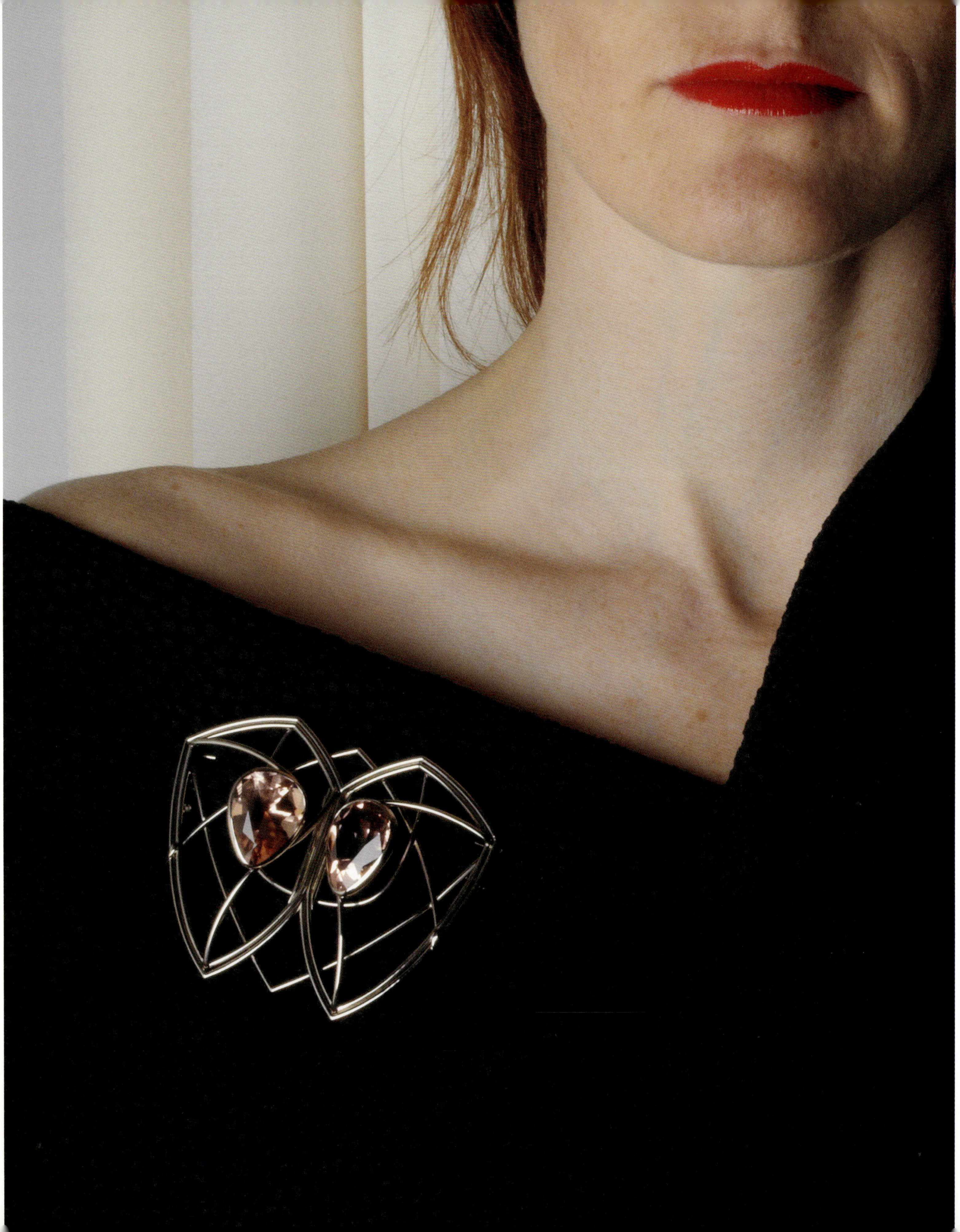

Double Valence Plus Brooch,
2017
white gold, morganites

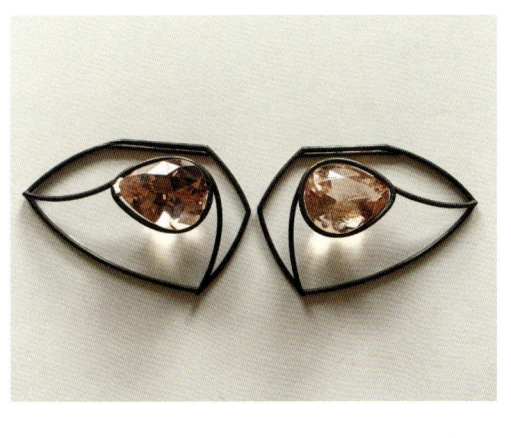

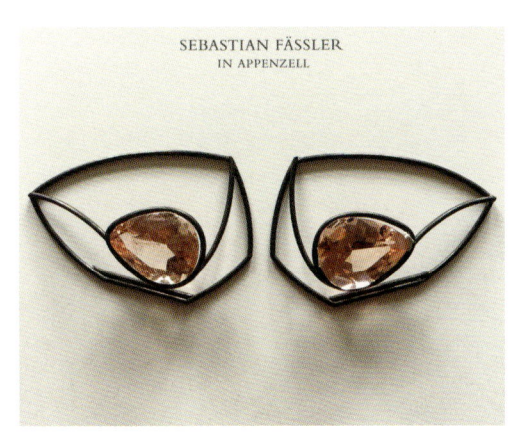

Prototype for the *Double Valence Plus Brooch* in different orientations, in blackened silver and morganites

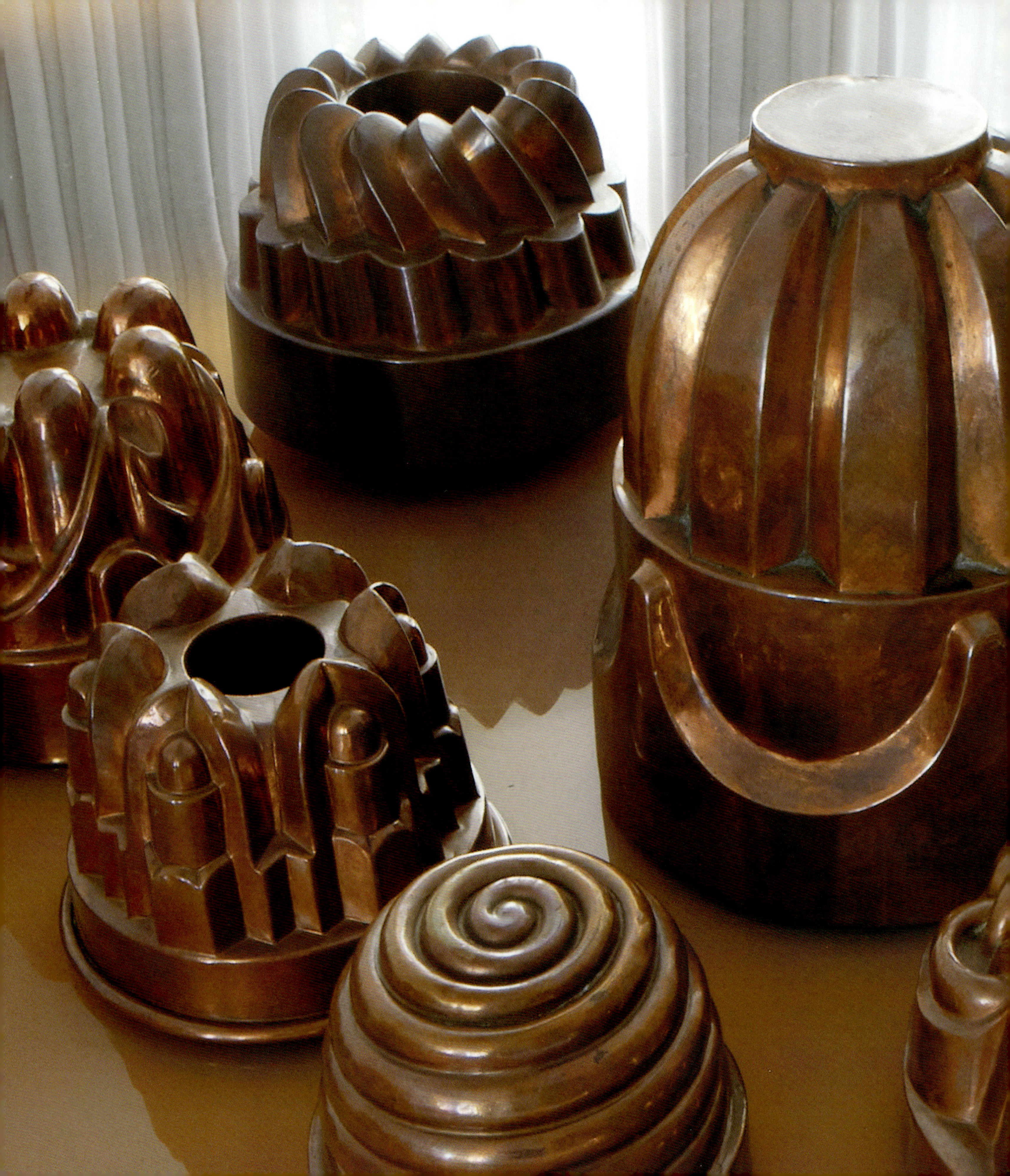

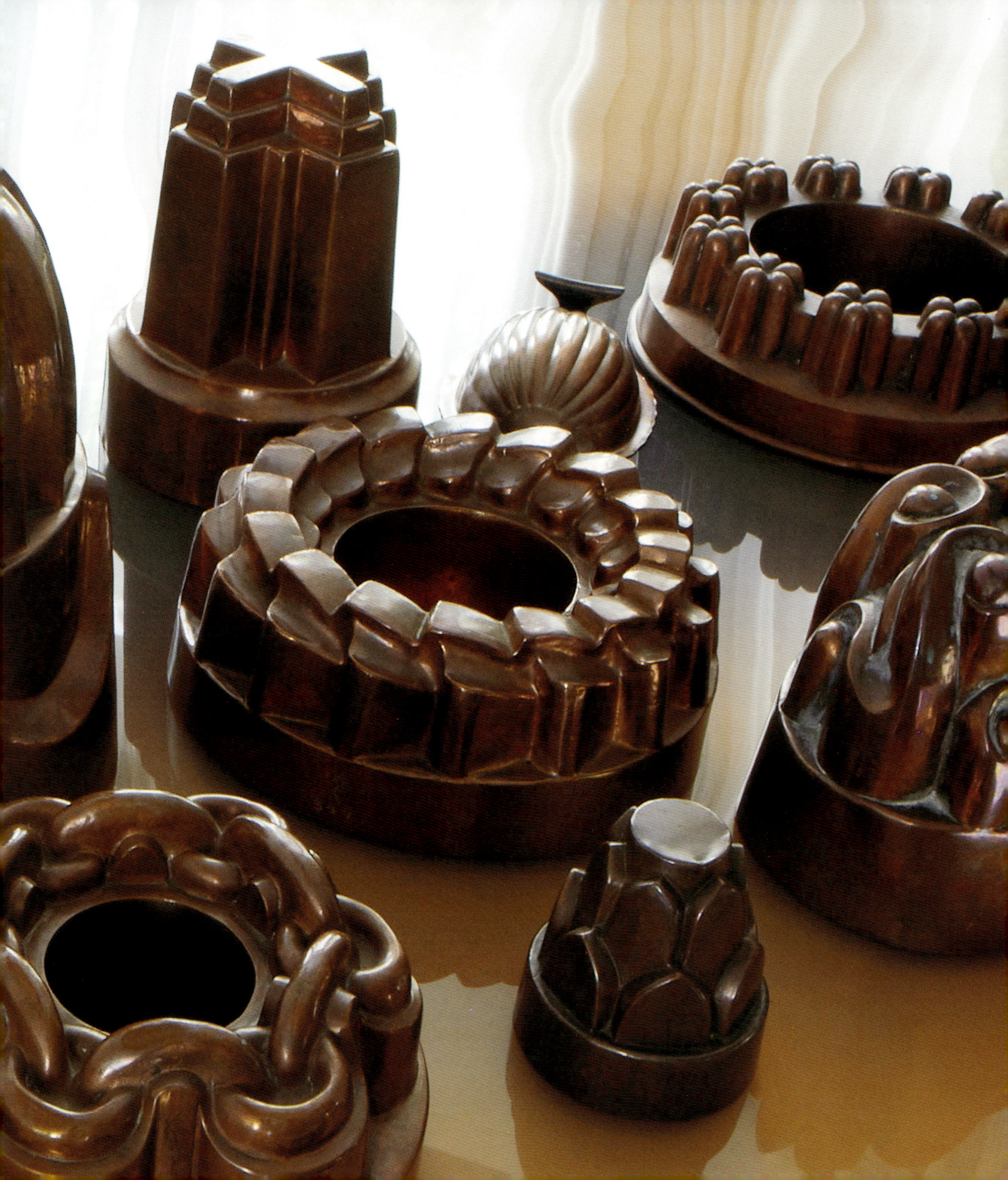

Decorated Gugelhupf from Café Schober (now relocated and renamed Café Felix), Zurich, 2008

Jelly Ring, 2022
platinum, chrysoprase, emerald
faux suede doily

COPPER MOULD

'Copper Mould' is Cora Sheibani's most popular collection. Childhood nostalgia played its part in framing the concept as her mother used to take her for afternoon tea at Café Schober in Zurich (made famous for its decorated Gugelhupf cakes) as a treat after her violin lessons.

The inspiration for the collection came about years later when her goldsmith Sebastian took her to a local café for a mid-morning break and they ordered coffee and pastries. Cora's imagination was instantly fired by the shapes and decorations, and she started drawing cakes as jewellery on her sketchpad.

'When my goldsmith saw what I had drawn he showed me a copper cake mould and said, "Hey, isn't that an amazing shape" and he went away and made a mini brass mould exactly like the one he had shown me that day.'

When the brass mould was completed, they both agreed that it looked too perfect, and realised quite quickly they needed to create a prototype that looked less like something which belonged in a doll's house. A second, more stylised, prototype was made as a ring in the shape of a Gugelhupf (a type of Bundt cake).

Delighted with the results, Cora went on a designing spree and soon had enough pieces to open a patisserie. The original Bundt cake design was embellished with diamond sprinkles and later became a jelly if a clear gemstone was used. The collection evolved further to include ice cream cones, cupcakes, Christmas puddings, berry tartlets, *Linzer Torten, Spitzbuebn* (biscuits filled with jam), cream tartlets, a pretzel necklace, a terrine brooch and a Prussienne (puff-pastry biscuit) brooch. Cora even designed a Jammy Dodger biscuit ring (with a heart in the middle) for an English friend, the artist Kate Daudy in exchange for one of her artworks.

The development of the 'Copper Mould' collection was again a close collaboration between Cora and her goldsmith Sebastian Fässler who made all the prototypes in brass and wood, weighing-in with advice when necessary. An example of their productive, problem-solving relationship occurred during the development of the *Ice Cream Ring*. The prototype was made originally with three scoops of ice cream, but it didn't look right, so Sebastian suggested using two scoops to make a cross-over ring instead. He made a new model; it was a big improvement, and the *Ice Cream Ring* became one of two best sellers in the collection.

Contact sheets of Cora's antique copper moulds shoot for *Copper Mould Collection Cookbook* by Paola Petrobelli, 2008

The 'Copper Mould' collection was fashioned in gemstones and materials chosen to resemble the colour of the food portrayed. Puddings, tarts and jellies were consummated in gold set with ebony, chrysoprase, green opal, cacholong opal, nephrite and lapis, and then decorated with diamond sugar sprinkles or ruby berries or a spinel cherry on top. The utilisation of such a diverse range of designs and materials was made possible by stone dealer Gustav Caeser, who was willing to carve stones for single pieces on a one-off basis. Over time, new pieces have been added and new materials made available to the extent that today customers can even select their own colour combinations.

The collection was launched in October 2008 in downtown New York at a friend's studio space (Mike Latham, who founded the Arts Corporation design firm). Cora later learned that downtown New York is a good place for art but not ideal for selling jewellery. To make matters worse, the show was held two weeks after Lehman Brothers filed for bankruptcy and between the Jewish holidays of Rosh Hashanah and Yom Kippur, which to put it mildly, was not great timing!

Cora sold only two pieces, but the buyer was a great art and jewellery collector who became a good customer. The event was also written up in the food section of *The New York Times*, so it wasn't all bad. After the show, Cora's father told her not to worry, saying 'You know when I did my first Pop Art exhibition in 1965, I sold one multiple to Max Bill (the Swiss Bauhaus artist)...it doesn't mean anything.' Bruno Bischofberger had works by Roy Lichtenstein and Andy Warhol in that exhibition; and all he sold was a print for 43 Swiss francs. For Cora, this felt like the first time her father had properly offered encouragement since choosing her career as a jeweller. 'I felt he believed in me now and this meant a great deal.'

Cora produced a 'Copper Mould' cookery book featuring recipes for cakes, jellies and confections alongside images of the jewellery (each with a list of ingredients) to promote the collection. Such was her enthusiasm for the subject that it manifested into something akin to an obsession to the extent that she amassed a vast collection of antique copper moulds and even enrolled in an historic jelly-making course. Her sister Lea once again helped to design the book, assisted by close friends Ashkan Sahihi, who photographed the food, and Paola Petrobelli, who photographed the jewellery.

Jelly-making workshop with Ivan Day, December 2008

COPPER MOULD

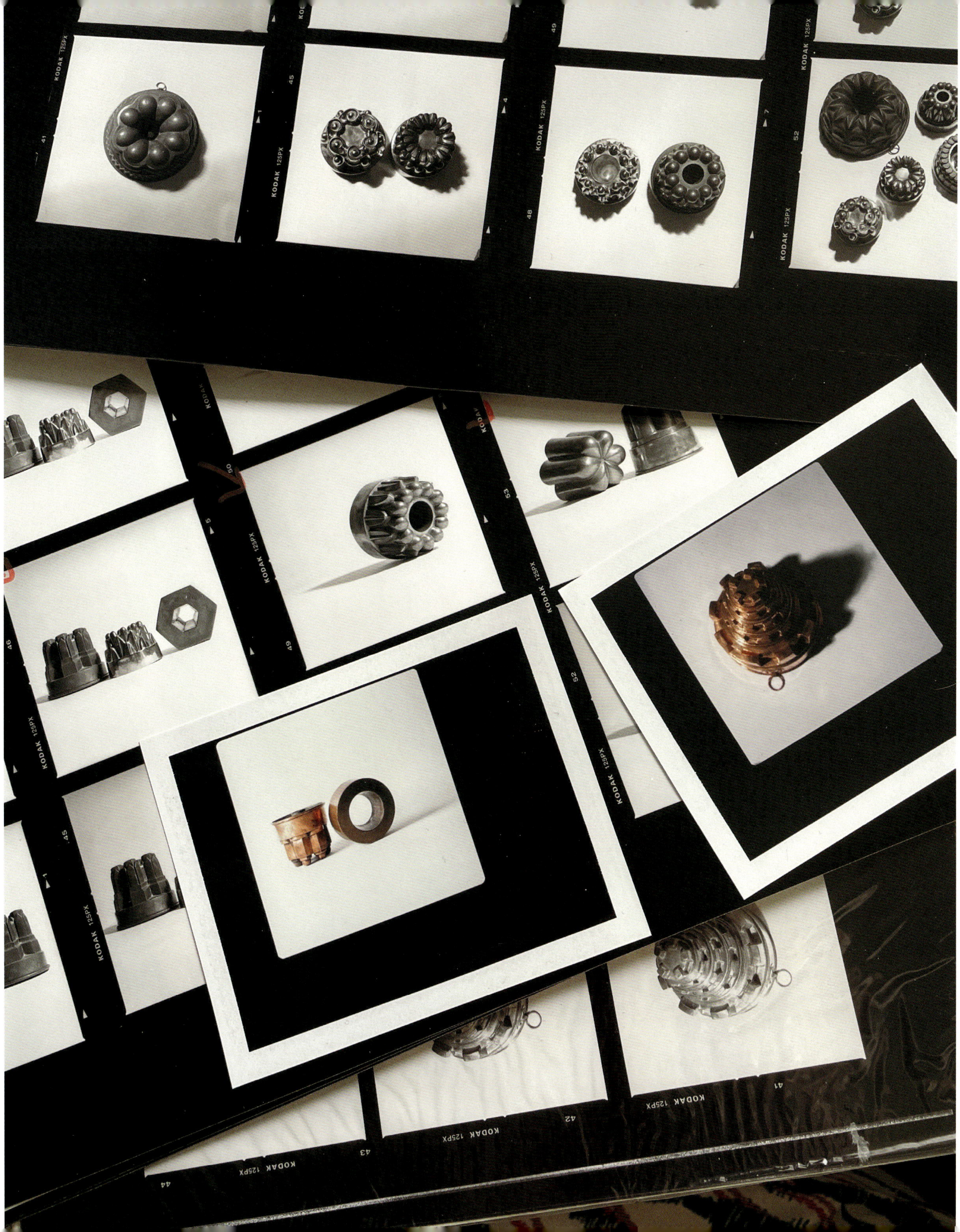
KODAK 125PX

BELOW LEFT
Carved stones for *Gugelhupf* and *Jelly* rings, 2022

RIGHT
Lemon Jelly Ring, 2014
yellow gold, citrine, ruby

BELOW RIGHT
Jam Tartlet Ring, 2013
yellow gold, carnelian

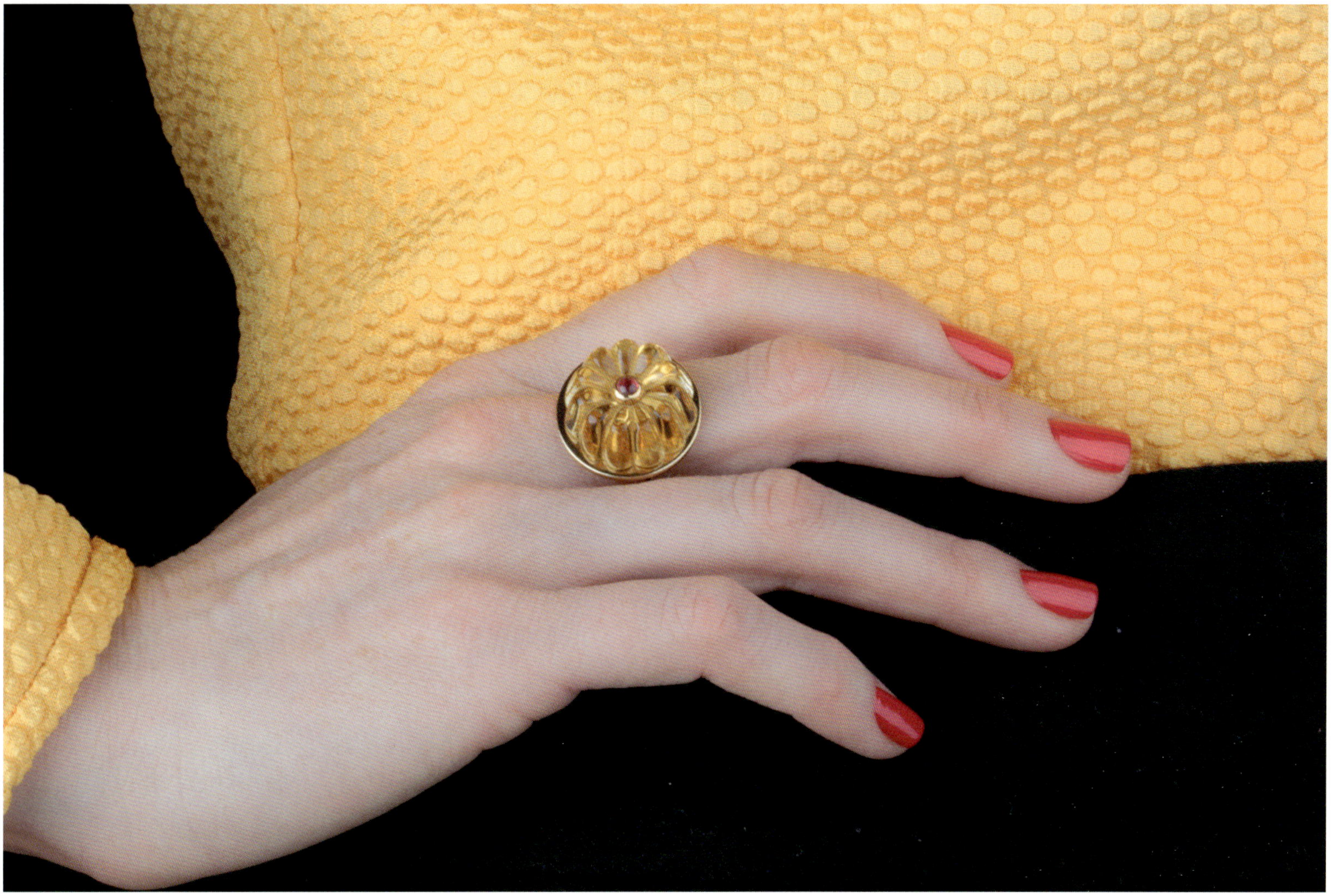

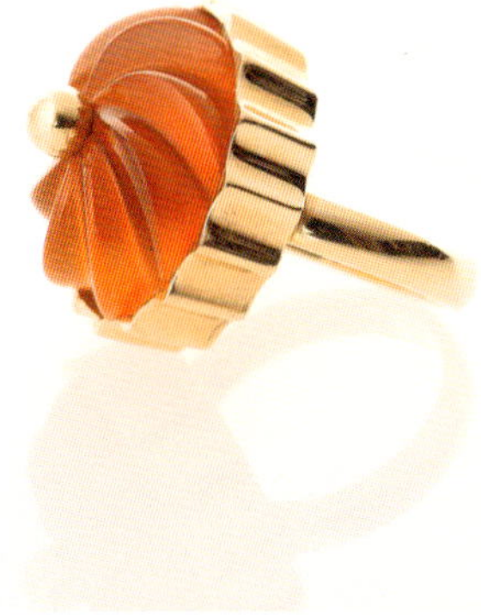

BELOW
FROM LEFT TO RIGHT
Strawberry Pudding Ring, 2020
rose gold, pink opal, pink sapphire

Mixed Berry Tartlet Ring, 2019
rose gold, cornflower blue sapphires, orangey-red spinels

Lime & Matcha Ice Cream Ring, 2022
white gold, green opal, malachite

Linzer Torte Ring, 2012
white gold, lapis lazuli

Layered Blancmange Ring, 2019
red gold, striped chalcedony, light pink diamond

Large Cupcake Ring, 2018
white and rose gold, pink opal, pink spinels

Decorated Gugelhupf Ring, 2019
rose gold, ebony, fluorescent brown diamonds

RIGHT
Designs for 'Copper Mould' collection rings and prototypes made in 2005, and *Copper Mould Collection Cookbook* printed in 2008

77

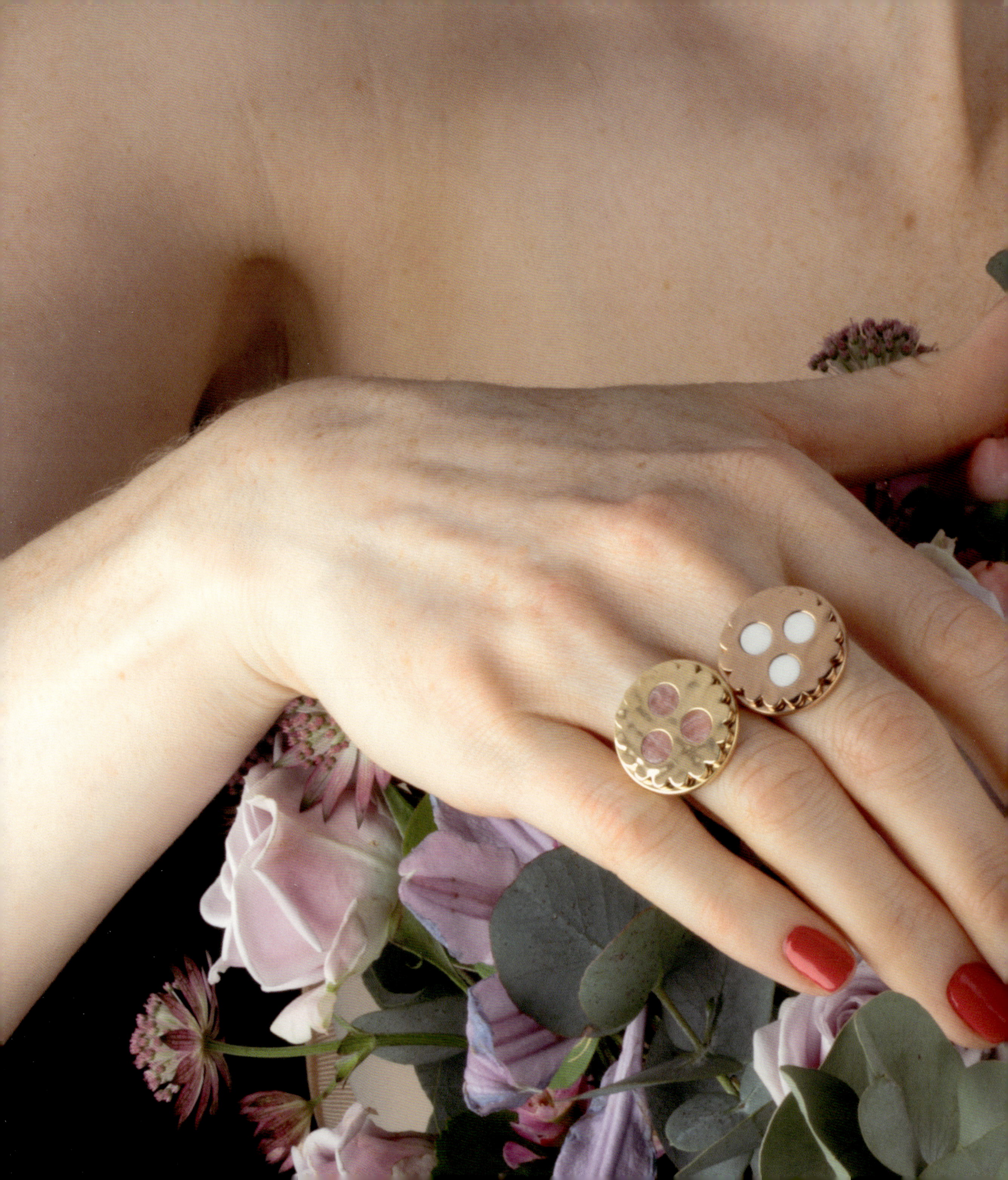

79

PP.78-79
Spitzbueb Ring, 2017
yellow gold, rhodocrosite

Spitzbueb Ring, 2017
red gold, cacholong opal

Decorated Gugelhupf Ring,
2006/2007
yellow gold, cacholong opal,
blue sapphires, rubies

ABOVE
Terrine Brooch, 2006
yellow gold, carnelian, peridots,
cacholong opal, rubies,
chrysoprase, ebony

BELOW
*Mint & Strawberry Ice Cream
Ring,* 2021
yellow gold, chrysoprase, pink
opal

RIGHT
Mixed Berry Tartlet Ring, 2019
rose gold, cornflower blue
sapphires, orangey-red spinels

79

PP.78-79
Spitzbueb Ring, 2017
yellow gold, rhodocrosite

Spitzbueb Ring, 2017
red gold, cacholong opal

Decorated Gugelhupf Ring,
2006/2007
yellow gold, cacholong opal,
blue sapphires, rubies

ABOVE
Terrine Brooch, 2006
yellow gold, carnelian, peridots,
cacholong opal, rubies,
chrysoprase, ebony

BELOW
*Mint & Strawberry Ice Cream
Ring,* 2021
yellow gold, chrysoprase, pink
opal

RIGHT
Mixed Berry Tartlet Ring, 2019
rose gold, cornflower blue
sapphires, orangey-red spinels

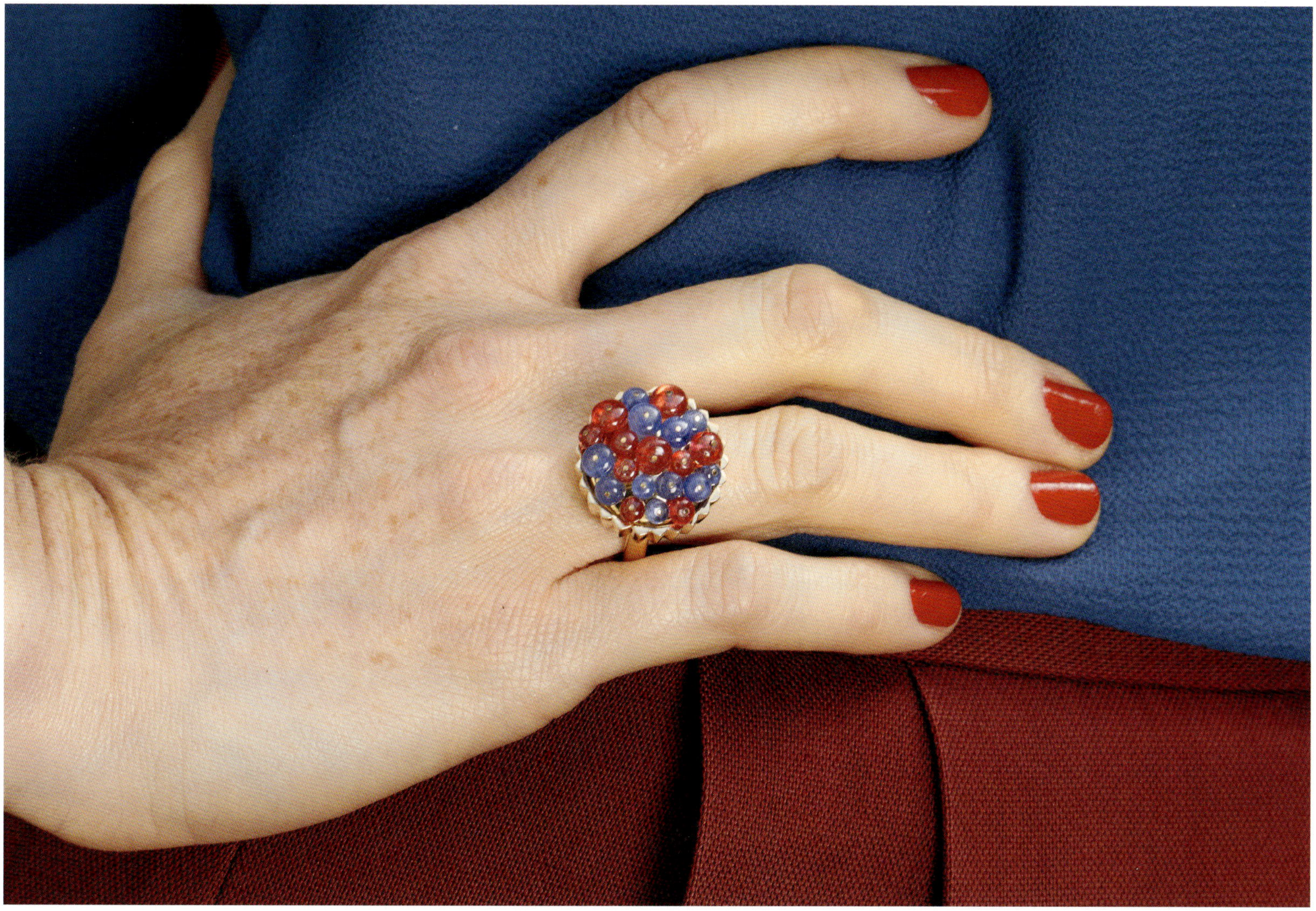

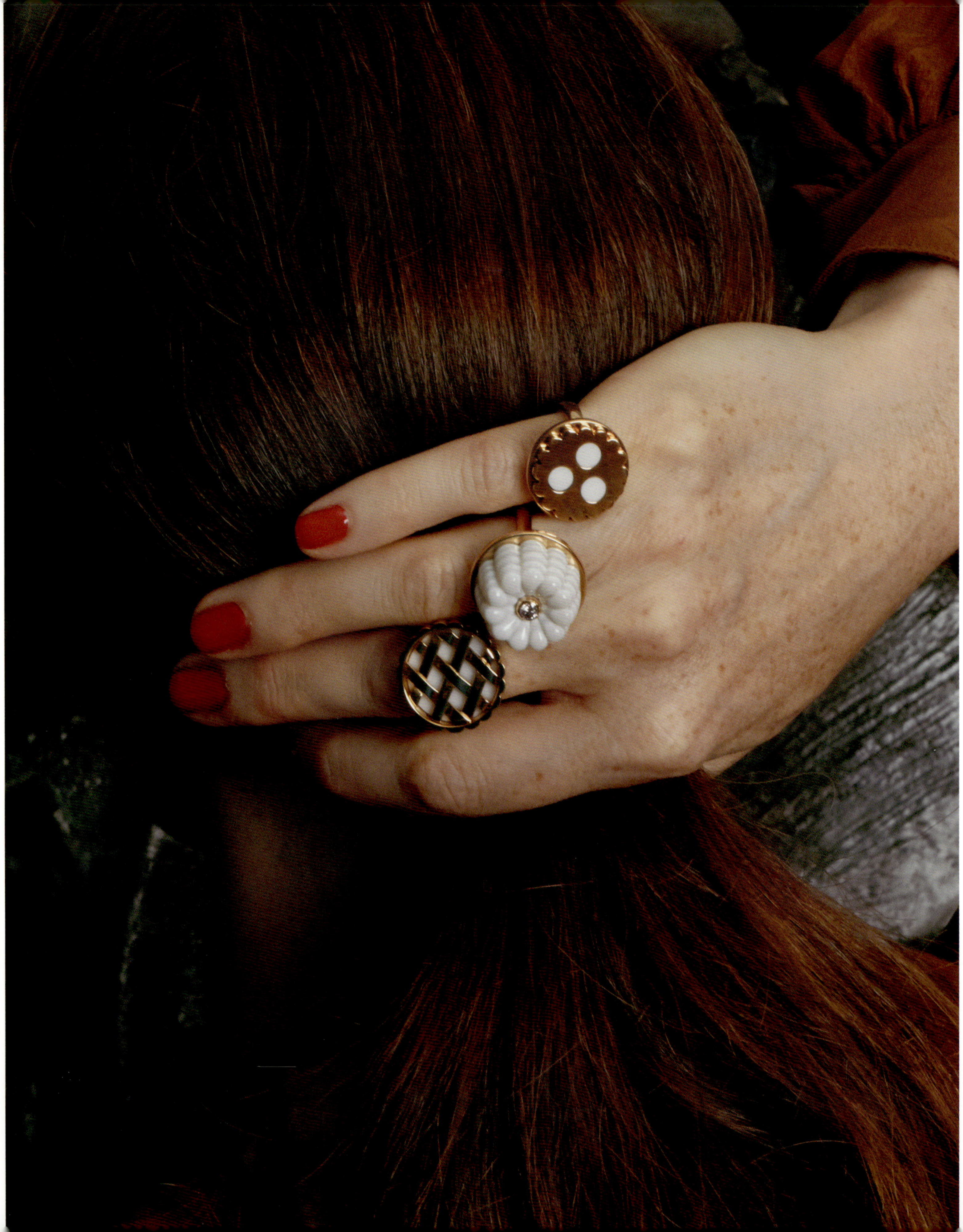

Spitzbueb Ring, 2017
red gold, cacholong opal

Layered Blancmange Ring, 2019
red gold, striped chalcedony, light pink diamond

Linzer Tart Ring, 2019
rose gold, pale pink opal

Pretzel Necklace, 2010
yellow gold

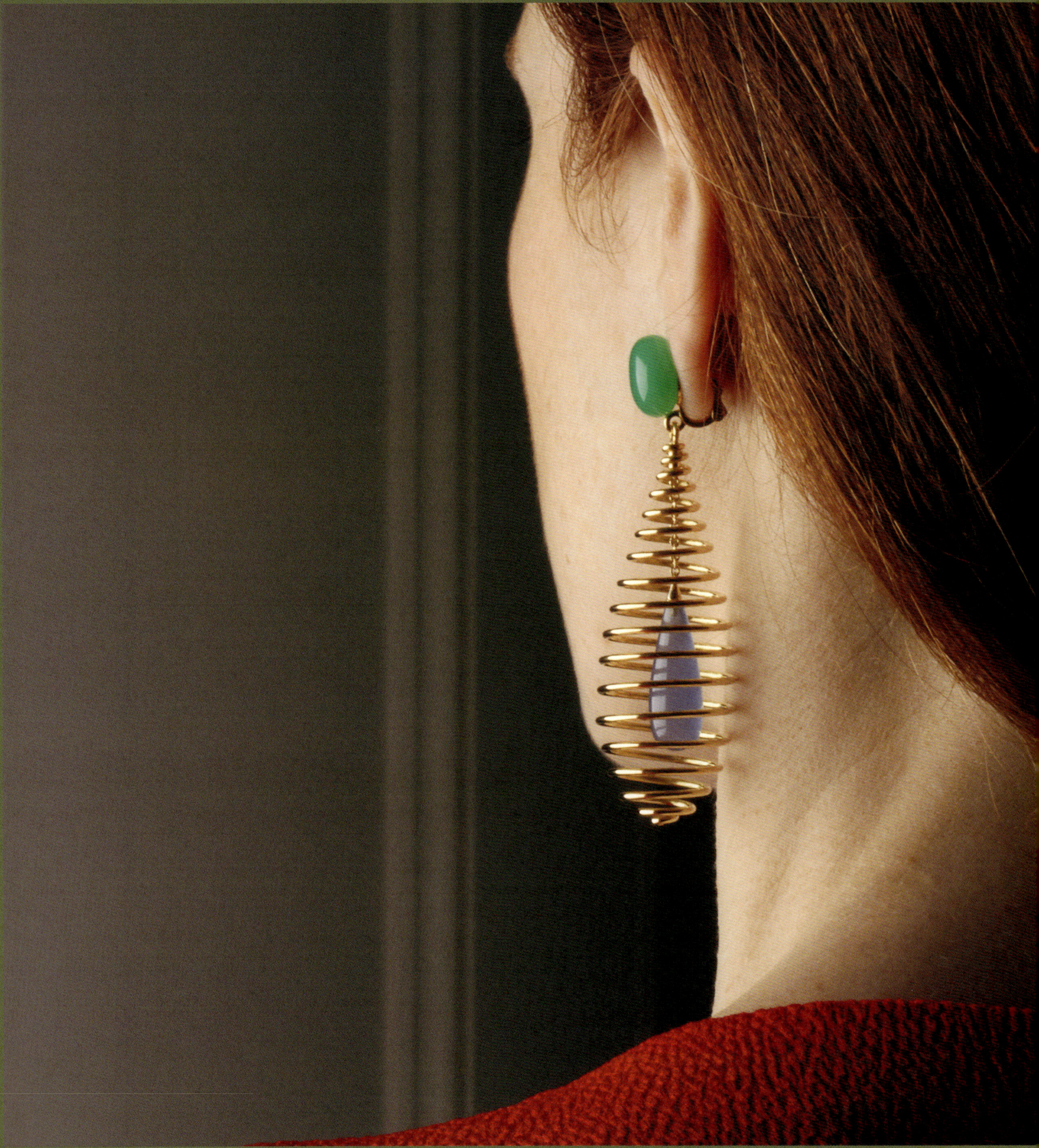

Cora Sheibani's sequence of *Spiral* earring designs was a precursor to the 'Valence' collection. Twelve pairs have been made over the years including, in 2018, this version in yellow gold, chrysoprase and blue chalcedony. Making the spiral drop was a big challenge because it required gold wire to be carefully wound around a shaped block. This resulted in a classic 'ship in a bottle' conundrum...how to then remove the block? The answer is that it had to be cut horizontally into very thin slices. *Spiral* is one of Cora's most popular earring designs and a frequently worn item in her personal collection.

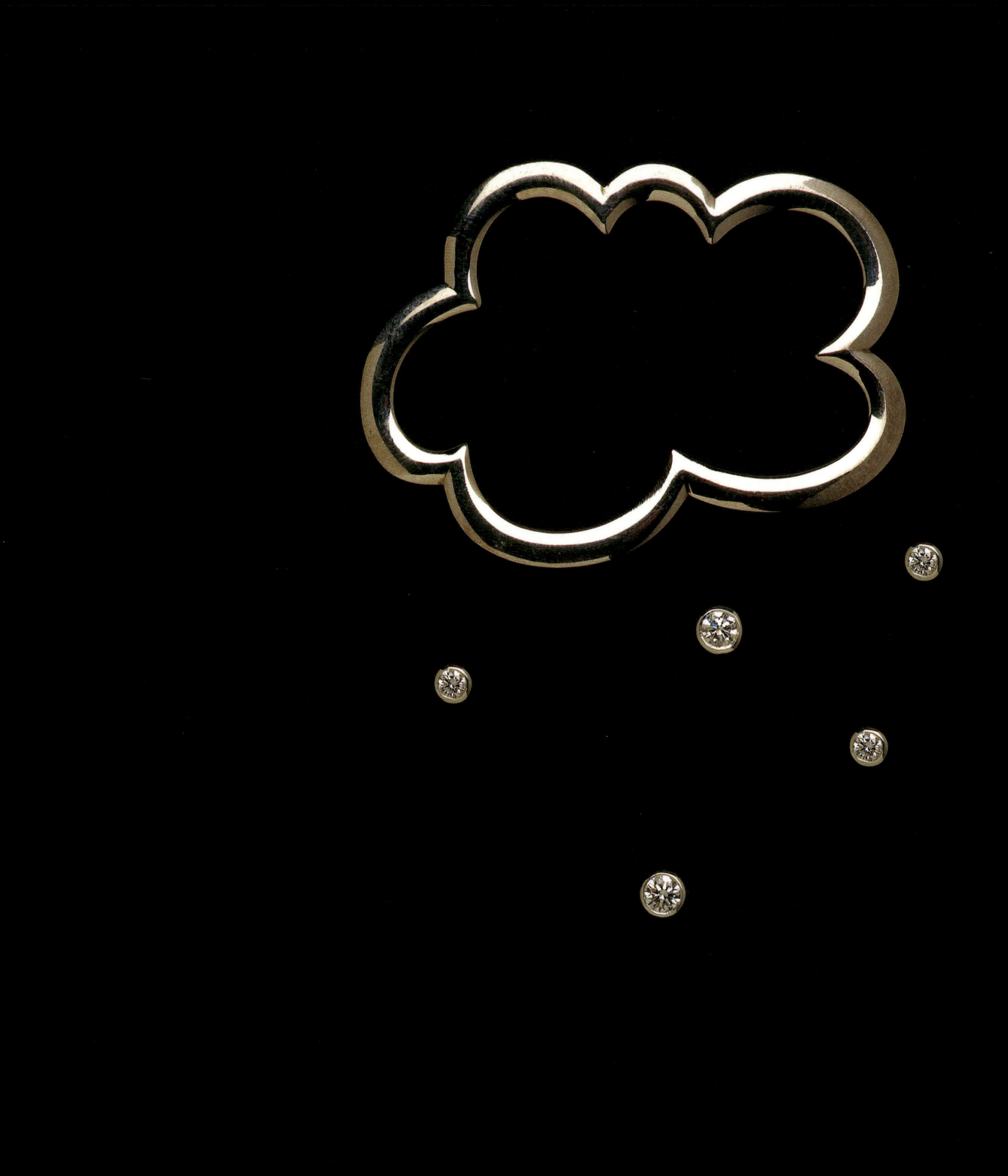

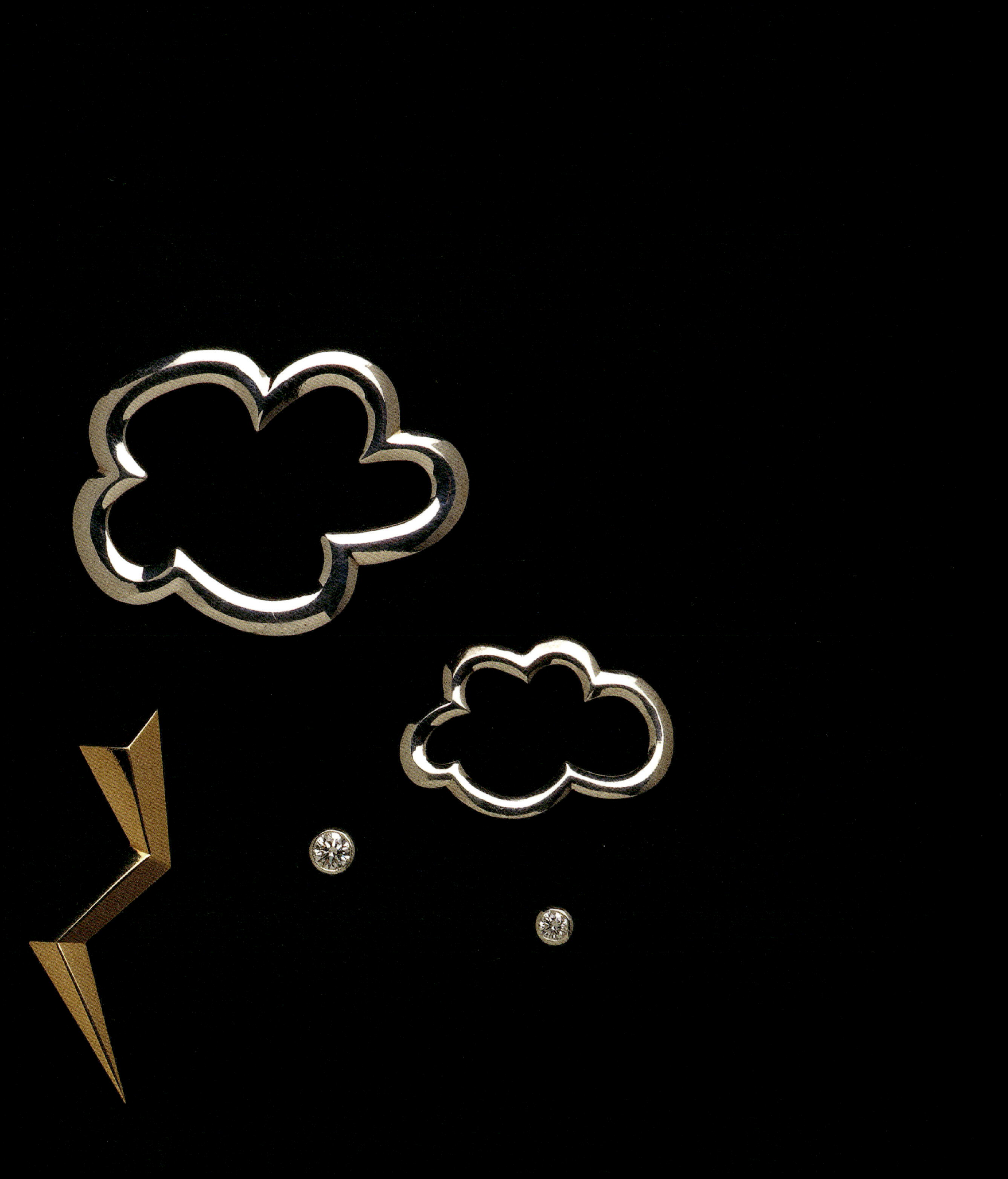

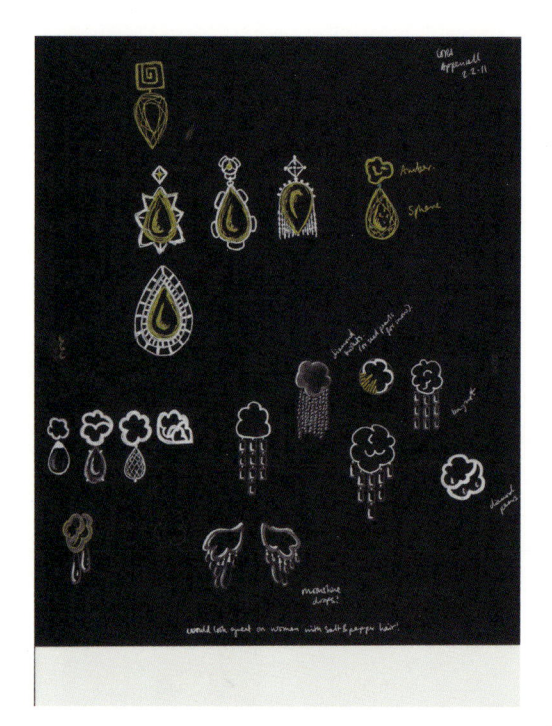

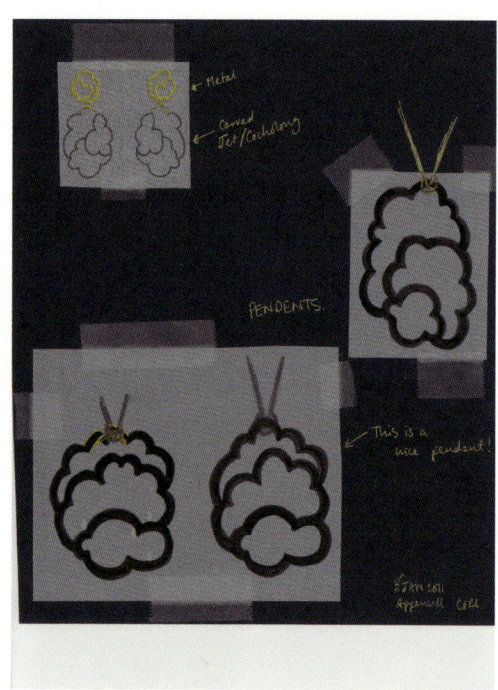

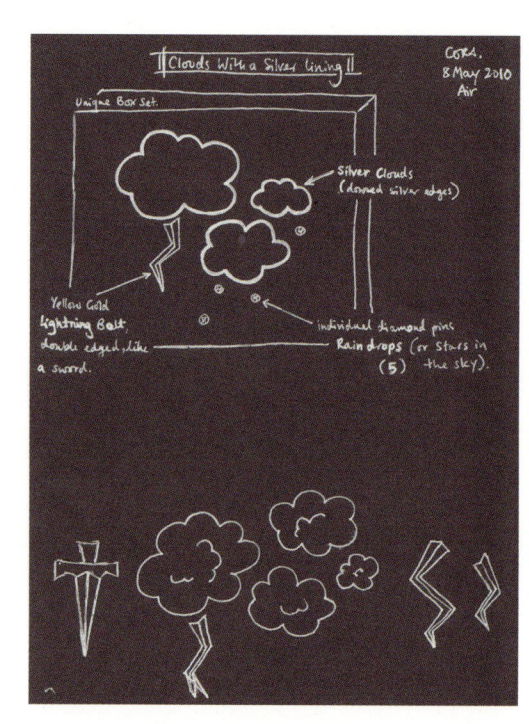

Sketches for 'Clouds with a Silver Lining' jewels, 2010-11

CLOUDS WITH A SILVER LINING

The idea for the 'Clouds' collection originated in a rather circuitous manner from a request by Cora's maternal grandmother, Ella.

'My grandmother asked me to design a tiara for her and I was thinking she now lives in a granary just outside of Vienna with no central heating...what does she want a tiara for?'

Later, on a trip to India, Cora noticed that on all the new high-rise buildings in Mumbai the shiny steel had already turned black, like silver when it tarnishes.

This set her thinking about her grandmother's brief, so she drew a skyscraper tiara in her sketchbook and then, on the following page, a dress design inspired by the Mumbai skyline featuring skyscrapers, aeroplanes, clouds and stars at the top. Years later, she finally got round to making a skyscraper brooch but at the time, her mind kept drifting back towards the clouds.

'I guess that led me to thinking that skyscrapers go black, clouds go black, silver goes black and hence "Clouds with a Silver Lining".'

Later, back in London, Cora rigorously explored the subject, poring over such esoteric publications as *The Cloud Collector's Handbook* before translating her ideas into stylised motifs in white and silver pen on dark paper. These initially comprised designs for brooches, some earrings, a *Raindrop Cloud Ring* and a *Cloud Collar Necklace*.

The early pieces were made in silver with the intention that they would oxidise to resemble darkening rain-clouds, 'but I soon realised that silver doesn't go from silver to black when it tarnishes...in between it goes yellow' so instead Cora decided to make the rain-clouds in mostly matt white gold, rhodium plated to become black or grey and the 'good weather' clouds in polished yellow or rose gold. Raindrops and rays of light were added using diamonds, pearls, jelly opals, moonstones and sapphires. The finishing touch to the collection was a flock of golden birds 'to go with the good weather clouds', allowing the wearer to arrange her own skyscape using the different pieces.

Atypically for a designer who identifies as a colourist, 'Clouds with a Silver Lining' is a virtually monochromatic collection featuring black and white as the principal colour palette. 'I loved the stark contrast between black and white, and between matt metal clouds and shiny diamonds.'

This time Cora did not produce a book but instead collaborated with fashion designer Edeline Lee who designed a collection to be worn with the jewels. 'I wanted to show people how modern and cool brooches are and not just something your grandmother would wear.'

The 'Clouds' collection was launched in 2011 as a fashion show at the Paradise Row gallery in Fitzrovia, London. The show featured models wearing a new collection by Edeline Lee, accessorised with Cora's jewels. To complement the theme of clouds, Edeline introduced the idea of using her now signature 'bubble fabric', and soon after launched her eponymous fashion label. Their friend, writer-director Zeina Durra, produced a short film for the show.

A second launch took place at her father's gallery space in Zurich with the same concept of models wearing the new collection. The workload was exhausting but ultimately worthwhile. 'The atmosphere was extraordinary…great buzz, amazing people and for many years after people turned up to buy jewellery and they would still be talking about the show.'

LEFT
Cora and Edeline Lee at the collection launch, Paradise Row Gallery, London, 2011
both dresses by Edeline Lee
photograph by Marc Sethi

RIGHT
Cloud with Rays of Sunlight Brooch, 2011
silver, platinum, gold pin, diamonds
dress by Edeline Lee
photograph by Marie Kristiansen

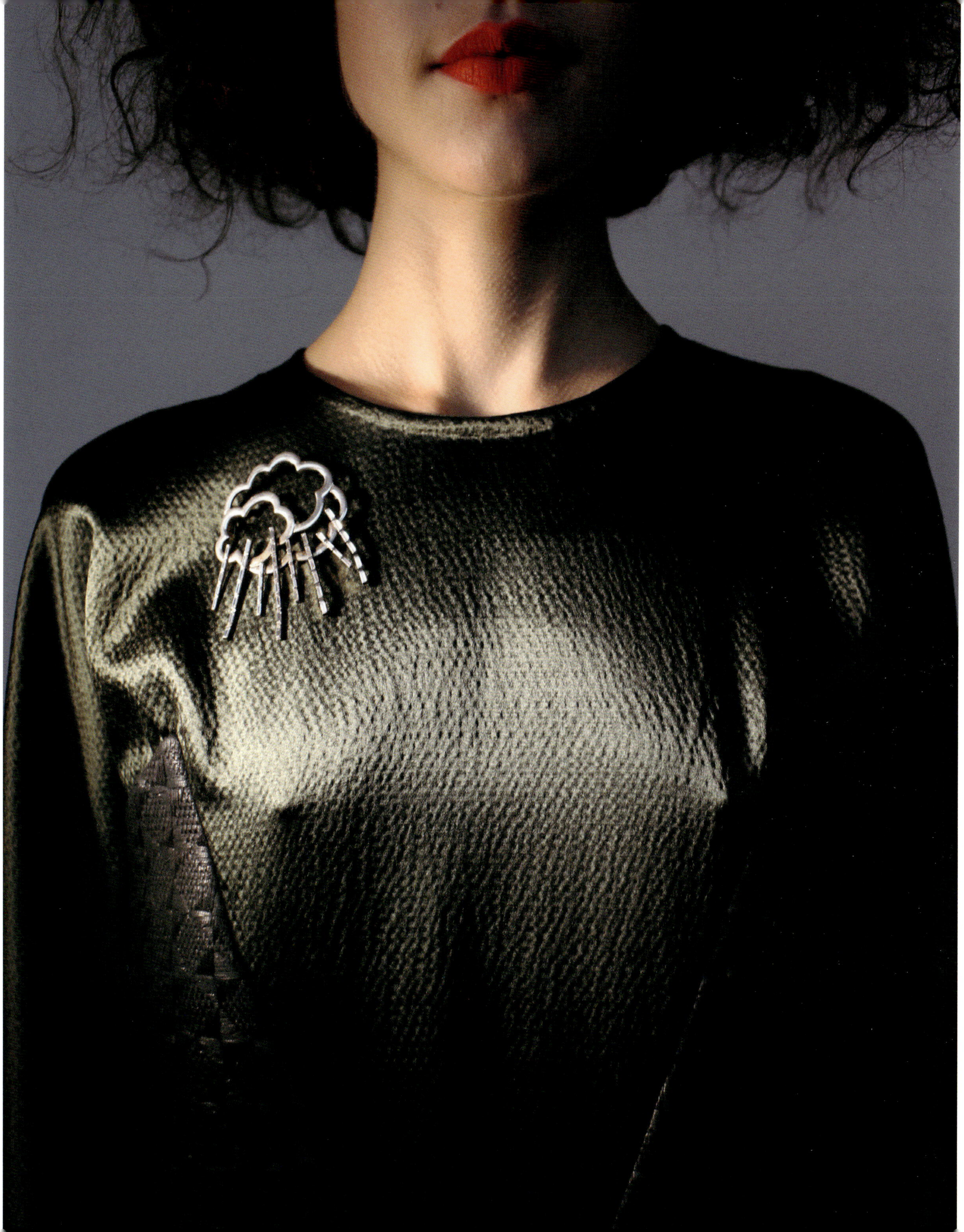

BELOW
Model line-up at Cora's 'Clouds with a Silver Lining' show, London, September 2011 wearing a range of 'Clouds with a Silver Lining' collection pieces
Dresses by Edeline Lee
photograph by Marc Sethi

RIGHT
FROM LEFT TO RIGHT
Bird pins, 2011
yellow gold

Good Weather Cloud Brooch, 2011
rose gold

Black Cloud Brooch Set (2 of 3), 2011
matt silver, rhodium plated in three shades of grey, gold pins

Cloud with Rays of Sunlight Brooch, 2011
silver, platinum, gold pin, diamonds

93

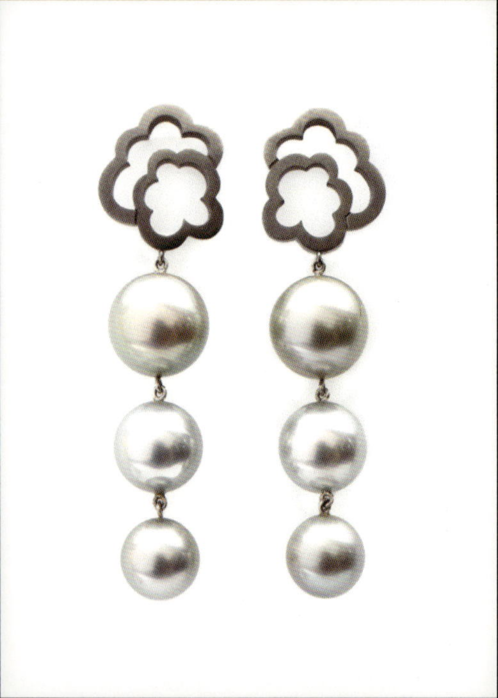
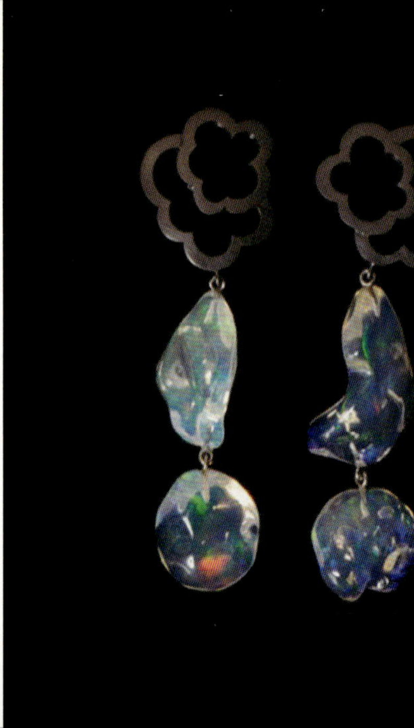

Black Cloud Brooch Set, 2011
matt silver rhodium plated in three shades of grey, gold pins, diamonds

Gugelhupf Ring, 2008
white gold, dumortierite, blue sapphire

jacket by Edeline Lee

LEFT
Snow Cloud Earrings, 2012
blackened matt white gold,
silver cultured pearls

Cloud and Ice Earrings, 2012
blackened matt white gold,
opals

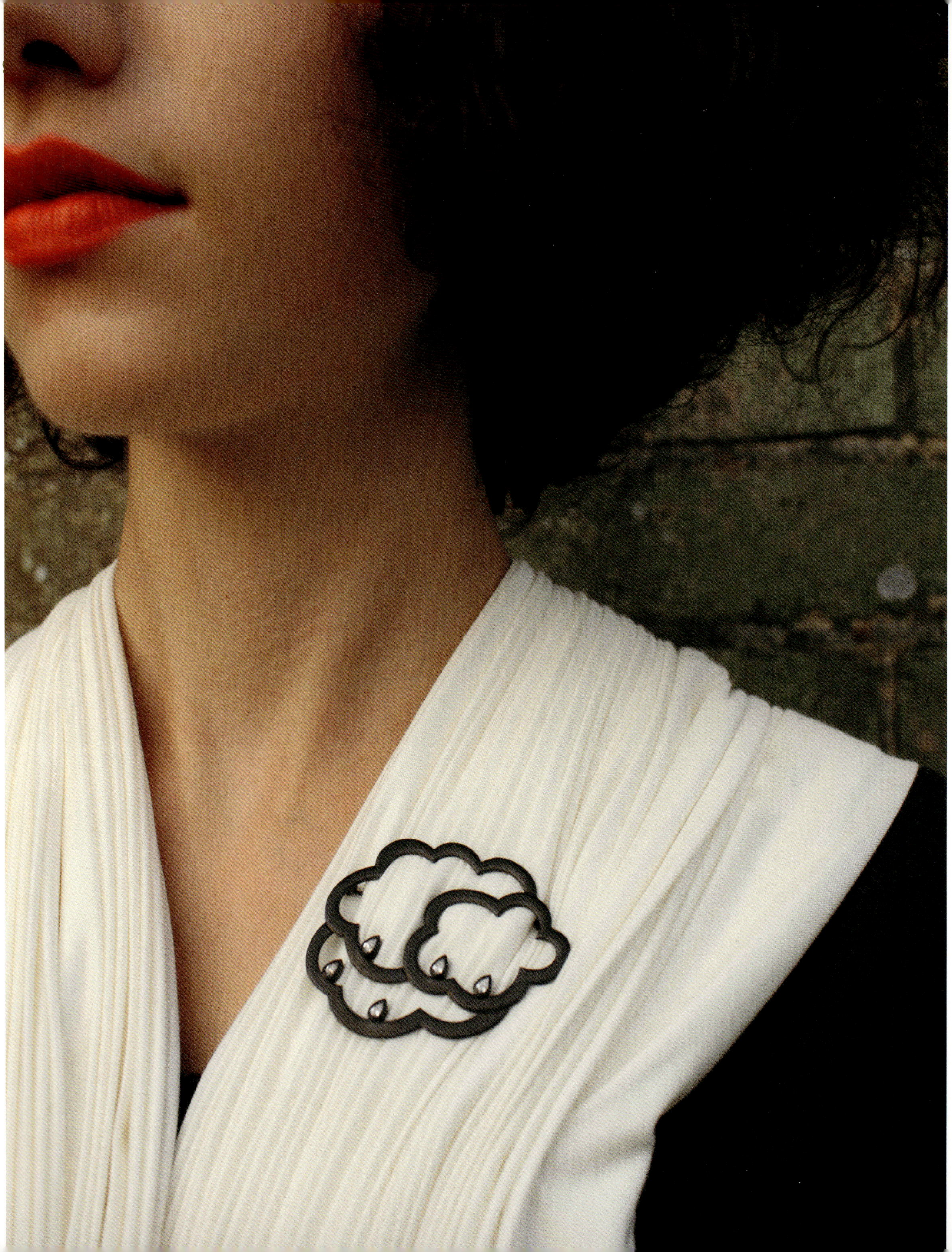

LEFT
Bad Weather Cloud with Rain Brooch, 2011
blackened matt silver, yellow gold pin, diamonds
dress by Edeline Lee
photograph by Marie Kristiansen

BELOW
Rain Cloud Earrings, 2011
white gold, platinum, diamonds

ABOVE
Blue Rain Cloud Brooch, 2012
white gold, blue sapphires

LEFT
Rain Cloud Brooch, 2019
matt gold rhodium plated grey,
diamonds

'Cloud' design sketches, 2010
see final pieces on pages 91 & 96

RIGHT
Bird pins in three sizes, 2011
yellow gold

Vertical Grey Cloud Brooch, 2022
matt silver rhodium plated grey,
gold pin

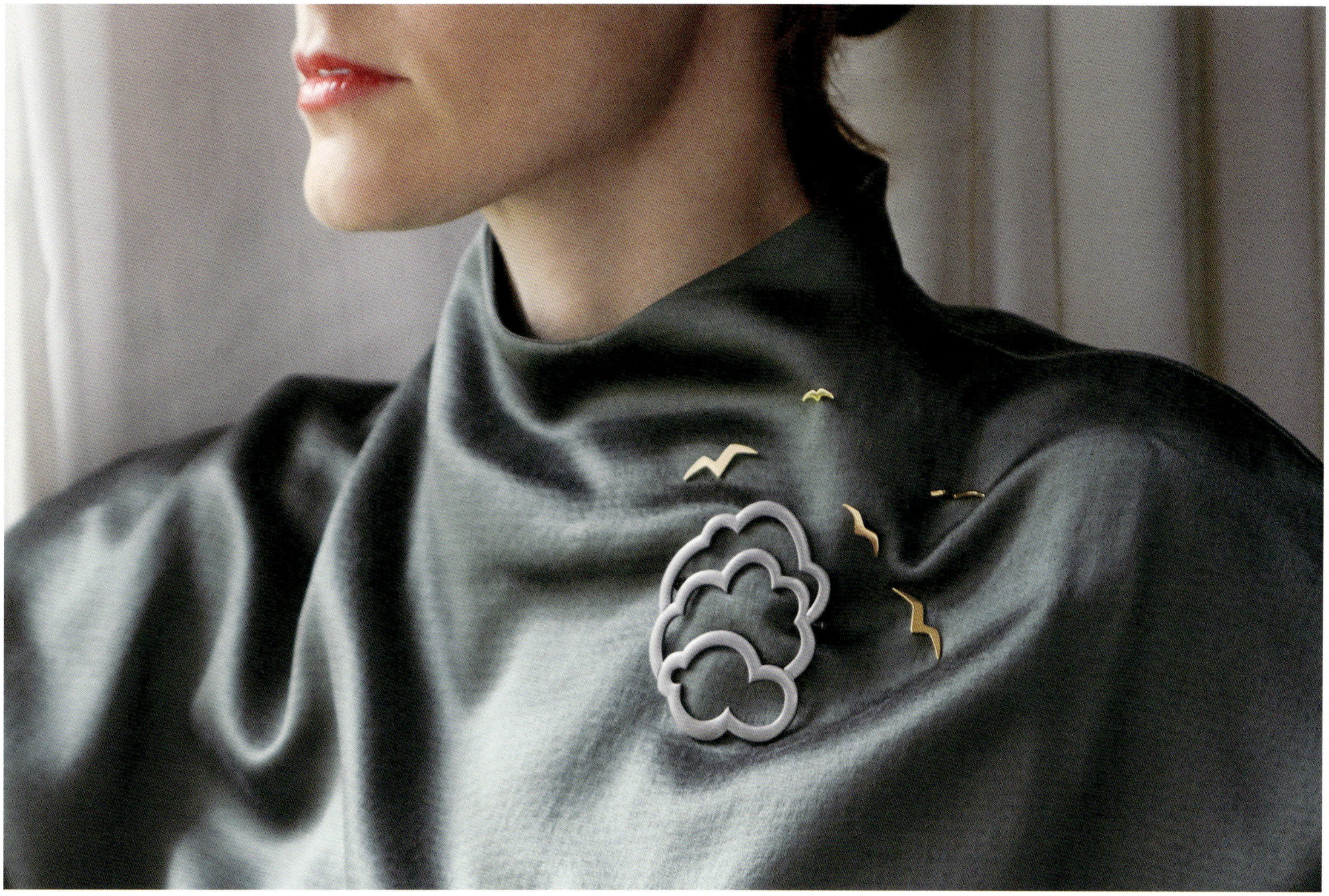

BELOW
Blizzard Cloud Earrings, 2018
white gold, greyish-blue spinels

Vertical Cloud Brooch, 2018
matt white gold rhodium-plated
grey, blueish-grey sapphires

RIGHT
Silver Clouds Collar, 2011
silver, white gold clasp

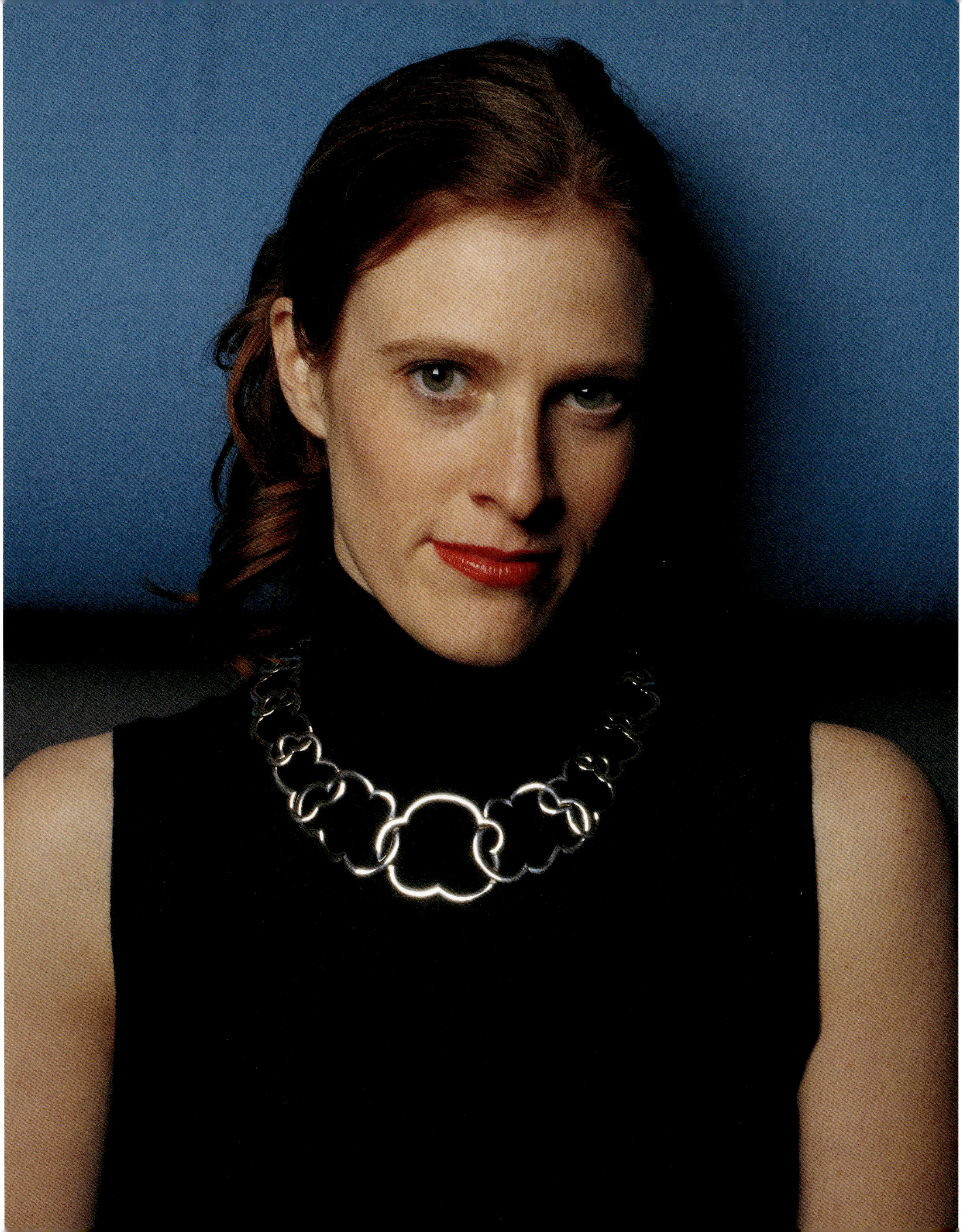

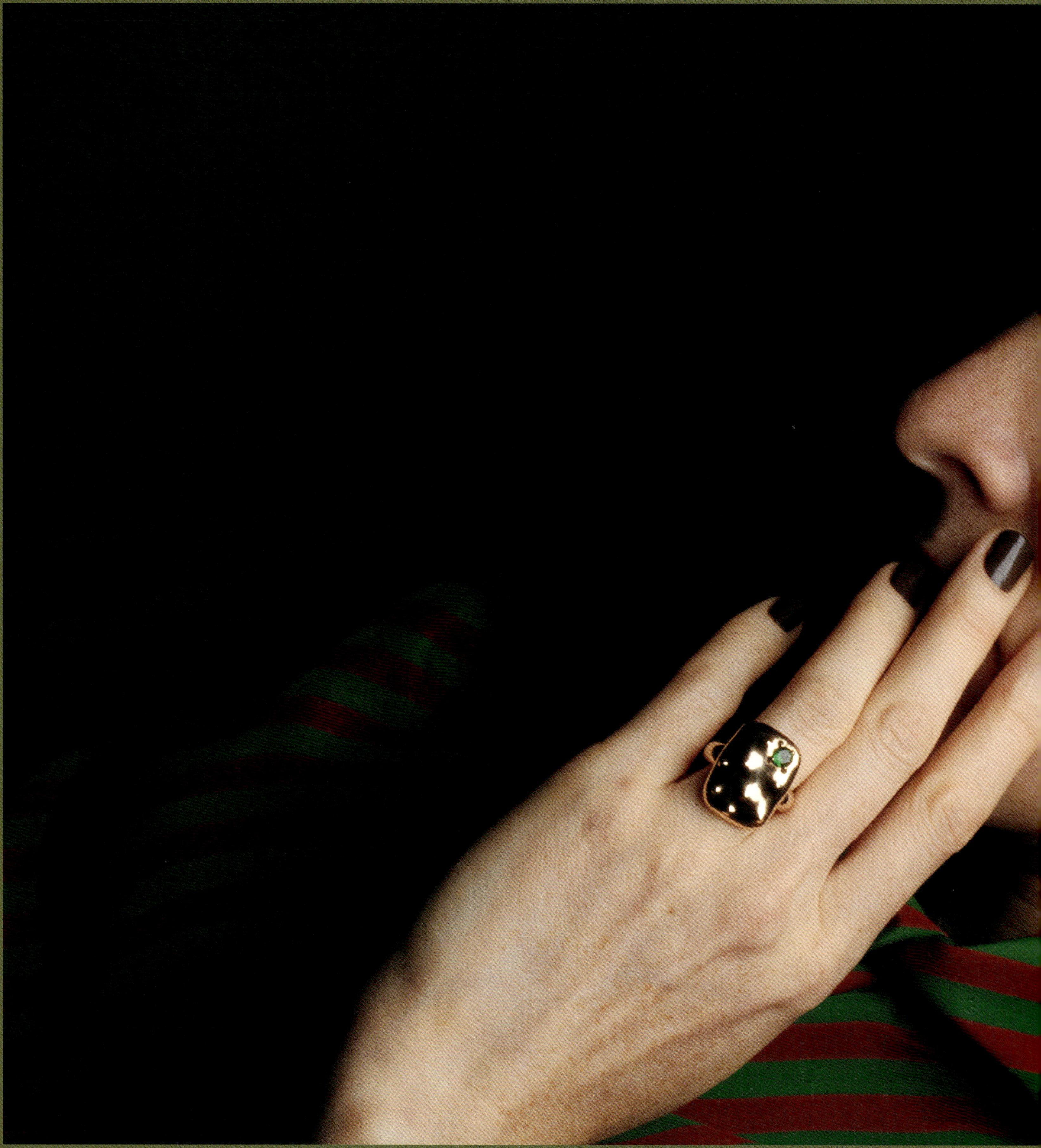

Cora Sheibani modelling her *Small Cactus with Flower Ring* (2018) in rose gold and tsavorite, and *Hoop Earrings* (2018) in rose gold, lavender jadeite, and rough-edged emerald slice. In 2017, Cora Sheibani was commissioned to design jewellery using a selection of diamonds owned by a client. Two matching diamonds were selected and set as earrings inside a pair of white jadeite hoops held by looped, gold wire prongs. They were the first in a series of pieces designed to feature these elements.

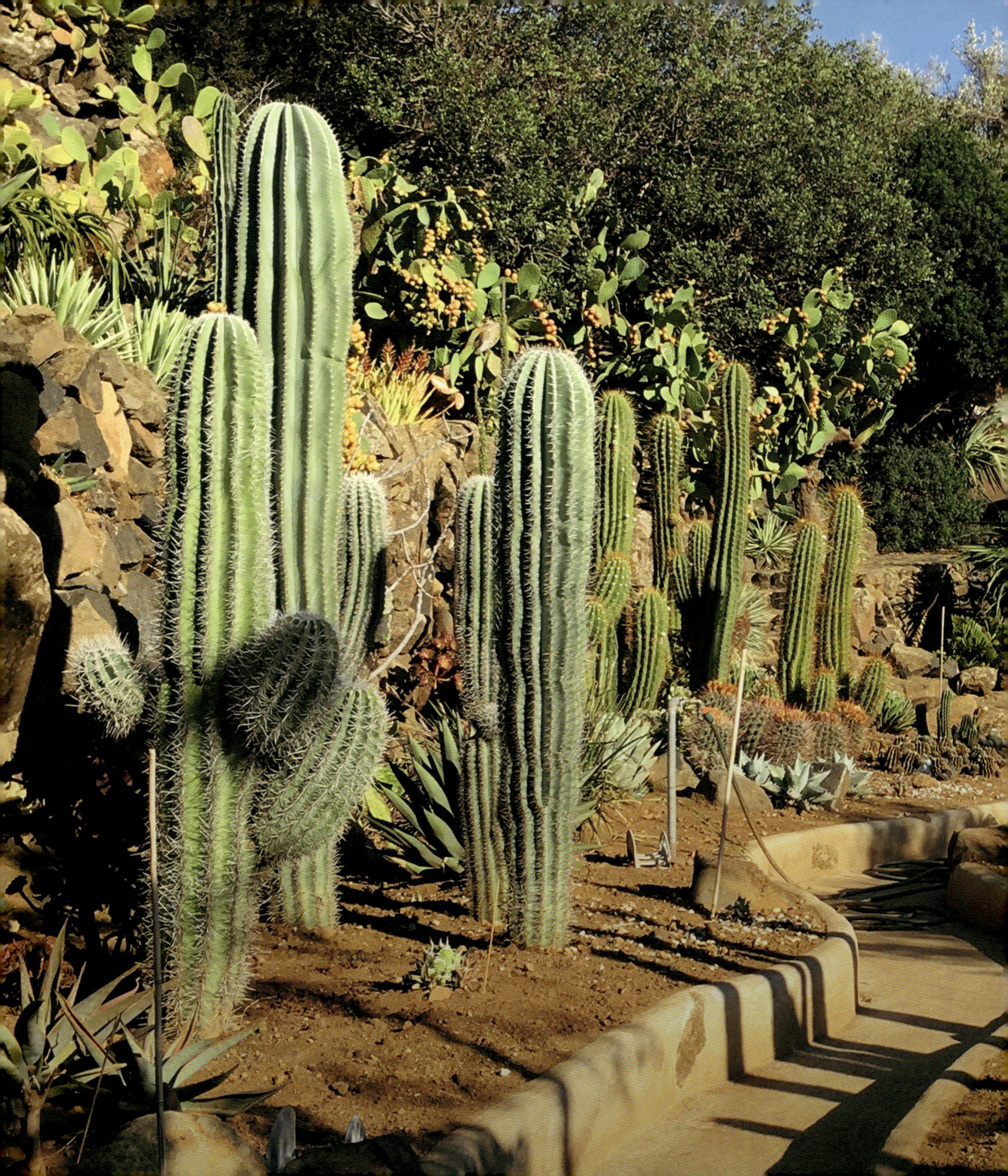

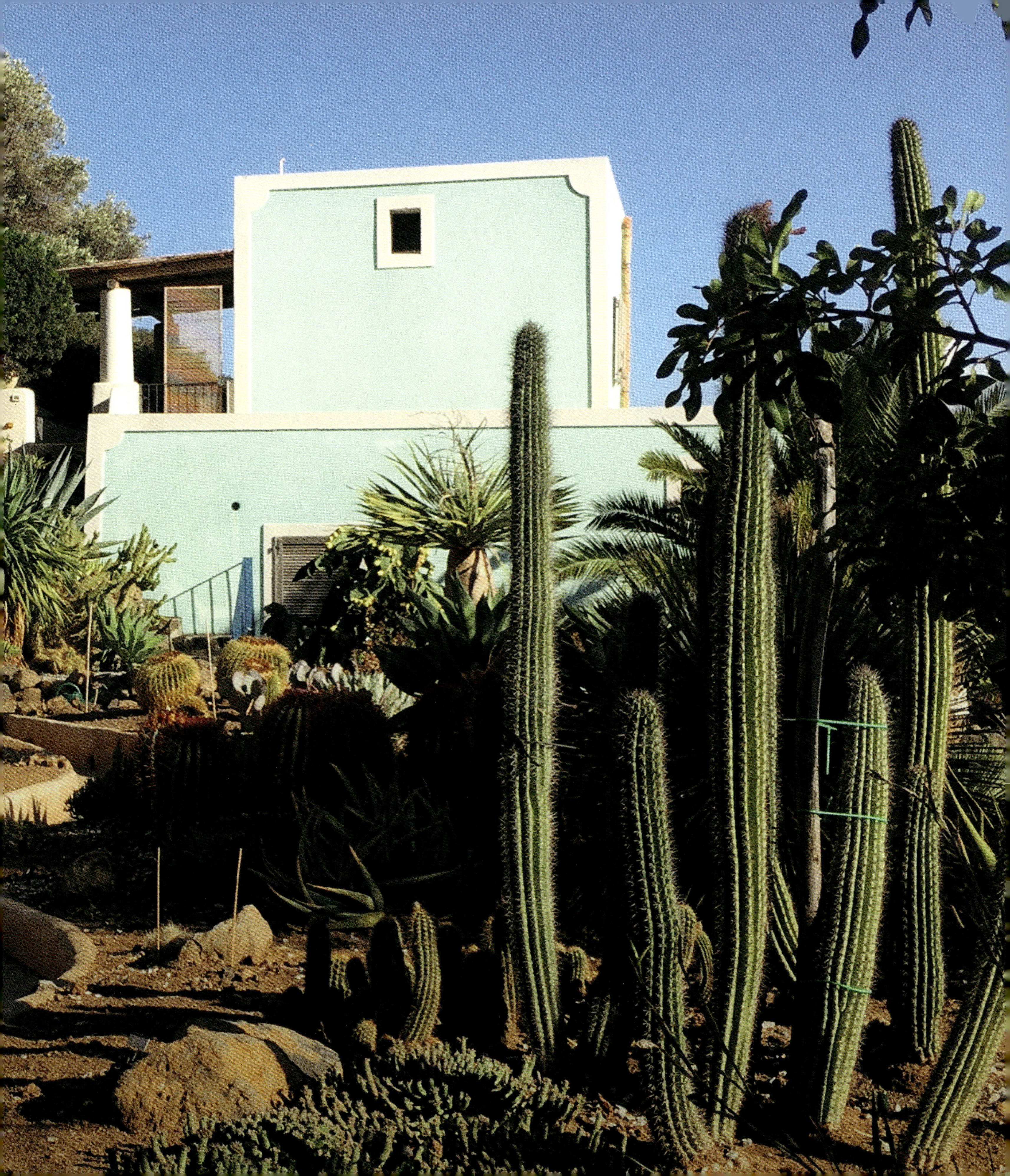

CACTACEAE

Green Texan Cactus Leaf Ring, 2020
yellow gold, nephrite, blue sapphires

The inspiration for the 'Cactaceae' collection was Filicudi, an arid, windblown island in the Aeolian archipelago off the northern coast of Sicily where Opuntia cacti (prickly pears from Mexico) grow in the wild and where her mother has cultivated an extensive cactus garden. The catalyst, however, was more prosaic – a window box of potted cacti outside a jewellery dealer's office in London. Immediately captivated, she began to plant them at home in south-facing window boxes where everything else seemed to have trouble thriving: 'I really like these little survivors that multiply in numbers, bloom at unexpected moments in an array of colours and have the most amazing graphic shapes.'

Cora started sketching ideas for the collection in October 2011 – initially for bracelets as there were none in her previous two collections. These were distilled into a few stylised cactus motifs and subsequently prototypes which could be used as the basis for cocktail rings and earrings or combined to form a bracelet. As with the 'Copper Mould' and 'Clouds with a Silver Lining' collections, the designs are graphic representations rather than realistic copies.

'Cactaceae' features a toned-down colour palette combining mainly green stones with yellow, rose and white gold. The collection comprising bracelets, rings and earrings was developed in Paris with goldsmith Michel Paullin who made prototype models first before casting them in gold. Michel, who was introduced to Cora by her friend Kate Daudy, spoke not a word of English so she communicated with him via drawings and a limited vocabulary until she took up French lessons to reacquaint herself with the language.

The initial stone chosen to represent the fleshy leaf of the cactus was Siberian nephrite, a translucent green type of nephrite jade with black inclusions individually carved by Gustav Caeser in Idar-Oberstein, Germany or by his Hong Kong partners. Alternative green-hued stones used later in the collection are amazonite and chrysoprase.

Other pieces are made in spikey yellow, rose and white gold or else set with an array of faceted green tsavorites. One of the most elegant rings in the collection (see page 102) is one that represents a prickly pear in bloom, cast in polished yellow gold and set with a single green tsavorite flower. Here Cora is playing her favourite game of contradiction by switching around the colours as they occur in nature – from a green cactus leaf and yellow flower to a yellow cactus leaf and green flower.

2012

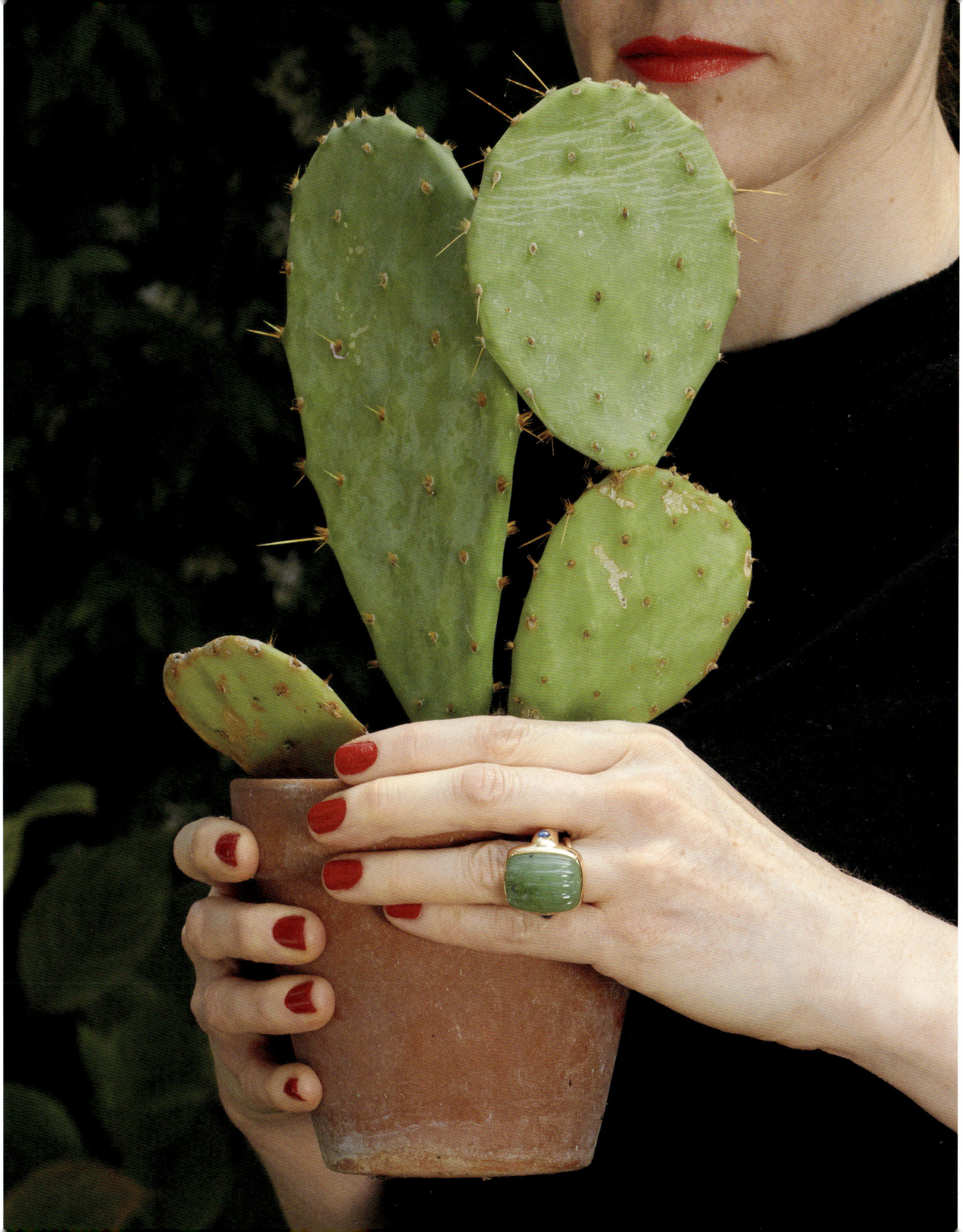

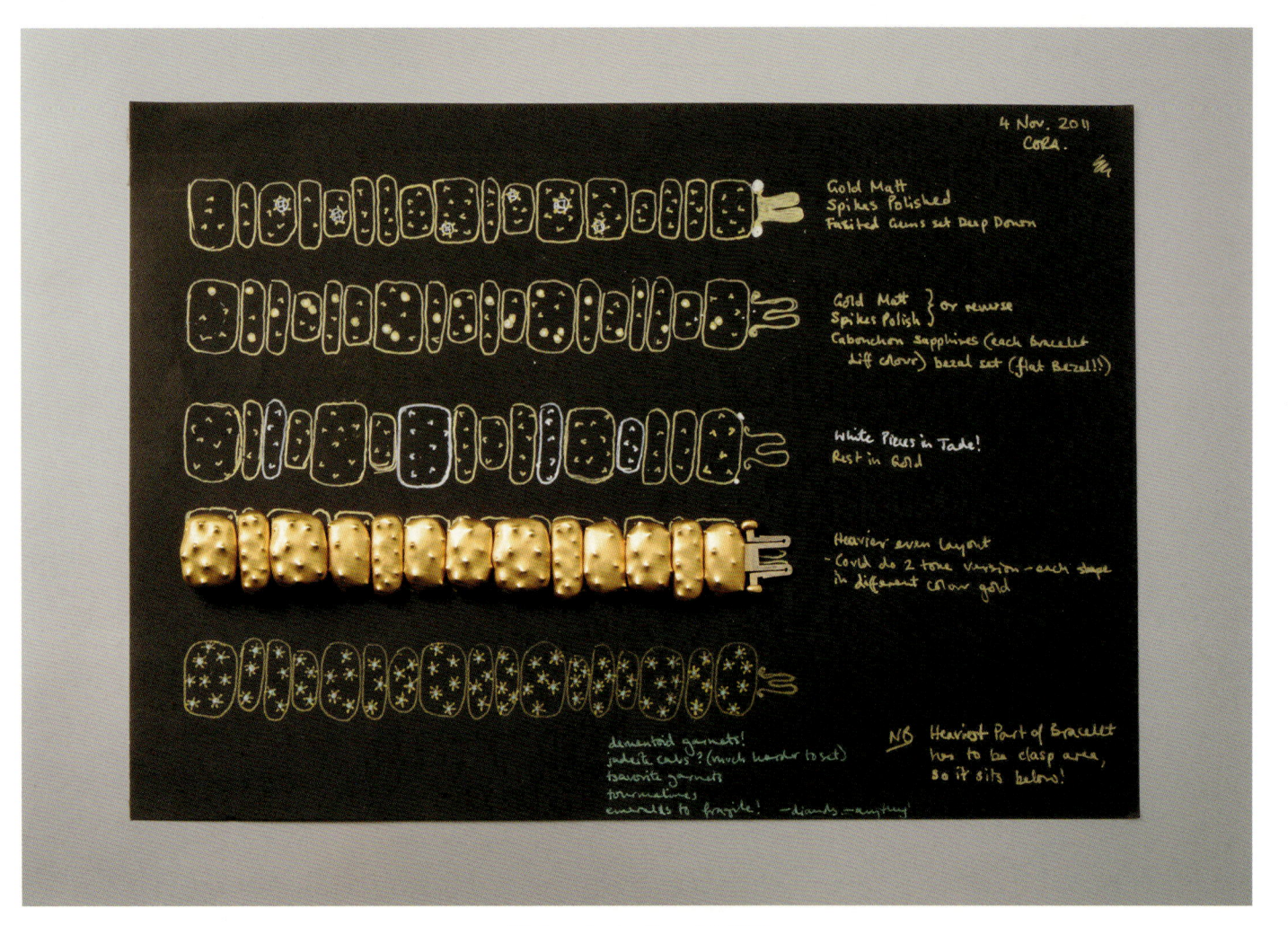

Mexican Cactus Bracelet, 2013
matt yellow gold
Cactus Bracelet sketches, 2011

CACTACEAE

The setting of small stones into polished gold can be messy, but Cora employed an 'Étoilé' technique used to great effect by Van Cleef & Arpels during the 1930s and 1940s to overcome the problem. The setter said he hadn't used such an 'outdated' method since his apprenticeship, but this didn't deter Cora, who admires the way jewellery used to be made and doesn't believe in cutting corners. Moreover, she knew this technique would lend itself to the collection because the engraved spiky grooves, made after setting the stones, could be elongated to conveniently mimic the spines on an Opuntia cactus.

'I used it because they look like cacti spikes, but the setter made them longer and thinner to look more spikey than usual.' 'Cactaceae' was launched in Basel, Switzerland at a townhouse belonging to Galerie von Bartha. It was a soft launch and much of the collection was produced later over an extended period of time. The collection was later accompanied by a 'gardening' book designed by Carolina Vargas with photography by Gisela Torres. In exchange for doing the photography, Cora collaborated with Gisela on a short surrealist movie 'Moonlight Cactus'. The film was shot in Cora's house and her children, returning from school, were highly amused to find their mother posing in front of the camera wearing a scuba diving-like top and pretending to eat a cactus leaf.

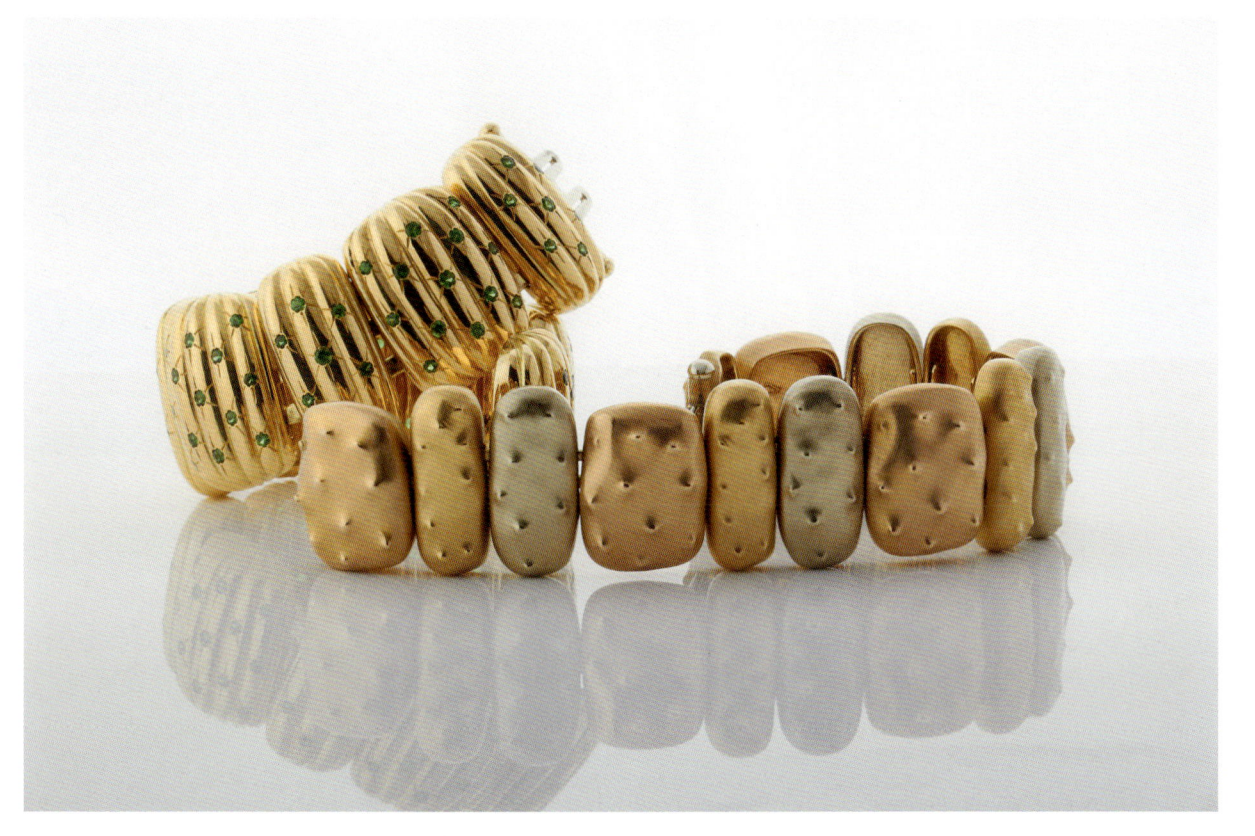

Texan Cactus Bracelet, 2019
yellow gold, tsavorite garnets

Mexican Cactus Bracelet, 2019
matt white gold, rose gold, yellow gold

Cactus Head Ring, 2018
rose gold, pink spinels

Mexican Cactus Bracelet, 2019
white gold, rose gold, yellow gold

BELOW
FROM LEFT TO RIGHT
Petra Cactus Earring, 2012
yellow gold, tumbled green tourmaline

Cactus Head Ring, 2012
white gold, diamonds

Mexican Cactus Bracelet, 2012
matt yellow gold

Green Leaf Cactus Ring, 2013
rose gold, nephrite

Texan Cactus Bracelet, 2012
matt rose gold

Mexican Cactus Ring, 2012
matt white gold, tsavorite garnets

Cactus Cufflink, 2012
yellow gold

RIGHT
Sketches for *Cactus* necklaces, 2012

CACTUS
16.3.2012

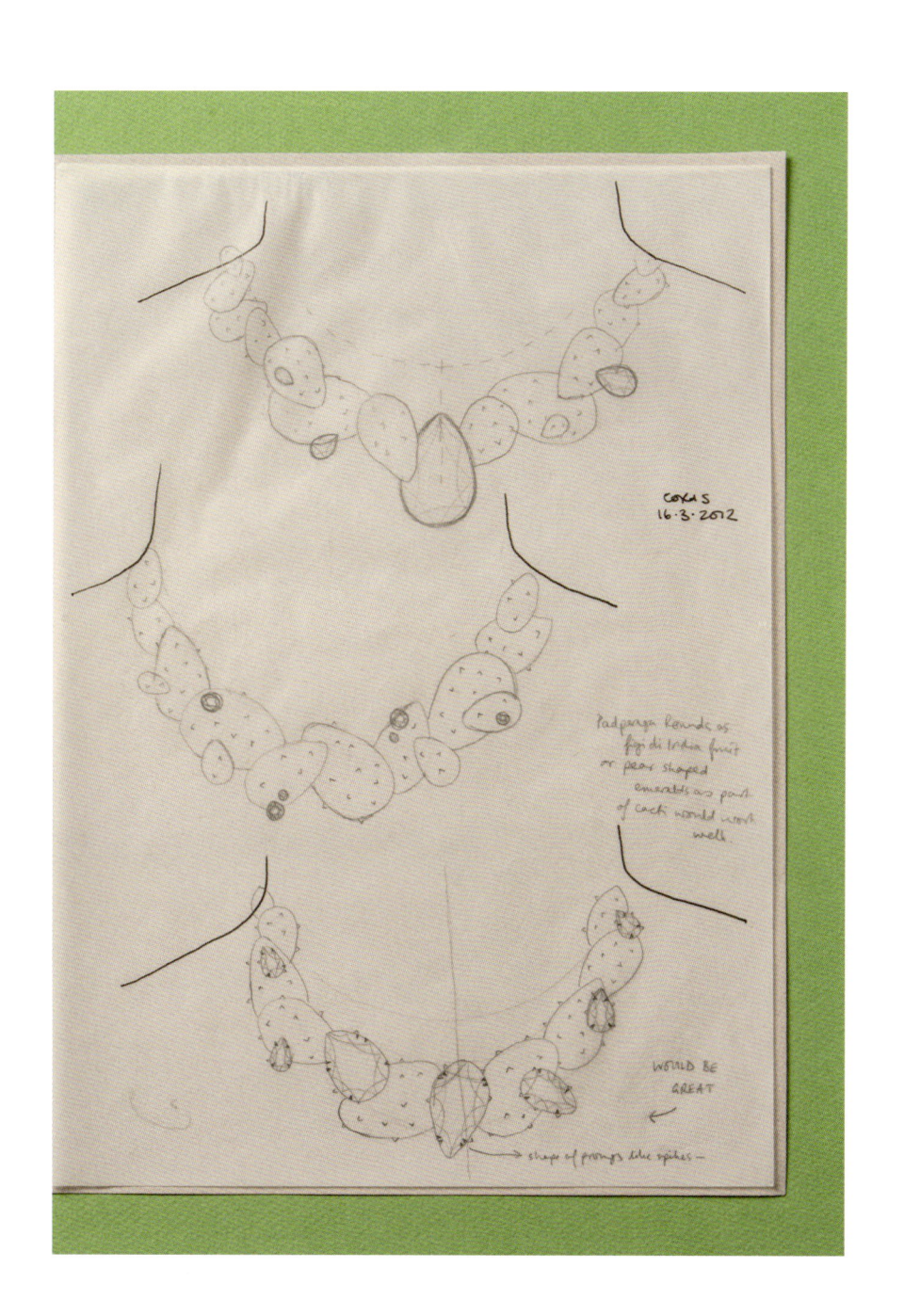

Padparga Rounds as figs di Indian fruit or pear shaped emeralds as part of cacti would work well

WOULD BE GREAT ←

← shape of prongs like spikes →

113

114

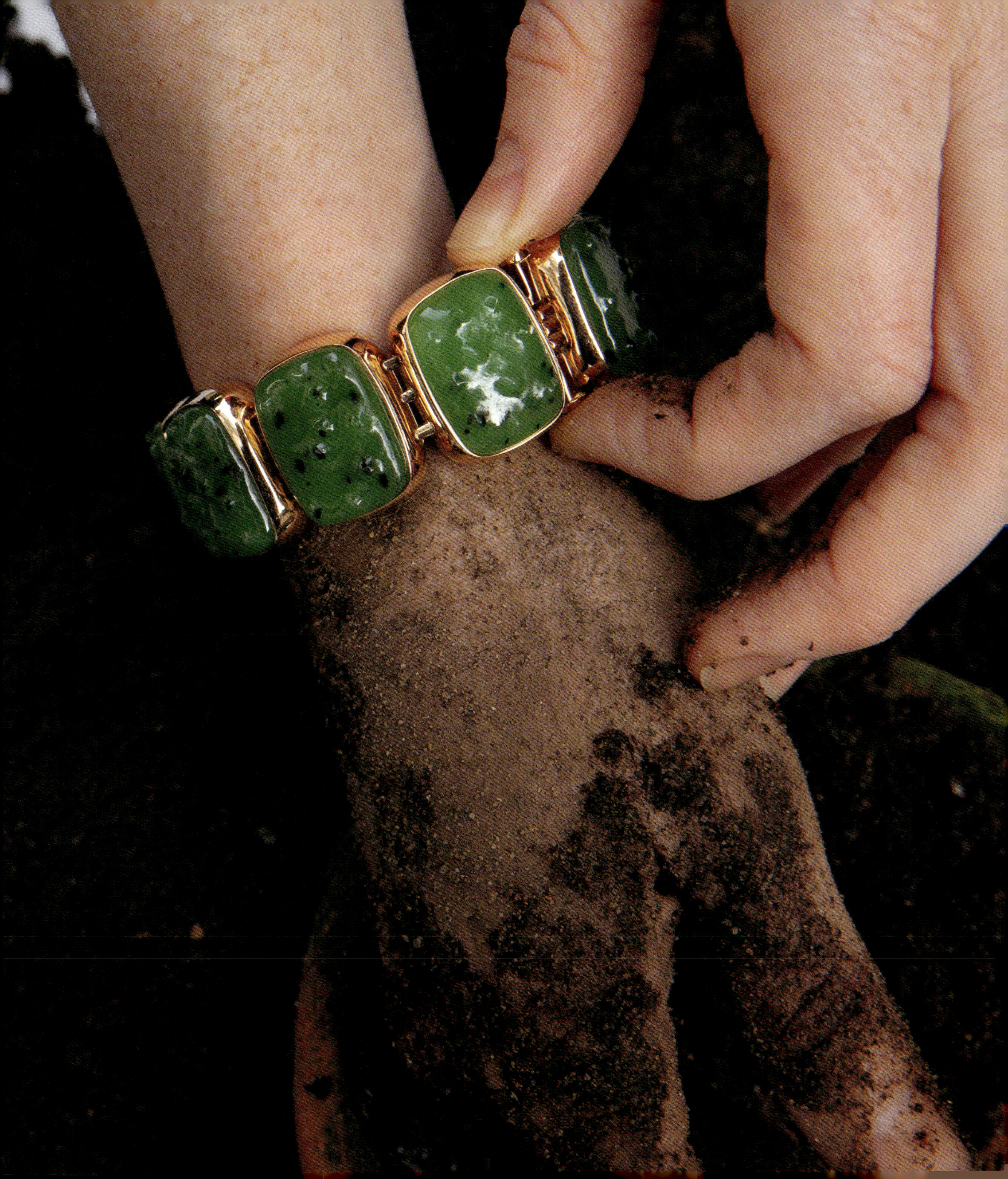

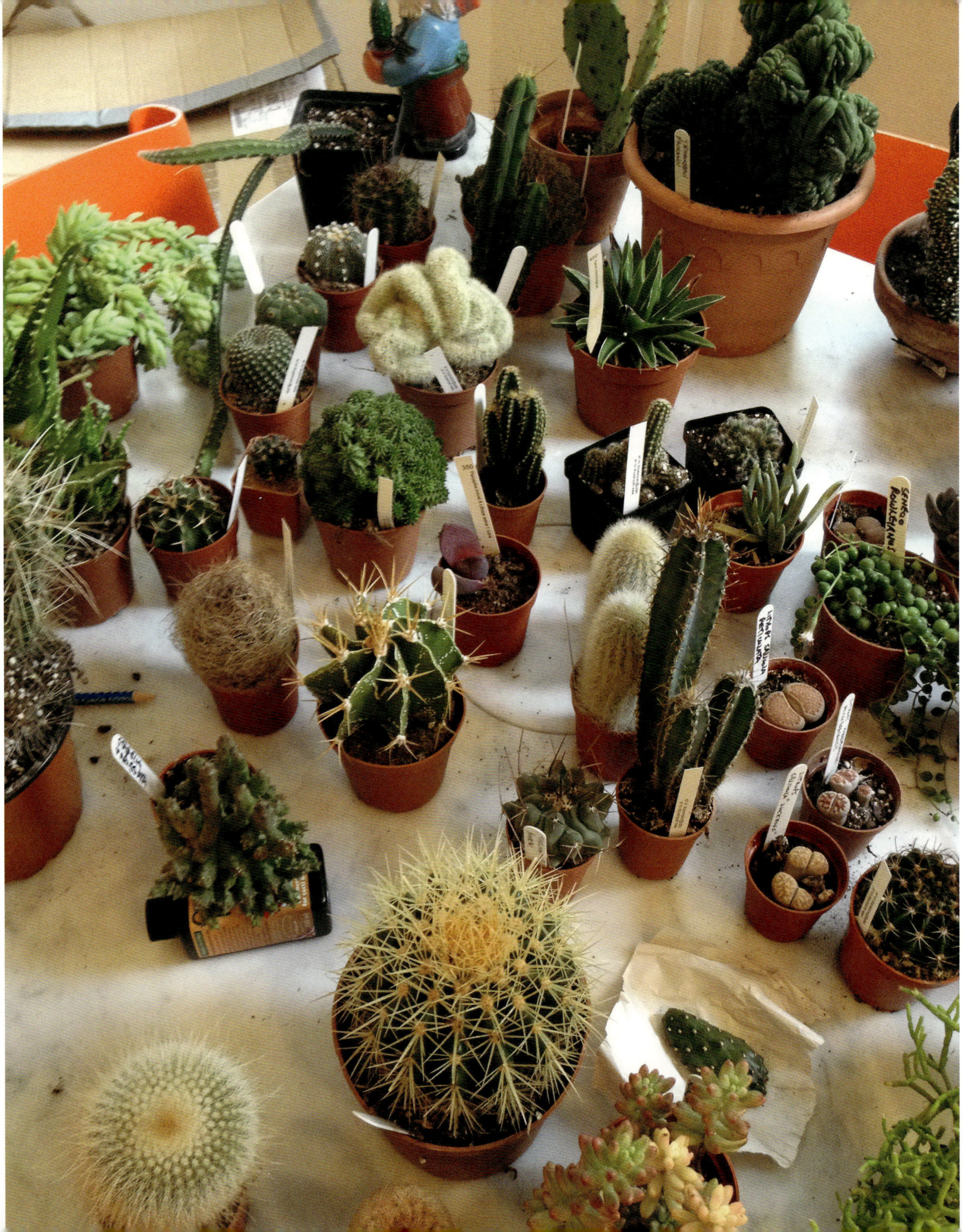

PP.114-115
Mexican Green Cactus Leaf Earrings, 2020
yellow gold, nephrite

Mexican Green Cactus Leaf Bracelet, 2012
rose gold, nephrite

LEFT
Cacti on Cora's kitchen table to be photographed for the *Cactaceae Collection Book*, London, 2012

RIGHT
Green Texan Cactus Leaf Bracelet, 2018
rose gold, nephrite

NEXT PAGE
Image from collection catalogue picturing *The Observer's Book of Cacti and Other Succulents* by S.H. Scott

Cactus Cufflinks, 2012
yellow gold

Plate 36. *Lophophora Williamsii*. P.71

length of the stem. A particularly attractive species, dark green with whitish tubercles on the outer face of the leaves.

Haworthia Reinwardtii. Forms elongated rosettes. The leaves are triangular with a narrow base, dark green with numerous white tubercles arranged in regular transverse lines. A beautiful species.

Haworthia coarctata. The leaves form a spiral rosette the length of the stem, dark green, with small tubercles on raised longitudinal lines. The outside or back of the leaves is only sparsely covered with tubercles.

Haworthia attenuata. Has quite narrow, elongated leaves, with white tubercles in more or less broken transverse rows, more numerous on the outer face.

Haworthia fasciata. Similar to the preceding species. The rosettes are stemless, making many offsets. The leaves are numerous, up to $\frac{1}{2}$ inch broad and $1\frac{1}{2}$ inches long, rather shiny green with elongated pearly tubercles, which join together in transverse bands.

Haworthia limifolia. Forms rosettes, the leaves of which are about $1\frac{1}{2}$ inches long and $\frac{3}{4}$ inch broad at the base, lanceolate, and concave on the inner face. They are marked on both sides with 15 to 20 raised wavy transverse lines. The plant is dark green in colour.

Haworthia tessellata. Cape Province. The leaves are arranged in three series in stars, and are 1 to $1\frac{1}{2}$ inches long, by about $\frac{1}{2}$ inch broad, recurving from the base. The upper surface the leaf is almost transparent with darker transverse and longitudinal veins, the edges finely toothed. This species is one of the most charming varieties of the genus.

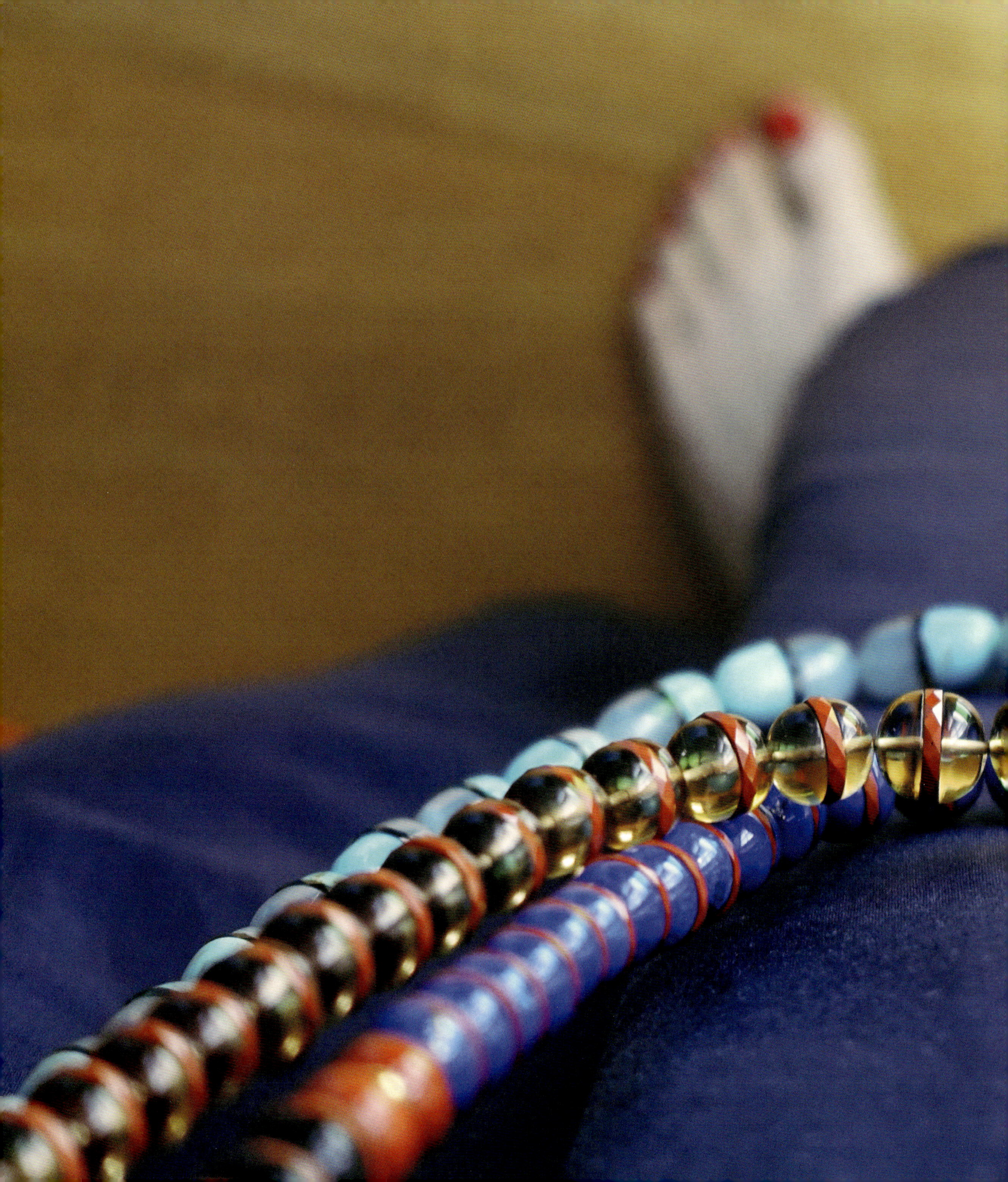

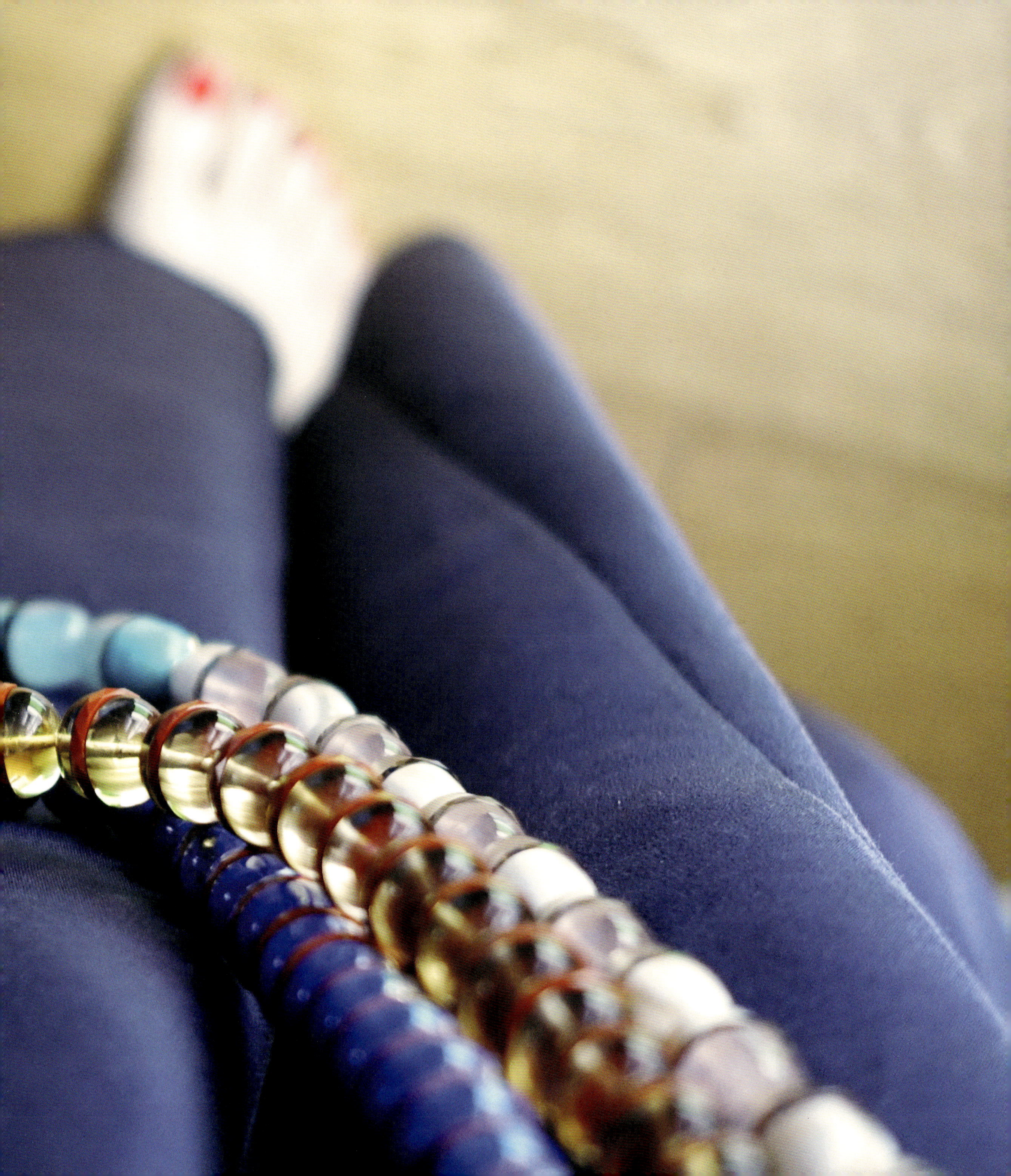

There was a four-year gap following the launch of back-to-back collections in 2011 and 2012. In the intervening period Cora Sheibani had her third child, Dara, and began to explore new themes and ideas while her friend, Carol Gardey, helped to promote her work and widen her client base.

The initial sketches for 'Colour & Contradiction' were undertaken in October 2014 but the collection took longer than usual to develop as the process required lengthy and detailed collaboration with stone dealers to source and cut stones to Cora's specifications. It was also the first time Cora had developed a collection with Anne Westhoff working full-time in the business.

'I think that allowed me to develop things in a much deeper way than I could on my own.'

'Colour & Contradiction' is different from other collections in that it is more about stone design than metal design and seizes on the contradiction of using faceted gold with polished stones rather than the other way round. The theme of contradiction was further explored by combining faceted opaque stones with polished clear stones when again the convention was to do the opposite.

'I liked the idea that usually you would facet the gemstone but here the metal was faceted rather than the clear gemstone.'

Having worked out the 'contradiction', Cora then turned her attention to the 'colour' by juxtaposing bold, contrasting stone combinations to create a collection where each piece is unique but equally where the potential for innovation is limited only by imagination and the variety of different materials available.

This edited excerpt comes from the introduction written by Cora in the accompanying colouring-in book and illustrates the process of inspiration, trial and error, and productive collaboration with goldsmiths and stone dealers necessary to realise the 'Colour & Contradiction' collection:

'In the spring of 2012, my Parisian goldsmith showed me a necklace that he had been asked to repair. It was made of brass and semi-spheres of rose quartz, intersected by slices of faceted smoky quartz. The necklace was large, heavy and imperfect, but it dazzled me. Later, analysing what so appealed to me about the necklace, I realised that I loved the faceted edge of the large discs of which only a sliver was visible.

'Inspired by this necklace, I started drawing many different types of jewellery with faceted discs cutting through curved

RIGHT
Early models and prototypes, 2014–15

BELOW
Cut-steel brooch, early 19th century
Cora's personal collection

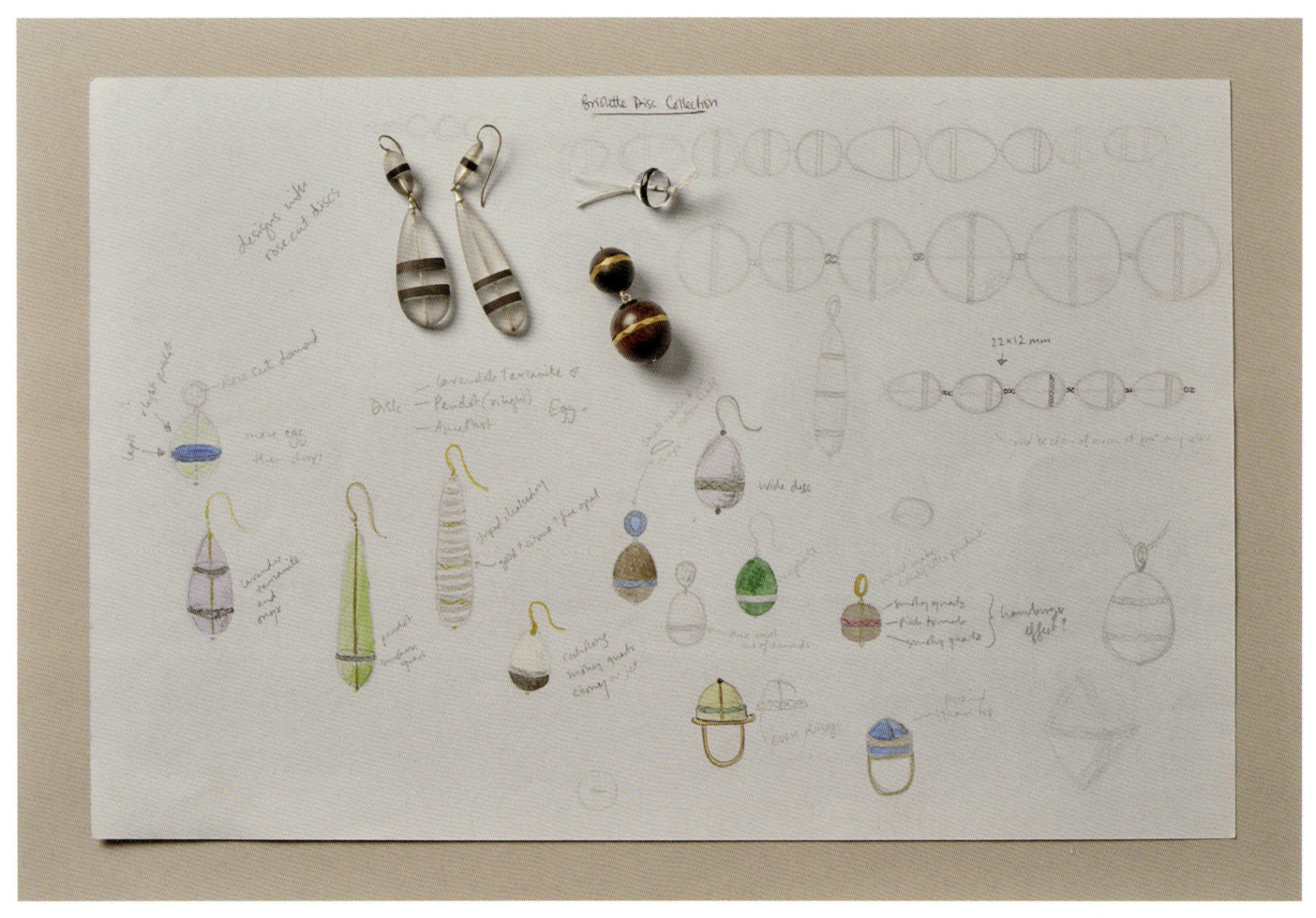

Prototypes and sketches for 'Colour & Contradiction' pieces, 2014

spaces. I bought wood beads and Perspex discs and tried out endless combinations but however much I tried, my initial results seemed heavy and old-fashioned compared to the quartz necklace I had seen. For a while I thought I would need to set aside the idea of contradicting form and texture, and not make the collection at all.

'Then I had the idea of faceting metal as well as stones. This idea came from cut-steel jewellery of the late 18th and 19th century that I first saw at the Victoria and Albert Museum. This jewellery is constructed out of hundreds of faceted steel nail heads, assembled together to mimic little sparkling diamonds or gemstones.

'When the first stone samples arrived after the summer, my desire to make a big chunky necklace like the one that inspired me disappeared and I was seized by the idea of wearing metres of small strands of coloured beads in rows, like Cleopatra. I thought up endless colour combinations and

COLOUR & CONTRADICTION

persuaded my stone dealer to make me samples of every possible stone we could use (24 different stones were delivered initially). We spent (and still spend) countless days in the office trying out endless different combinations. Opaque, clear and translucent stones can be matched in more ways than I had imagined.'

Each piece of jewellery in 'Colour & Contradiction' is made in a unique colour combination, as are all Cora Sheibani jewels. But with this collection an almost endless and wonderful variety of individual alliances of stones and beads is possible. The most striking pieces in the original collection are undoubtedly the triple-row 'C&C' *Acorn* and *Pill* necklaces, which are closed by an invisible gold bayonet clasp allowing the wearer to connect the separate strands together as one. Other standout designs include the *Lozenger Ring* and *Almond Earrings*.

The launch was held at Andrea Caratsch's Galerie space in Zurich. It is by far the largest collection to-date in terms of the number of models available.

The collection was then presented at Design Miami in a concept space featuring custom-made 'colouring-in' wallpaper designed to complement *Colour & Contradiction Jewellery: A Colouring Book,* which was launched to promote the collection at the same time. The idea was to allow visitors to take coloured pens that matched a template of coloured stones available and choose their own combinations on the wallpaper.

'Letting customers choose their own colour combinations has proven to be very popular...they have opinions and enjoy the process of customising their own jewellery.'

Later Cora made a collection of larger but more affordable necklaces made from wooden beads with faceted silver, bronze or copper discs. As this simple and inexpensive design did not allow for endless variations, Cora decided not to restrict the number of editions to be made and thus a new 'Unlimited' sub-brand was born.

An array of loose cabochon stones for *Lozenger* rings, 2019

Cora in her Curio colouring-in booth at Design Miami, November 2016
Visitors to the fair were encouraged to colour in jewels on the custom-made wallpaper
photograph by James Harris

A selection of various 'Colour & Contradiction' pieces displayed over an A3 photocopy of Cora's arm in her custom-made portable wireless display case

BELOW
FROM LEFT TO RIGHT
Cleo Ring, 2018
faceted yellow gold, striped blue chalcedony, lapis lazuli

Lozenger Ring, 2021
faceted yellow gold, nephrite, snowflake obsidian

Cleo Ring, 2016
faceted yellow gold, lapis lazuli, chrysoprase

Lozenger Ring, 2019
faceted rose gold, amethyst, silex jasper

Lozenger Ring, 2021
faceted yellow gold, malachite, green opal

RIGHT
Triple Pill Necklace, 2019
yellow gold, dumortierite, orange moonstone, faceted silex jasper

Lozenger Ring, 2019
faceted rose gold, blue chalcedony, silex jasper

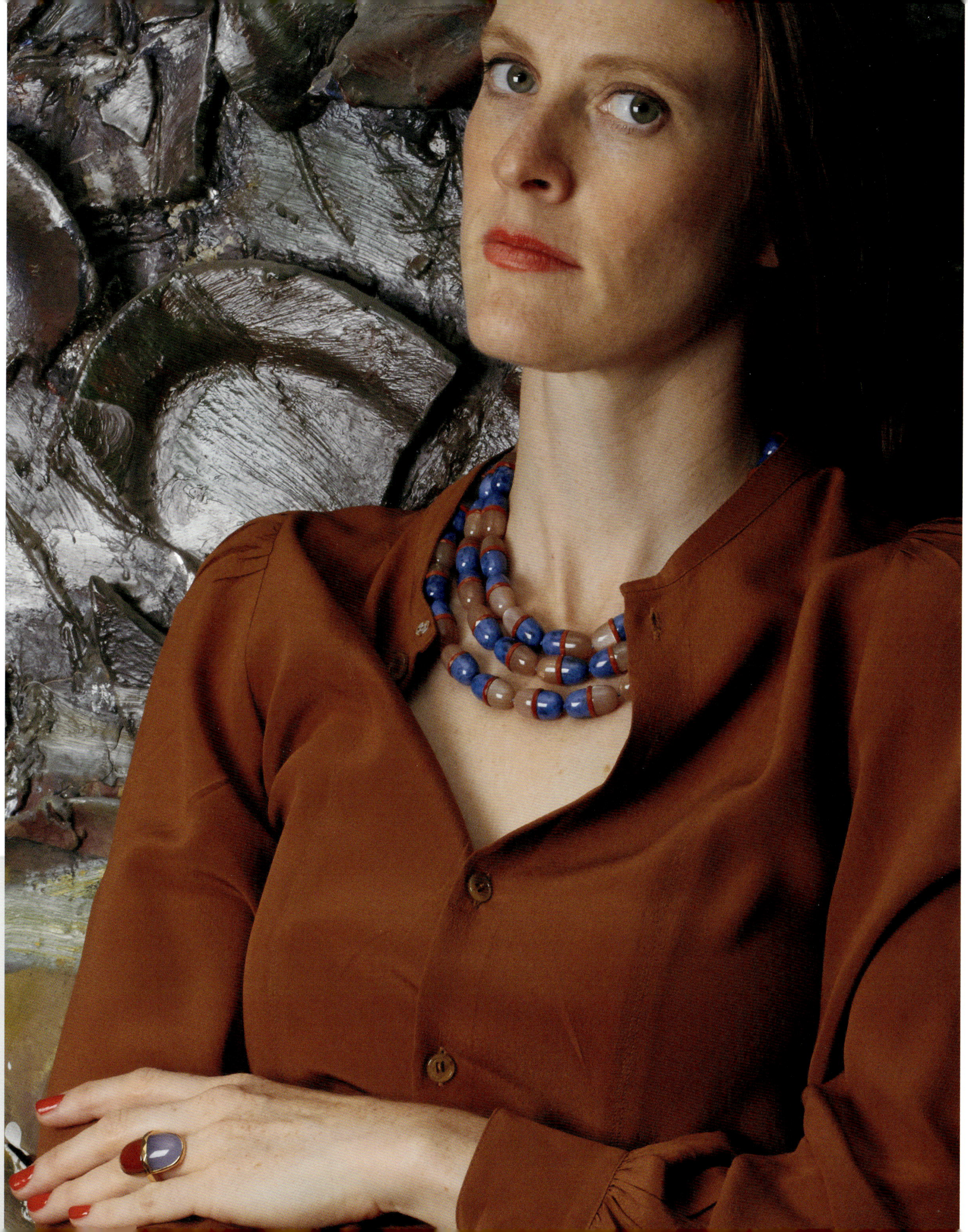

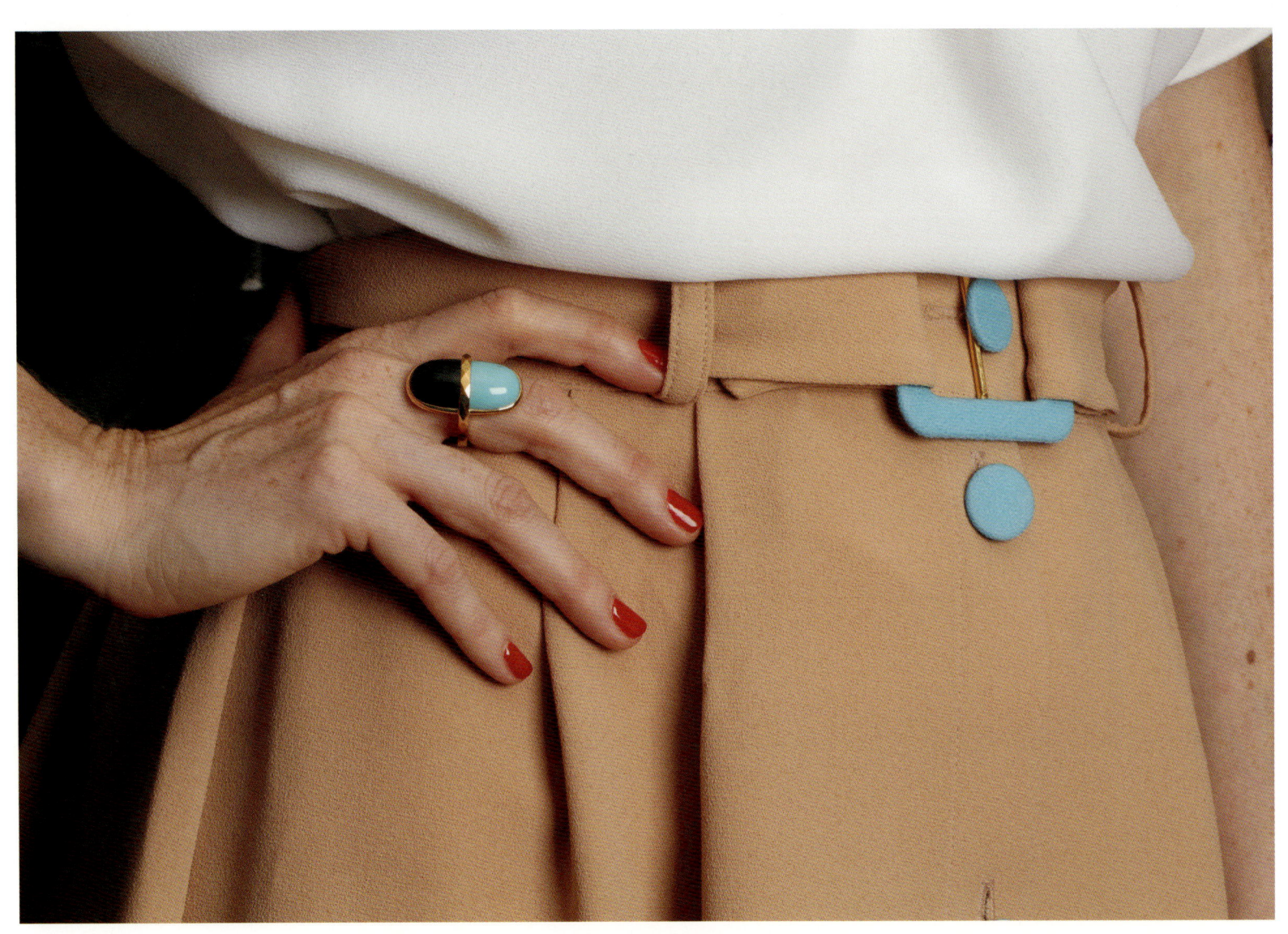

Lozenger Ring, 2015
faceted yellow gold, smoky quartz, turquoise

Triple Acorn Necklace, 2018
yellow gold, malachite, nephrite, faceted smoky quartz

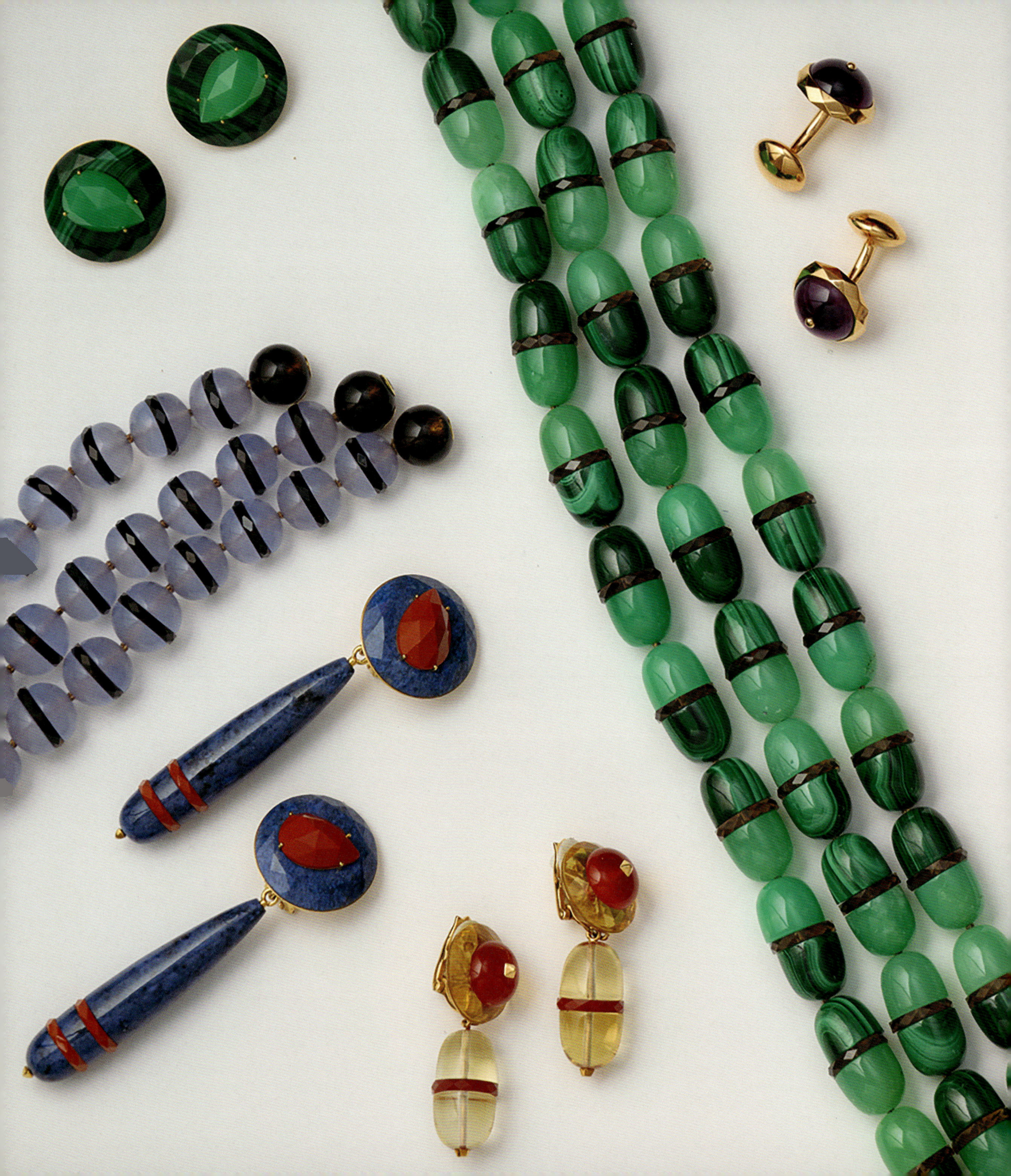

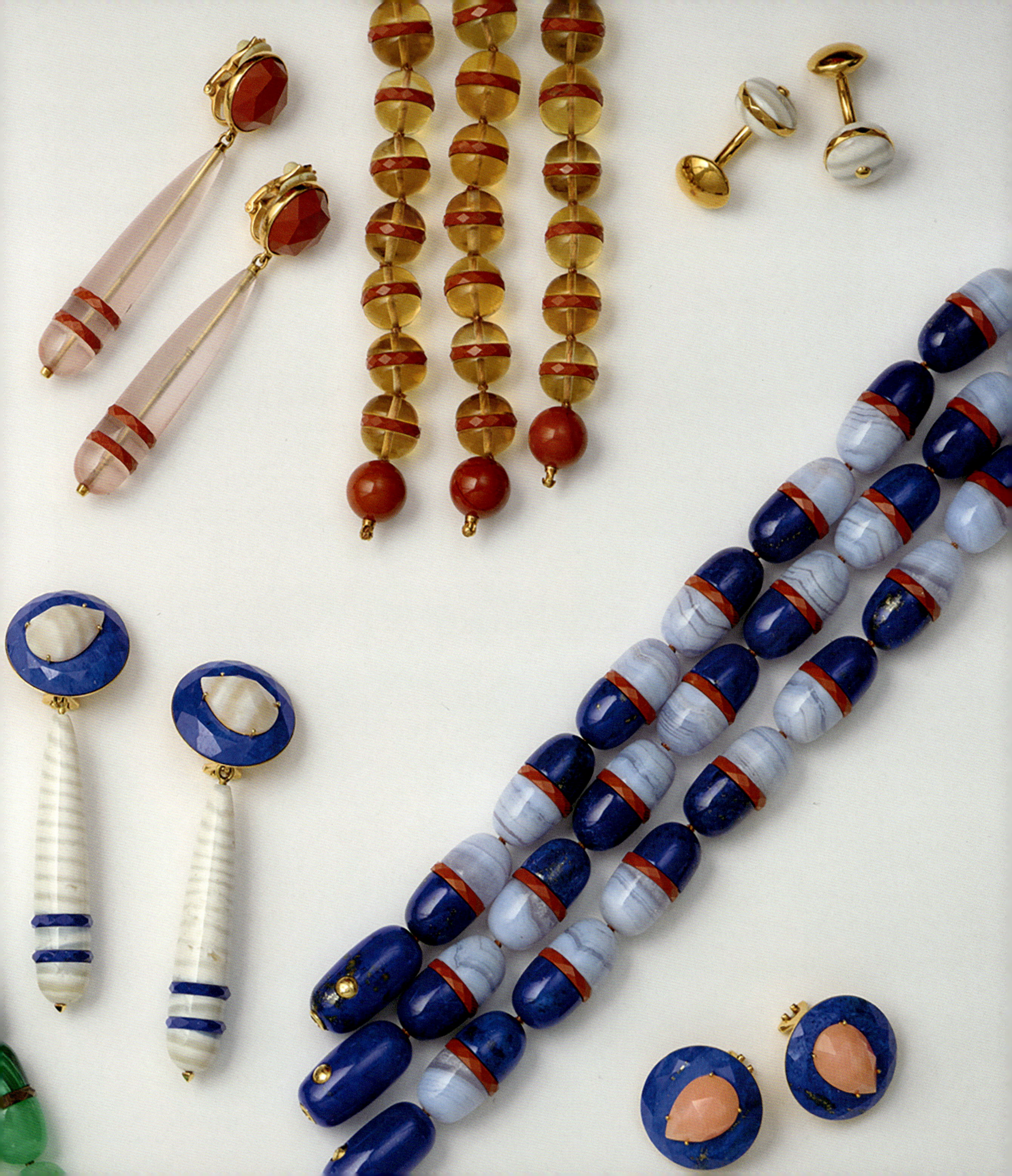

PREVIOUS PAGE
FROM TOP LEFT CLOCKWISE

Almond Earrings, 2019
yellow gold, faceted malachite,
rose cut chrysoprase

Triple Pill Necklace, 2022
yellow gold, chrysoprase,
malachite, faceted smoky quartz

Saucer Cufflinks, 2016
faceted red gold, amethyst

Long Drop Earrings, 2016
yellow gold, rose quartz, rose
cut and faceted silex jasper

Triple C&C Necklace, 2015
yellow gold, citrine, faceted silex
jasper

Burger Cufflinks, 2017
faceted yellow gold, striped
chalcedony

Triple Pill Necklace, 2021
yellow gold, striped blue
chalcedony, lapis lazuli, faceted
silex jasper

Almond Earrings, 2018
yellow gold, faceted lapis lazuli,
rose cut pink opal

Almond Long Drop Earrings, 2019
yellow gold, faceted lapis lazuli,
rose cut striped chalcedony

*Small Saucer with Pill Drop
Earrings,* 2016
yellow gold, citrine, carnelian

Almond Long Drop Earrings, 2019
yellow gold, dumortierite, rose
cut and faceted silex jasper

Triple C&C Necklace, 2019
yellow gold, blue chalcedony,
faceted smoky quartz

LEFT
Lozenger Ring, 2021
faceted rose gold, amethyst,
silex jasper

Cleo Ring, 2018
faceted yellow gold, striped blue
chalcedony, lapis lazuli

LEFT, BELOW
Burger Cufflinks, 2017
faceted yellow gold, striped
chalcedony

Two strands connected as one, of
a *Triple C&C Necklace*, 2015
yellow gold, citrine, faceted
silex jasper

Triple C&C Necklace, 2018
yellow gold, blue chalcedony,
faceted silex jasper

Triple Pill Necklace, 2015
yellow gold, silex jasper, faceted blue chalcedony

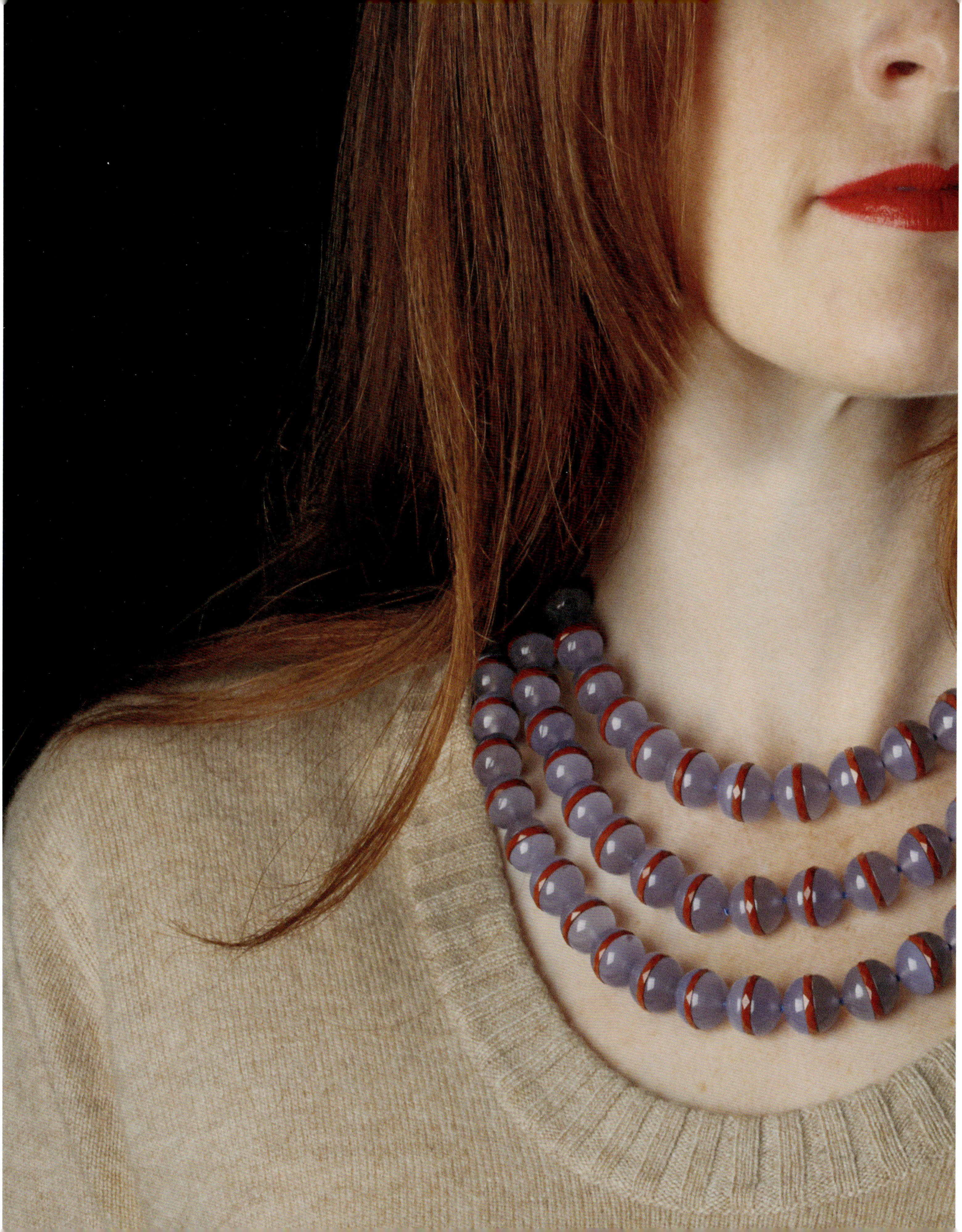

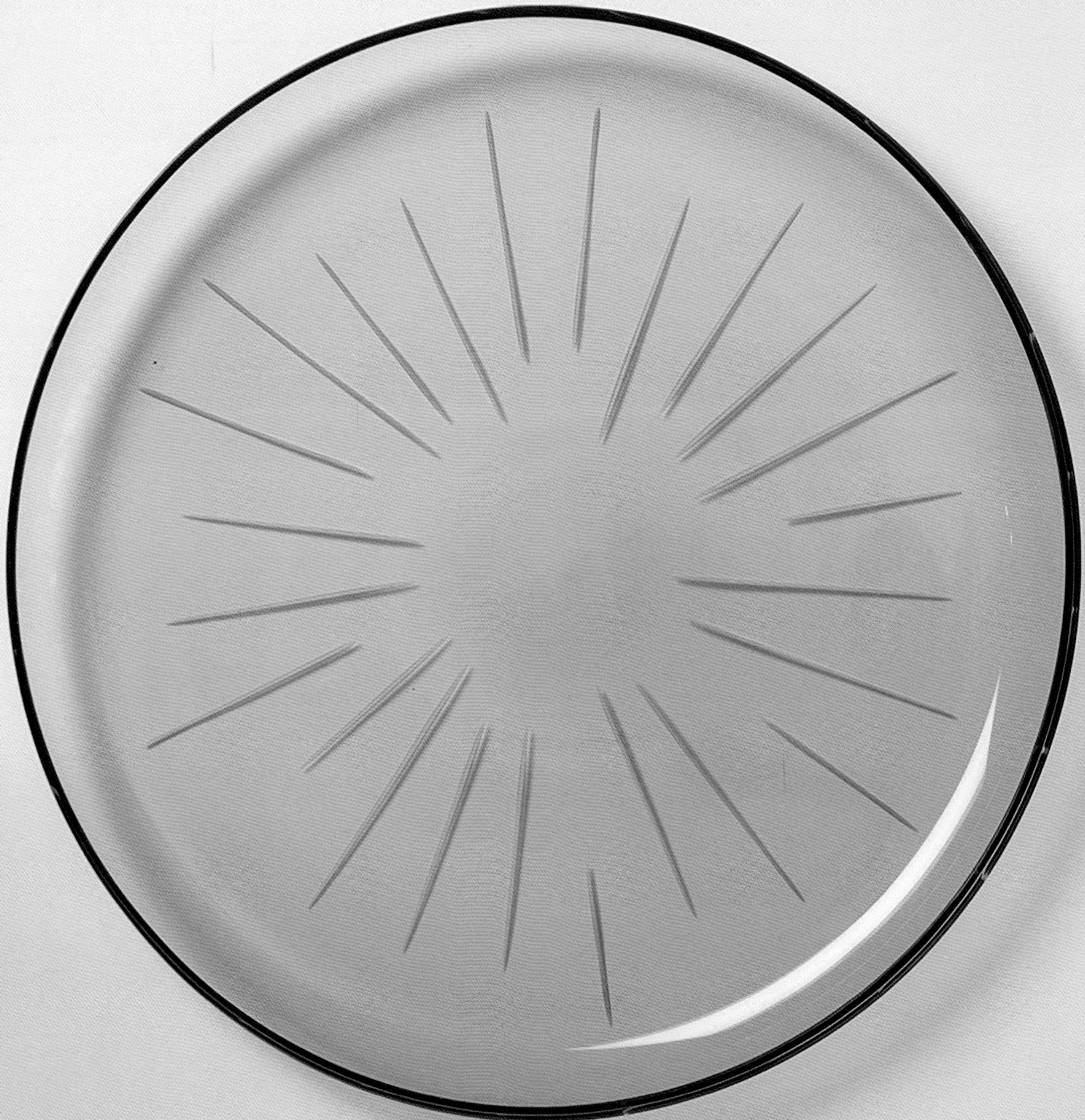

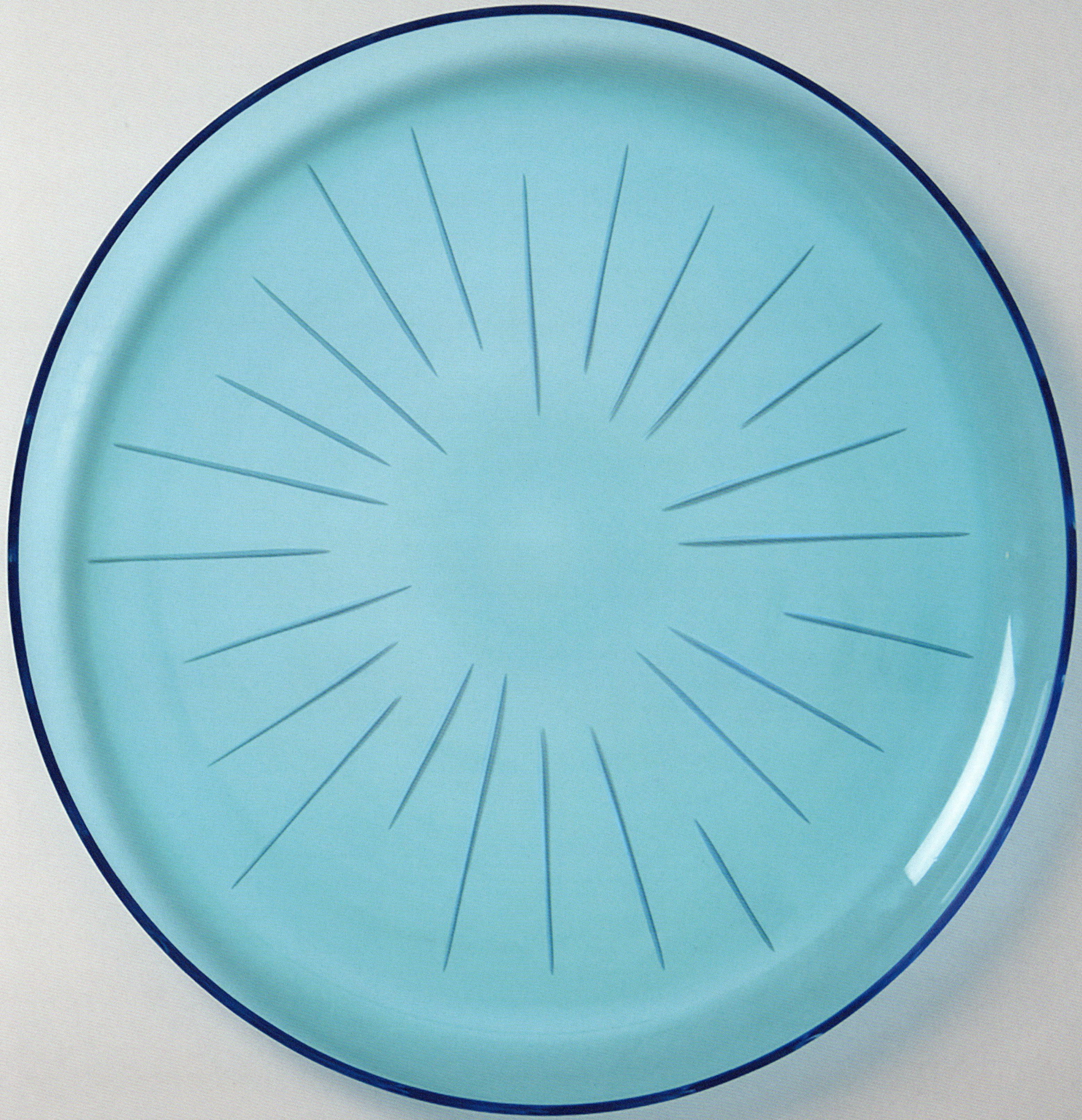

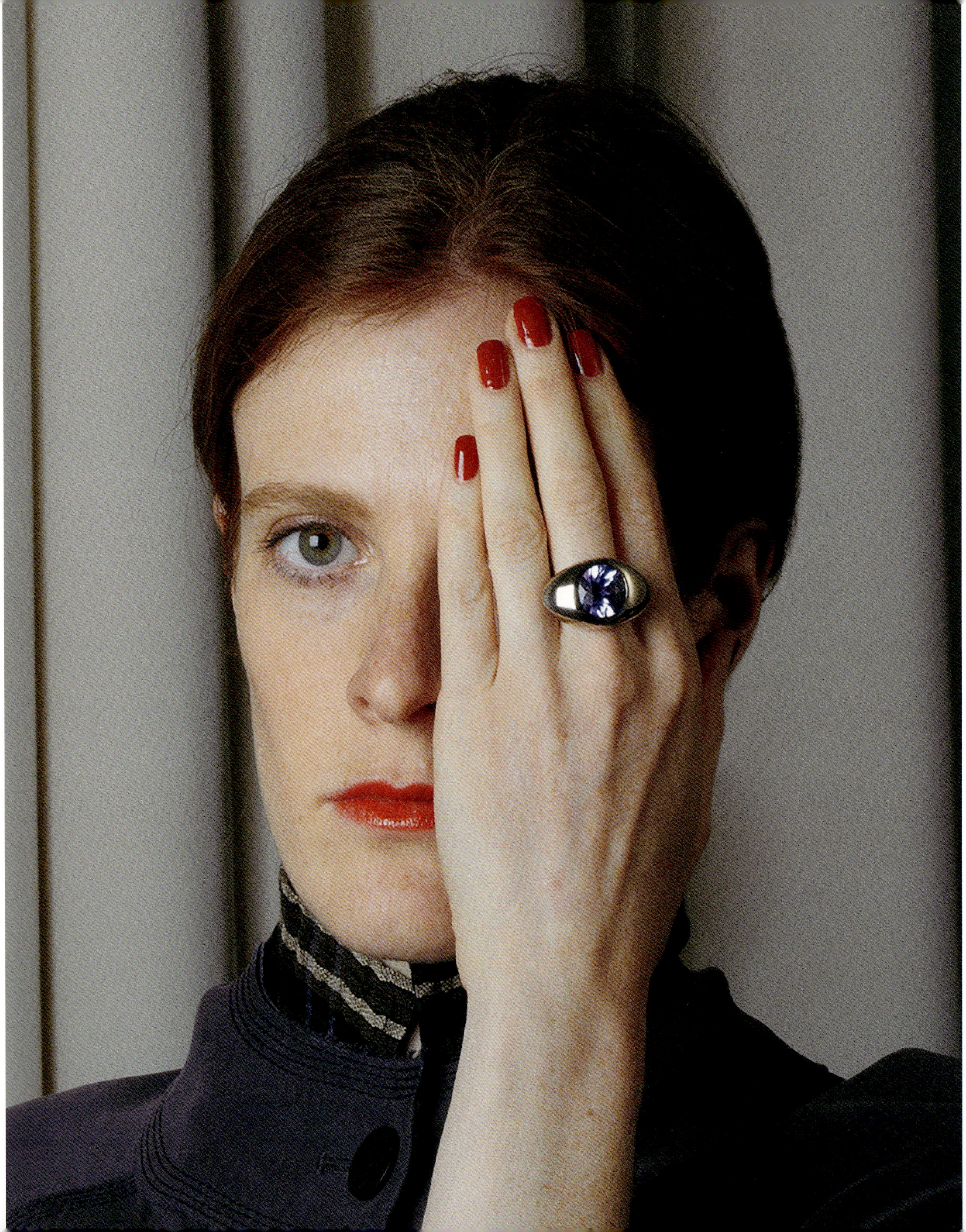

EYES

One day Cora was looking through her early sketchbooks and discovered a design for a silver tray.
'When you do Persian celebrations for weddings or New Year you set up a table and for this you require a large tray where you put different spices and such. And I remember for my wedding, my parents didn't have a big silver tray so in this early sketchbook was a design for a tray and I kind of felt that the design looked like an eye.'
This led to her designing a collection of silver holloware in 2014 featuring a central 'eye' in coloured Venetian glass. The inspiration for incorporating this material into the collection came from her friend, the artist Paola Petrobelli, who designs objects and lighting in Murano glass. Having made the first prototype silver tray, she set about designing a ring using a similar eye motif. It was at this juncture that Cora realised she did not have the money to manufacture nor the retail space to sell bulky items of silver tableware and decided to re-focus on what she does best – designing jewellery.
When embarking on a new collection, Cora is frequently motivated to design a piece she needs for herself so the initial idea for the 'Eyes' collection was to make a simple pinkie ring she could wear across the finger as ancient Greek rings were often worn. When it came to finalising the design, Cora was again inspired by rings from antiquity which often feature a double-faceted shank. She was also struck by the way a brilliant cut stone creates patterns not dissimilar to those seen in an iris.
The first pieces in the collection were a pair of 'pinkie' rings made in silver and set with synthetic blue sapphires. The idea was to wear them together, one on each little finger.
'We have two eyes after all so why not a pair of eye rings?'
Another reason for wanting to design a smaller ring was the realisation that large cocktail rings had become rather ubiquitous fashion accessories at the time. Using silver, however, proved to be too unstable and complicated to work with, so she quickly reverted to gold for future jewellery designs.
From here the 'Eyes' collection evolved from small rings to include larger and more elaborate rings, earrings and brooch-pendants featuring an array of different coloured gemstones set in yellow, rose and white gold. One of the things that occurred to Cora while developing the collection was that eye-shaped patterns occur in the animal kingdom – for example on a butterfly's wings. She also thought about

how at night, the only thing you see of nocturnal animals such as owls and wild cats are their eyes. These ideas were soon translated into animal eye-themed jewels.

Two pieces in the 'Eyes' collection were designed almost by accident. Cora had designed a *Butterfly Brooch-Pendant* (with three sets of 'eyes' on each wing) when it occurred to her that if you split the brooch in half the shape would work well as earrings. The *Butterfly Earrings* were conceived in a somewhat serendipitous manner but quickly became the best seller in the collection and her most successful earring design to date. Another beneficial outcome from this 'accidental' approach to design was that it was the first time Cora had made a pair of earrings that mirrored each other instead of being identical so the wearer's face was framed more beautifully. This was a valuable lesson learned and henceforth applied in future designs.

A second 'accidental' design for the 'Eyes' collection came about when Cora had two brown diamonds in the office to be used for a commission and was playing around with these and some newly arrived eye-motif waxes.

'We had these stones and Sebastian was coming to London with the rest of the prototypes for the collection. We placed them both on a larger piece he had made, and it looked like a mask and so a *Mask Ring* came about. It's a bit of an outlier in the collection but unlike a big jewellery house where everything has to fit into a box, I have the freedom to go off-piste like that.'

Further, more whimsical pieces in the 'Eyes' collection include a cross-over ring with two pear-shaped eye motifs, offset like the eyes in a Picasso painting; elongated, pear-shaped earrings which resemble fish fins; and *Owl Earrings* comprising quizzical, gold engraved 'eyebrows' perched above large, round 'wide-awake' eyes.

The full collection is based mainly around rings and earrings plus two additional brooch-pendant designs. A wide array of round, faceted gemstones have been used thus far to represent the iris (the coloured part of the eye) including brown diamonds, tourmalines, garnets, aquamarines, yellow beryls, a range of different coloured zircons and cat's eye chrysoberyl. The 'Eyes' collection was launched at a space in London at The Design Museum in September 2017.

P.140
Cyclops Ring, 2016
white gold, tanzanite

BELOW
Small Eyes Ring Set, 2018
yellow gold, reddish-brown spinels

RIGHT
Cora's home office with inspirations for the 'Eyes' collection

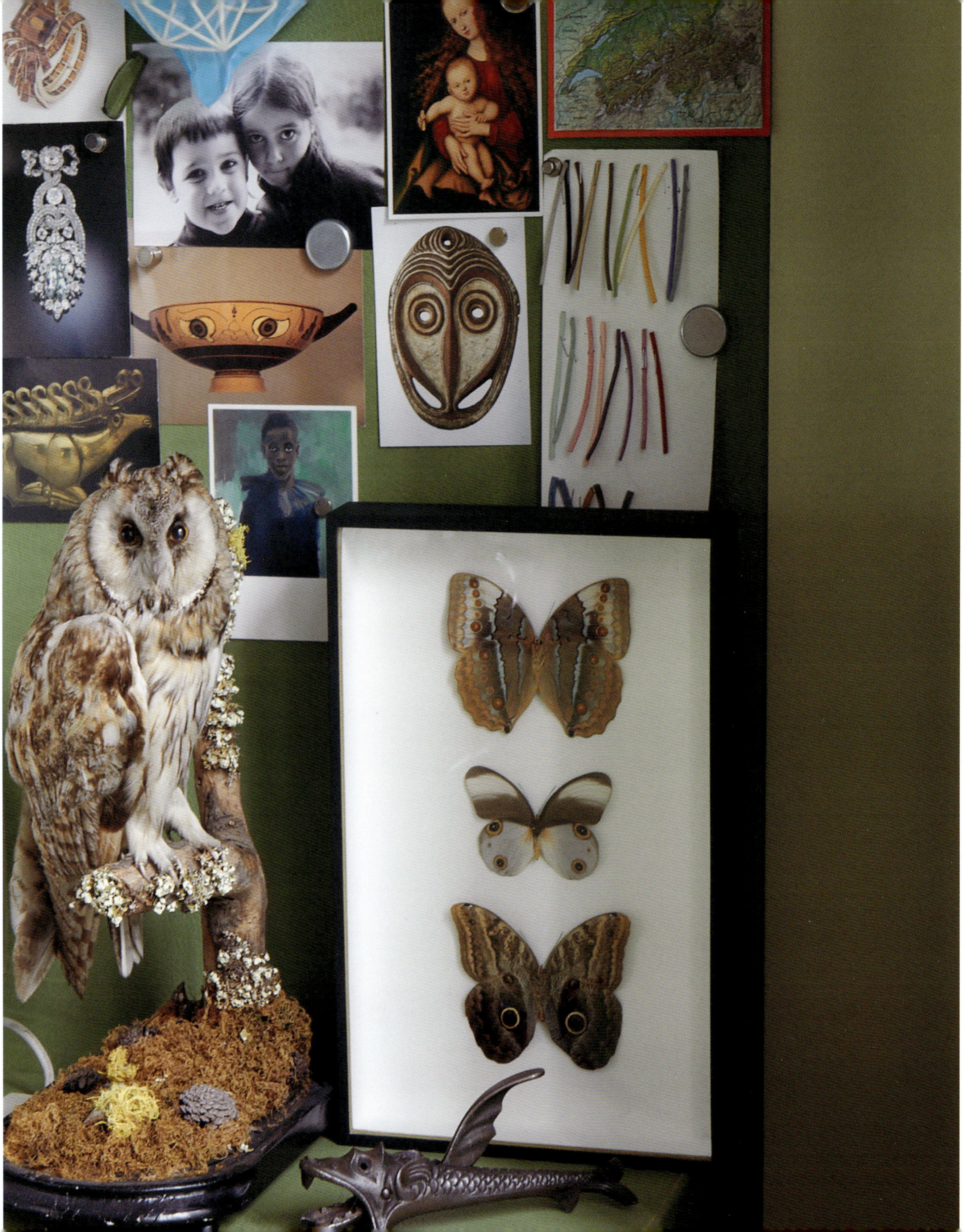

LEFT
Owl Earrings (with engraved eyebrows), 2018
yellow gold, peridots

BELOW
Wax models and prototypes for 'Eyes' pieces, 2016

Small Eyes Ring Set, 2017
white gold, spessartine garnets

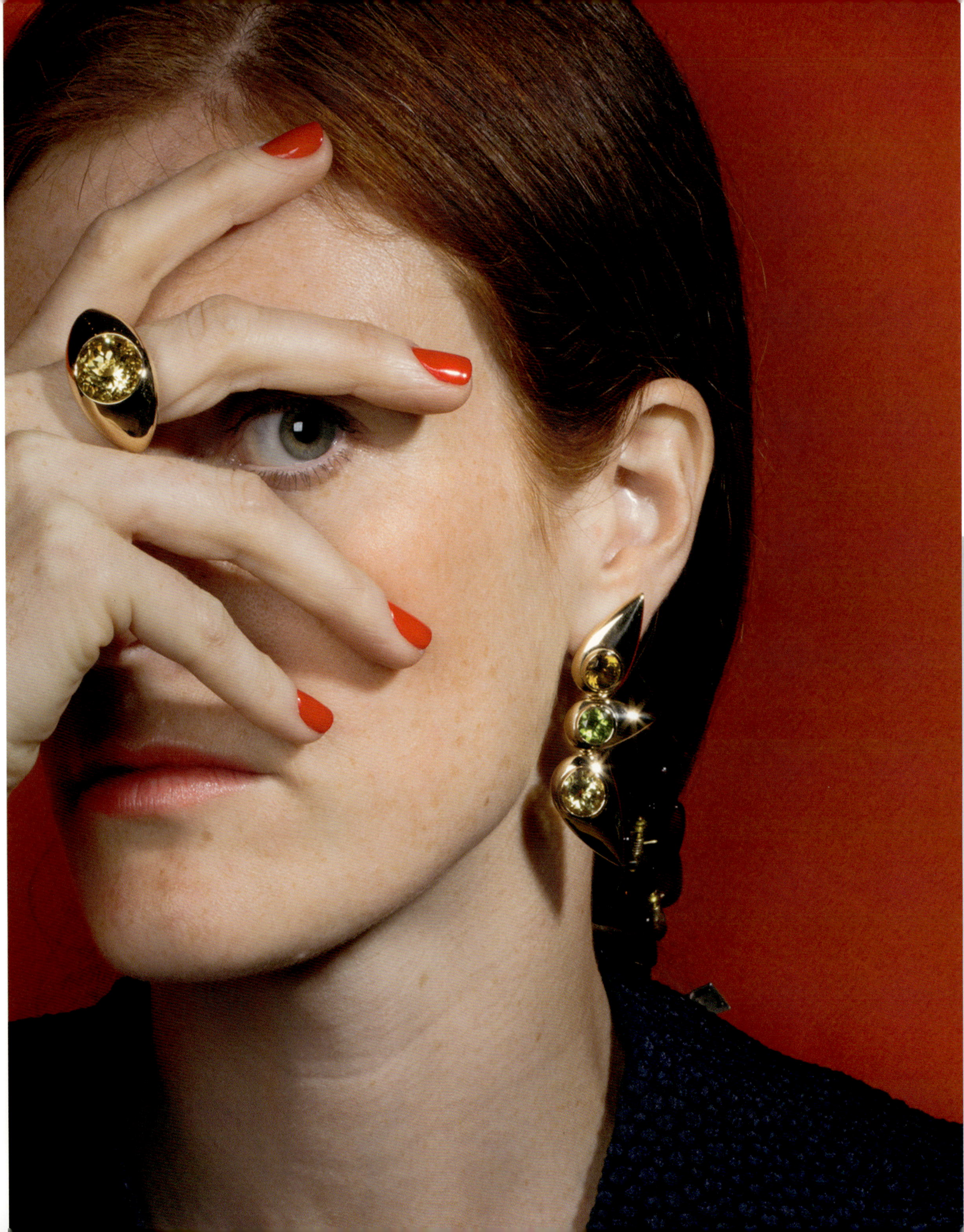

LEFT
Cyclops Ring, 2017
yellow gold, heliodor

Butterfly Earrings, 2017
yellow gold, brown garnets,
peridots, heliodors

BELOW
FROM LEFT TO RIGHT
Fish Fin Earrings, 2018
rose gold, aquamarines

Butterfly Earrings, 2021
yellow gold, aquamarines,
peridots, heliodors

Picasso Ring, 2019
Name © Succession Picasso 2022
rose gold, brown diamonds

Bird Brooch/Pendant, 2017
yellow gold, orange tourmalines,
light and dark green tourmalines

Mask Ring, 2017
yellow gold, spessartine garnets

Green Michelin Mask Ring, 2017
engraved yellow gold, tsavorite garnets

Butterfly Earrings, 2018
yellow gold, amethysts, green tourmalines, yellow garnets

BELOW
Butterfly Earrings, 2017
white gold, aquamarines,
blue zircons

BELOW & RIGHT
Butterfly Brooch/Pendant, 2017
white gold, amethysts,
brownish-pink zircons, pink
tourmalines

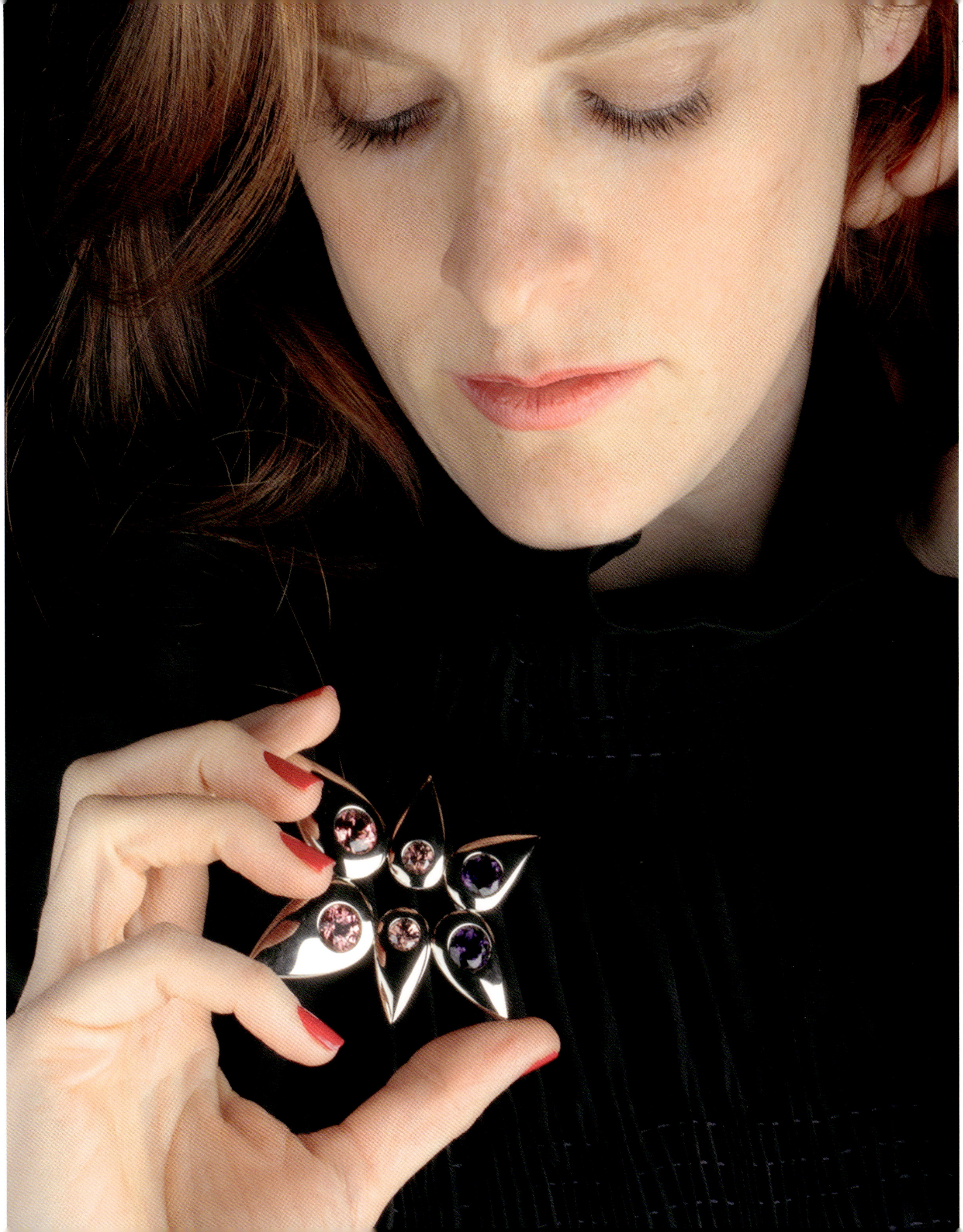

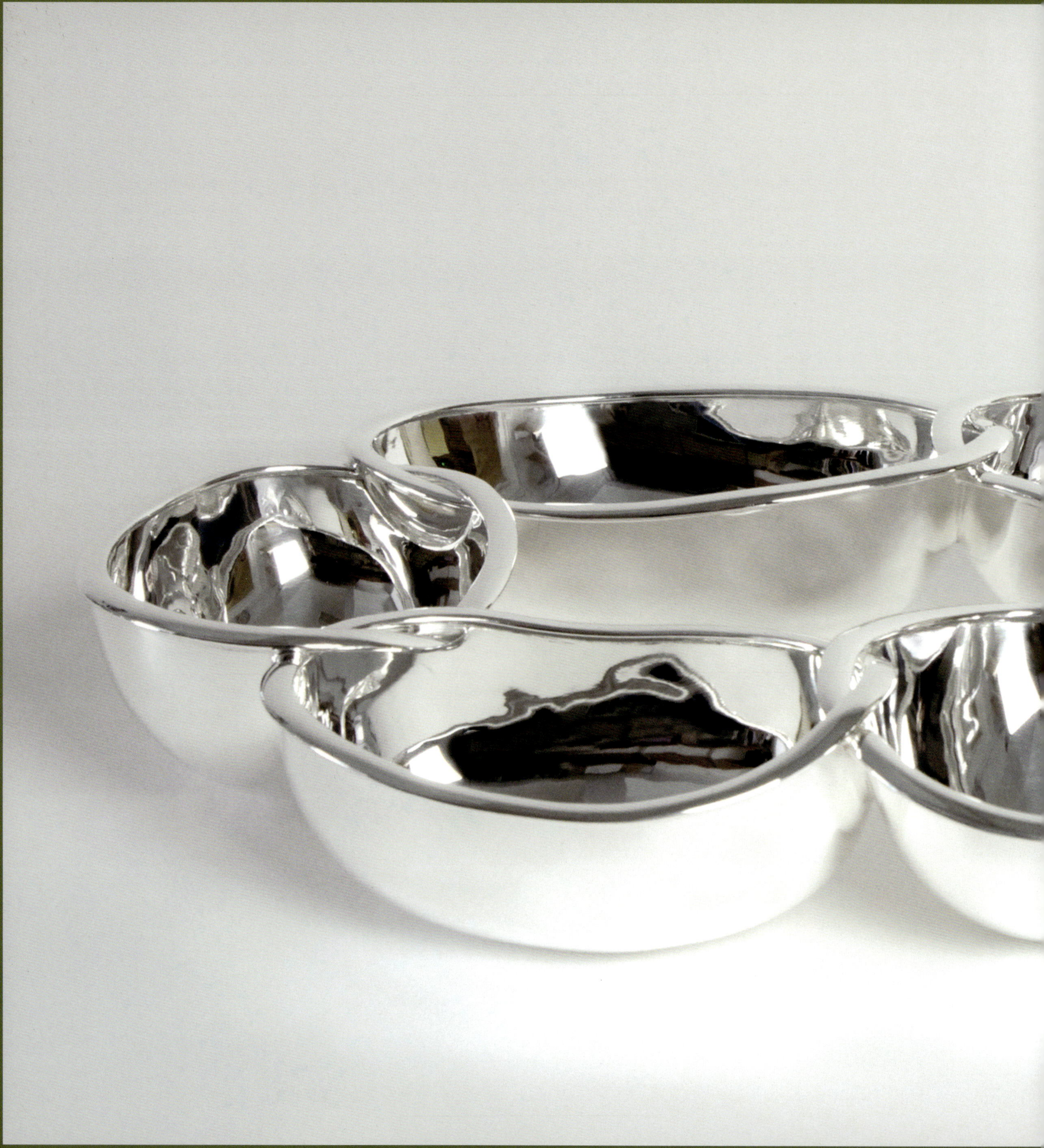

In 2015, Cora was commissioned by *Wallpaper** magazine to collaborate with Hamilton & Inches to design a silver table jewel to be featured in their annual 'Handmade' issue and then exhibited at the 'Handmade' show in Milan. The concept is a 'chain of bowls' comprising seven silver candy bowls, each hand raised and linked by a master chain – a jewel for the home, rather than the body. The finished piece was hand crafted by their master goldsmith in Edinburgh who insisted on making it exactly as designed (with seven differently shaped bowls rather than the three suggested by Cora as a compromise to simplify the process).

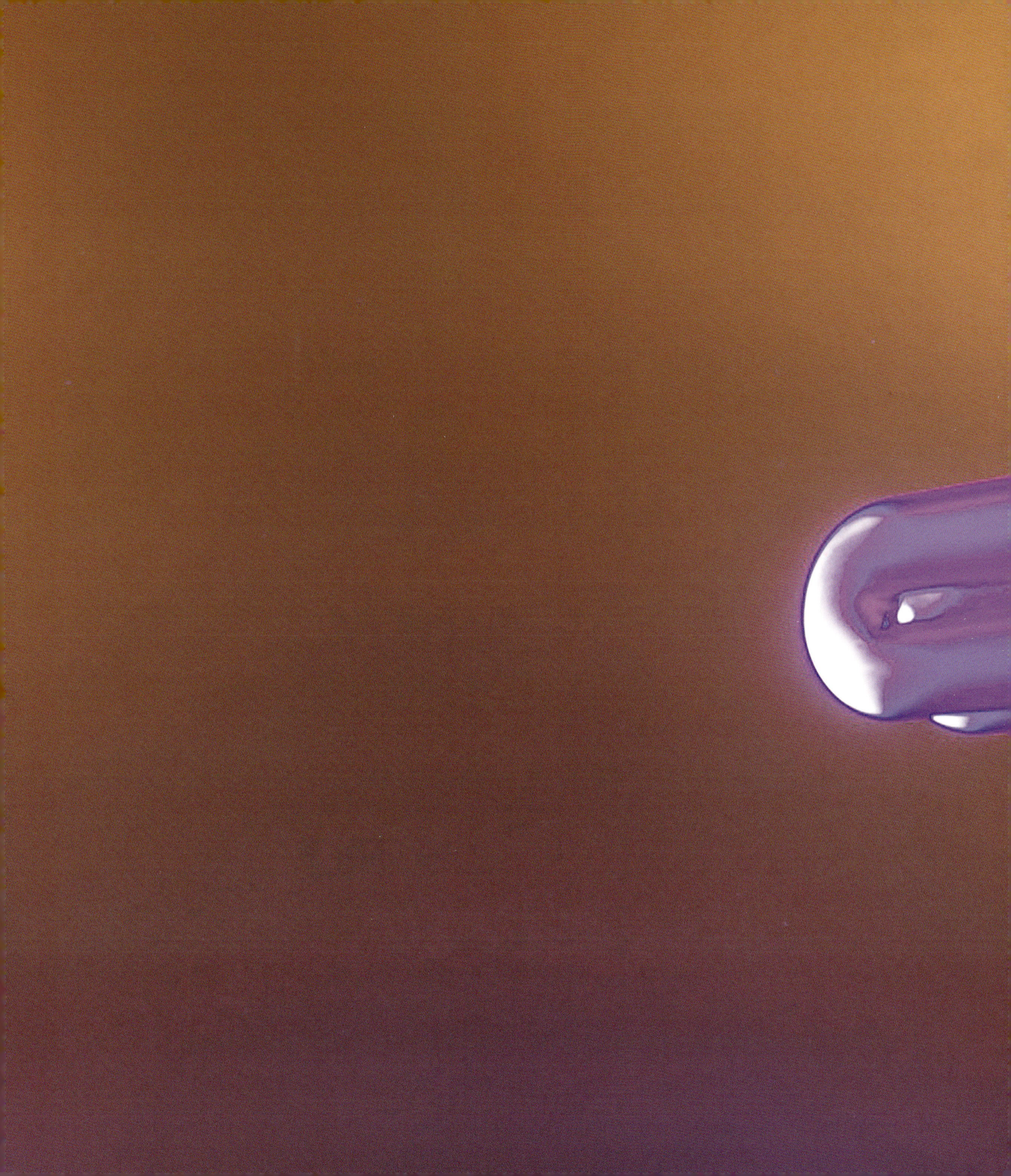

'I read a book called *Buried Treasure: Travels Through the Jewellery Box* by Victoria Finlay, and in the book she talks about how rubies from Myanmar always fluoresce and how the fluorescence is part of their hallmark that makes them special and glowing and more expensive than rubies from elsewhere and I thought "Hang on…in diamonds that's supposed to be bad…this is kind of nuts" so I thought "Fluorescence is just a cool phenomenon…let's do a collection that really celebrates that".'

Cora mentioned this project to an old friend, Louisa Guinness (whose husband Ben Brown had lent Cora his gallery space a decade earlier), who said 'I'd love to do a show with you. Can't you delay the launch by six months and do it at my gallery?' Louisa had been working with artist's jewellery for fifteen years at her Conduit Street gallery but this was to be the only solo show dedicated to a jeweller who was not also an artist. 'Glow' became a kind of 'fluorescent retrospective' whereby Cora remade some of her iconic pieces from previous collections and designed a few new pieces using fluorescent stones which glow when exposed to UV light, the kind of light you might get in a nightclub or a disco.

Cora started researching all the different stones and minerals that fluoresce, and in the process discovered many fascinating new insights. For example, that under UV light some blue and yellow sapphires fluoresce red; some kunzites glow orange and certain varieties of fluorite (a naturally fluorescent mineral, hence the name) turn an electric blue. She began to assemble a collection of fluorescent stones and minerals from different sources and even managed to find someone to supply the mining-grade torches she would need later for the show.

Many of these gemstones and minerals looked amazing under UV and some even continued to glow when the light was removed but, in the end, she realised that no one would buy jewels that only looked good in a disco and therefore decided to focus exclusively on high-quality stones capable of dazzling under natural as well as UV light.

Pieces made up with fluorescent stones in the 'Glow' collection include *Frame* brooches, *Cloud* brooches, an *Arrow Ring* and a *Disco Ring* (both new designs), some of the *Decorated Gugelhupf* rings from the 'Copper Mould' collection and a *Cactus Bracelet* with rubies. Cora also discovered that some pieces in stock already had fluorescent stones, so these were integrated into the collection.

Reverse Orchid Valence Plus Pink Pendant, 2016
red gold, kunzite
photographed under UV light

BELOW
FROM LEFT TO RIGHT
mauve zircon, kunzite, green fluorite, grey Umba sapphire in front of ruby in zoisite boulder

THEN FROM LEFT TO RIGHT
under UV light from three mining-grade torches
zircon is yellow, fluorite is blue, kunzite is orange, grey Umba sapphire is red and rubies are pink

RIGHT
Clouds & Skyscraper Brooch sketch, 2010

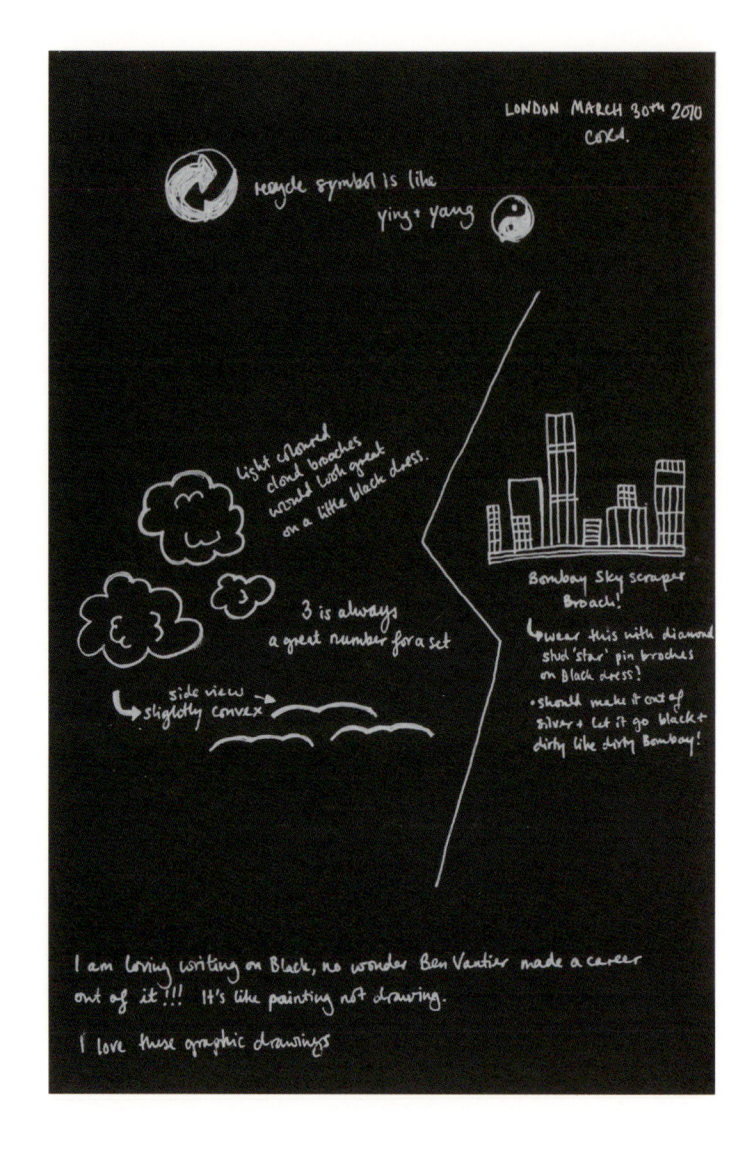

Notable stones sourced for 'Glow' include a large Marquise diamond which delivers an almost blinding glow under UV light, and 'Jedi' spinels, so named because they are a bright neon-pinkish red without the typical darker facets and are therefore 'untouched by the Dark Side'.

The launch was held at the Louisa Guinness Gallery in March 2019. Cora and Paola Petrobelli designed special stages constructed with integrated mining-grade UV torches to showcase the collection, and the exhibition was presented in semi-darkness. These mini UV stages were constructed by Mike Rundell & Associates for the main gallery space, and fluorescent minerals were sources for other displays in the back room.

Cora next presented the 'Glow' collection in Geneva at Gem-Genève's second edition in May 2019. It was here she discovered a little more about the history of how fluorescent diamonds had become undesirable (even though in daylight they look no different). Apparently, it was because Japanese buyers, buoyed by a booming domestic economy in the 1980s, had insisted on buying only 'pure' diamonds and for them, fluorescence was an imperfection. Another reason why this type of stone had fallen out of use was the tendency for celebrities to wear pavé-set pieces at discotheques and nightclubs where the UV light would show up roughly a third of these tightly packed diamonds as a multi-coloured patchwork of glowing dots, making the jewels appear dirty and uneven.

On the other hand, legendary French designer Joel A. Rosenthal (JAR), who happened to be passing by Cora's stand, commented, on noticing the diamond in her *Disco Ring*, that fluorescence like this was very rare and that he had been collecting such stones for years.

The lesson is clear. Fluorescent gemstones should be used by design rather than by accident.

Disco Ring, 2019
rose gold, diamond, pink 'Jedi' spinels from Mogok

LEFT
'Glow' show installation at Louisa Guinness Gallery. 'Mini-stage' showcases with UV torches were mounted on the walls to showcase how the jewels looked under UV light. London, March 2019
photograph by Tom Carter

BELOW
Disco Ring, 2019
rose gold, strongly fluorescent diamond and pink 'Jedi' spinels from Mogok, Myanmar (the diamond's fluorescence had to be toned down for this image under UV light, as it was so intense and distorted the image)

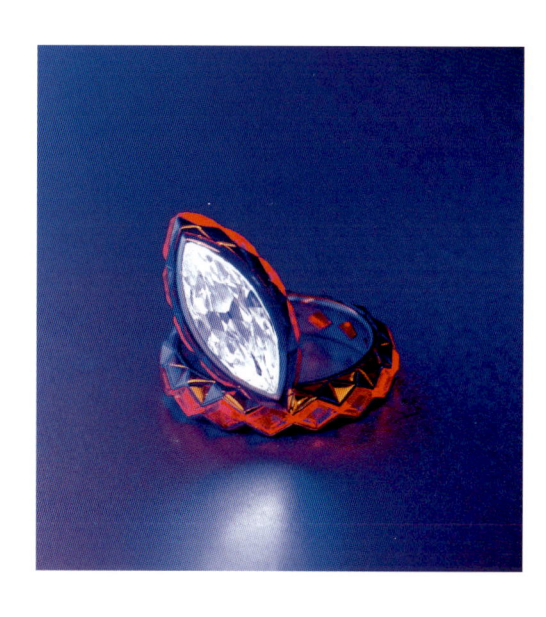

162

The 'mini-stage' showcases were designed with the help of Paola Petrobelli and
made by Mike Rundell & Associates
'Glow' show at Louisa Guinness Gallery, London, March March 2019

photograph by Tom Carter

Billowing Cloud Brooch, 2019
white gold, fluorescent diamonds

Skyline Brooch, 2019
matt white gold, fluorescent diamonds

photographed under UV light

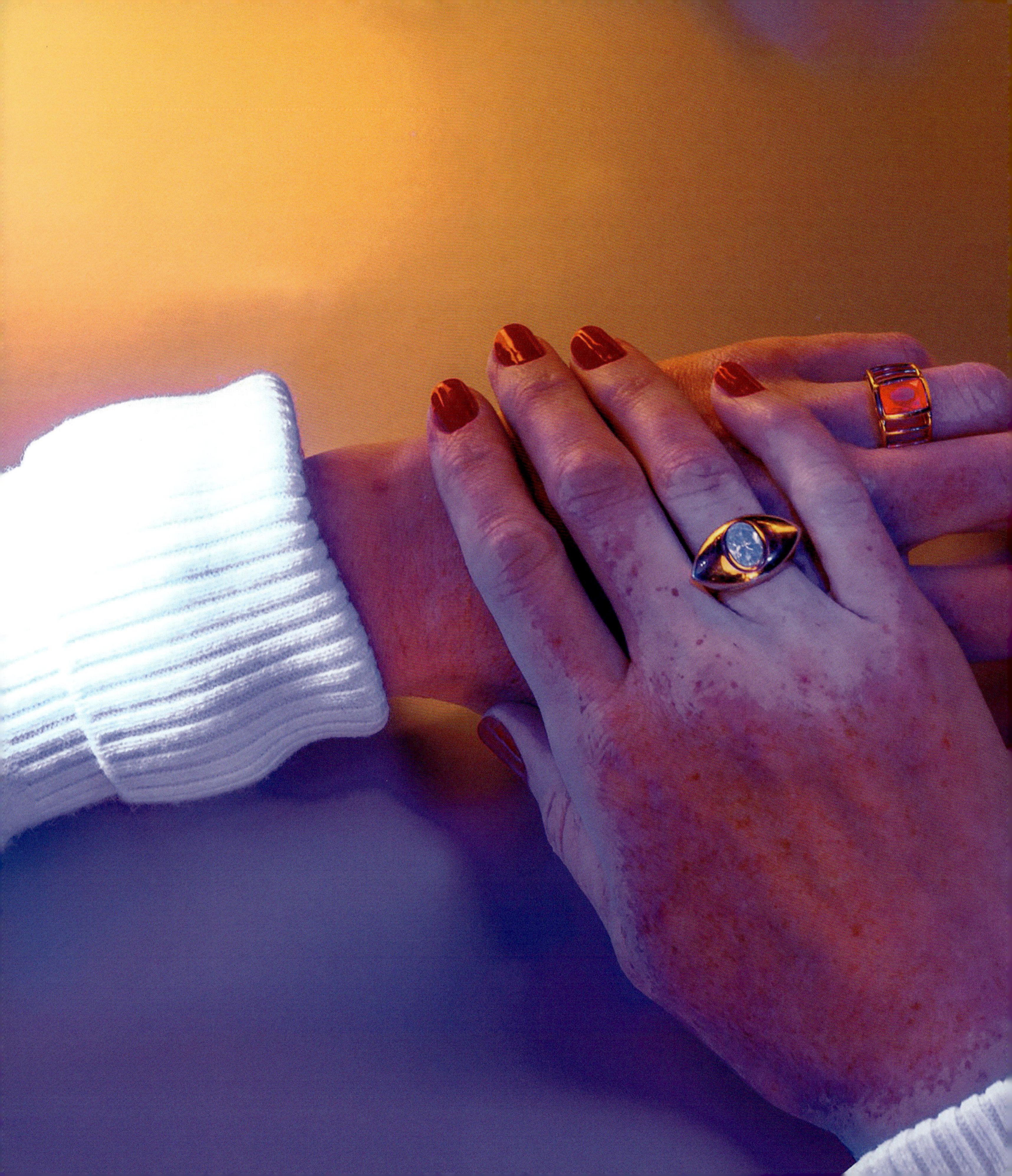

LEFT
Valence Plus Ring, 2014
rose gold, fluorescent intense pink sapphire

Small Eye Ring, 2018
rose gold, fluorescent light brown diamond

photographed under UV light

FROM LEFT TO RIGHT
Large Cupcake Ring, 2013
white and rose gold, pink opal, fluorescent pink spinels

Berry Ring, 2018
rose gold, fluorescent pink sapphires

Decorated Gugelhupf Ring, 2018
rose gold, ebony, fluorescent rubies

photographed under UV light

LEFT
Billowing Cloud Brooch, 2019
white gold, fluorescent diamonds

BELOW
Flowering Mexican Cactus Bracelet, 2019
rose gold, fluorescent rubies

FROM TOP TO BOTTOM
Reversible Highlighter Lentil Bracelet, 2019
white gold, fluorescent diamonds and yellow gold

Texan Cactus Bracelet, 2019
warm white gold, fluorescent rubies

Flowering Mexican Cactus Bracelet, 2019
rose gold, fluorescent rubies

photographed under UV light

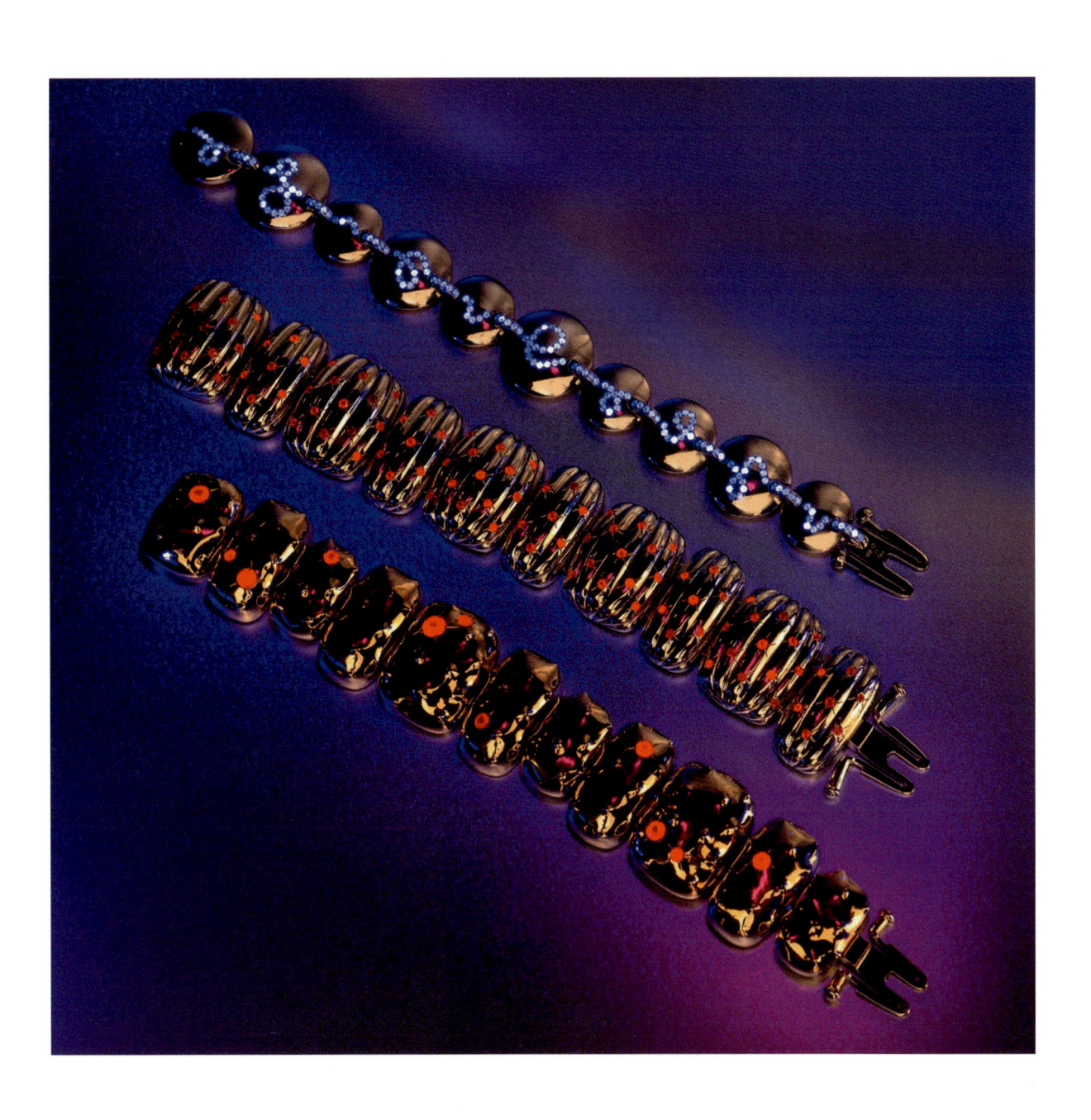

168

RIGHT
Decorated Gugelhupf Ring, 2018
rose gold, ebony, fluorescent rubies
photographed under UV light

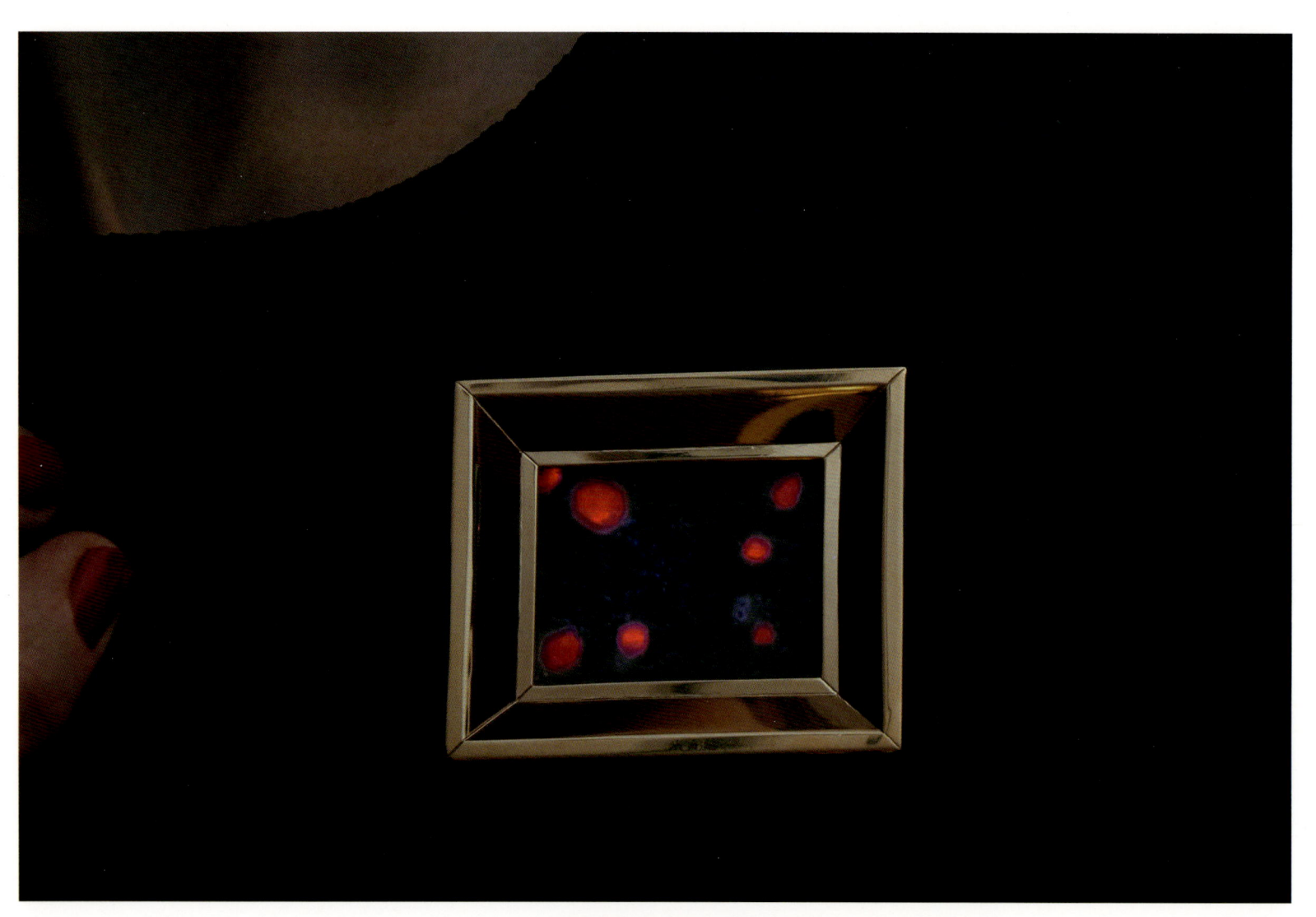

Simple Frame Brooch, 2019
yellow gold, fluorescent rubies in hornblende
photographed under UV light

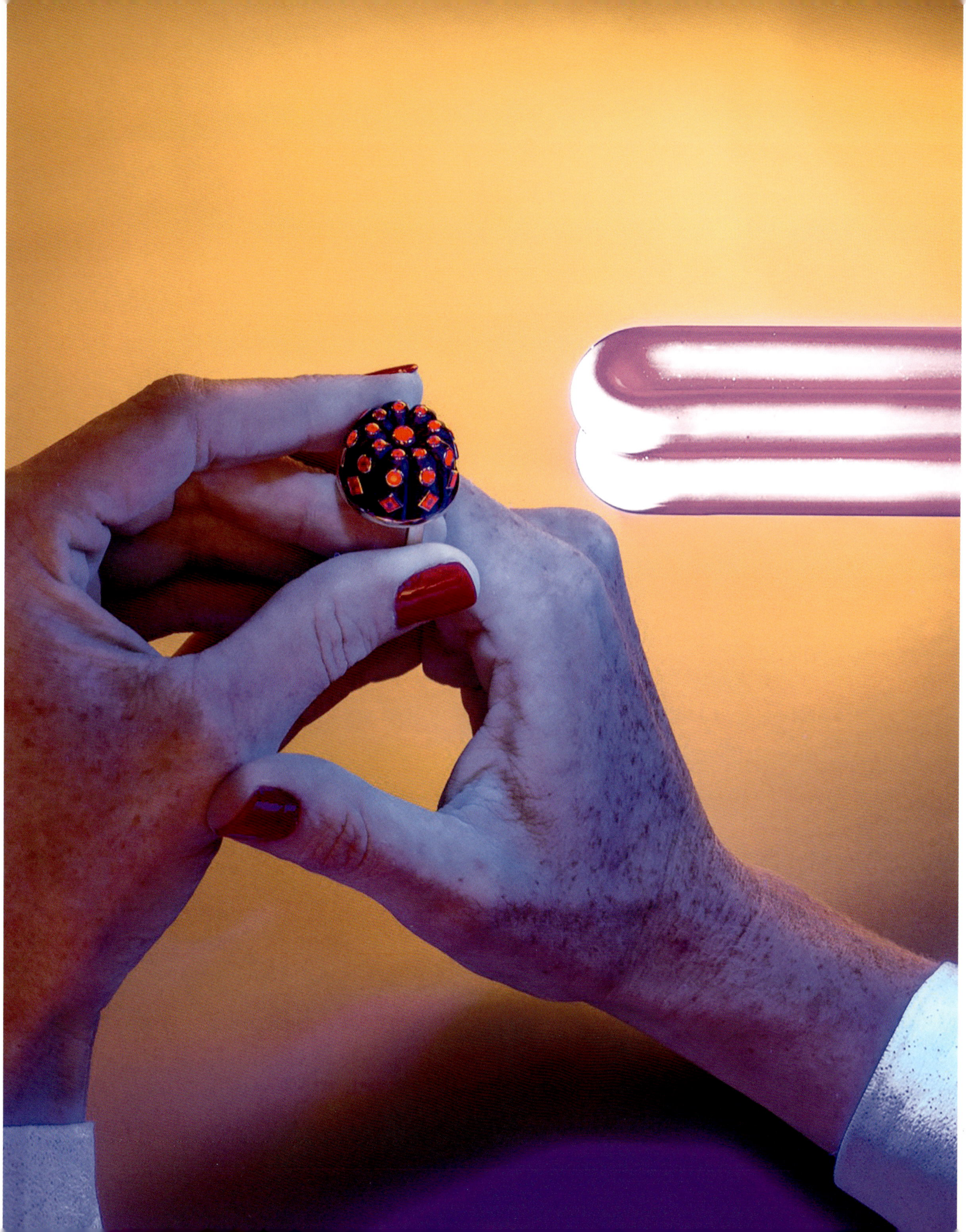

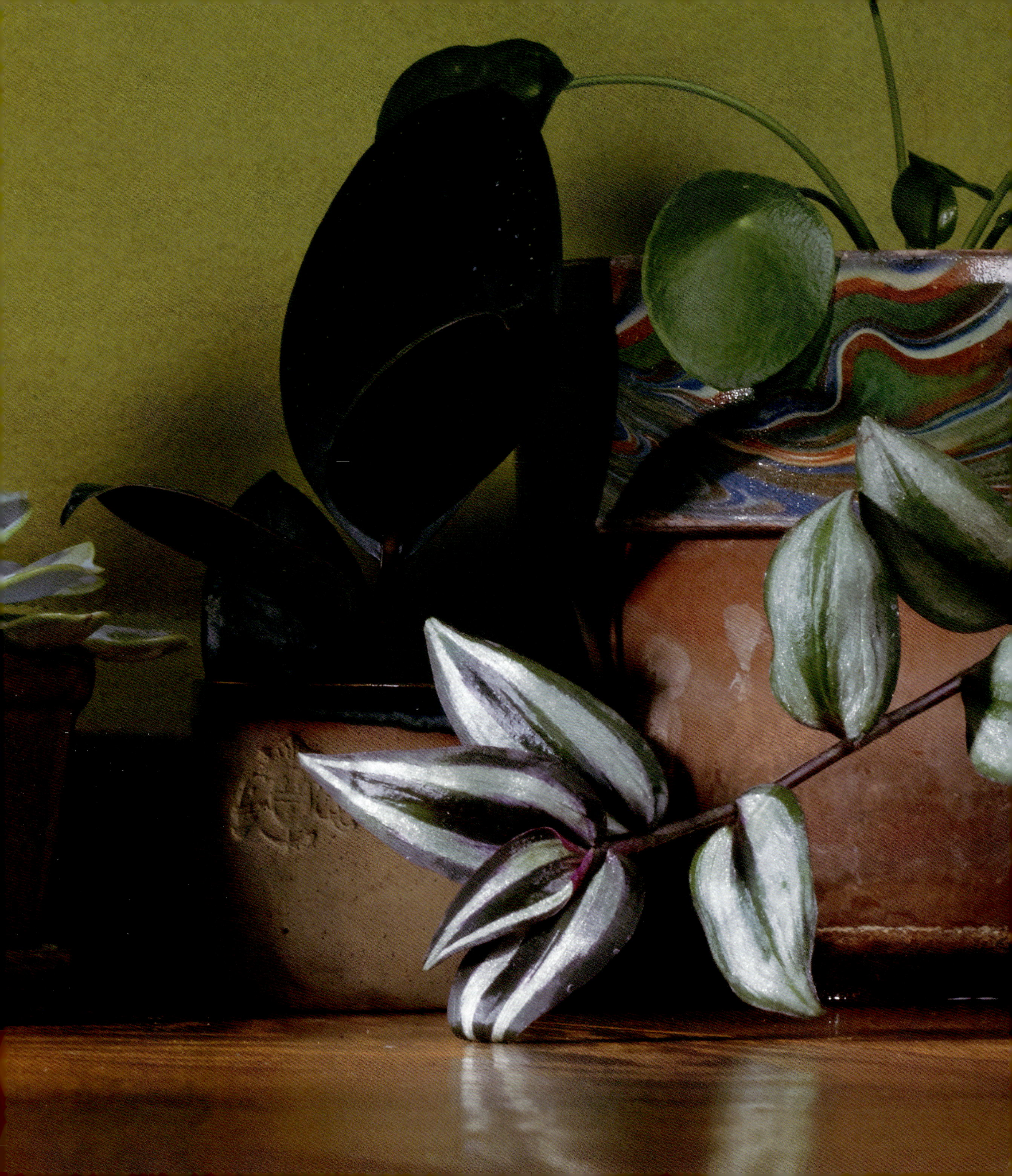

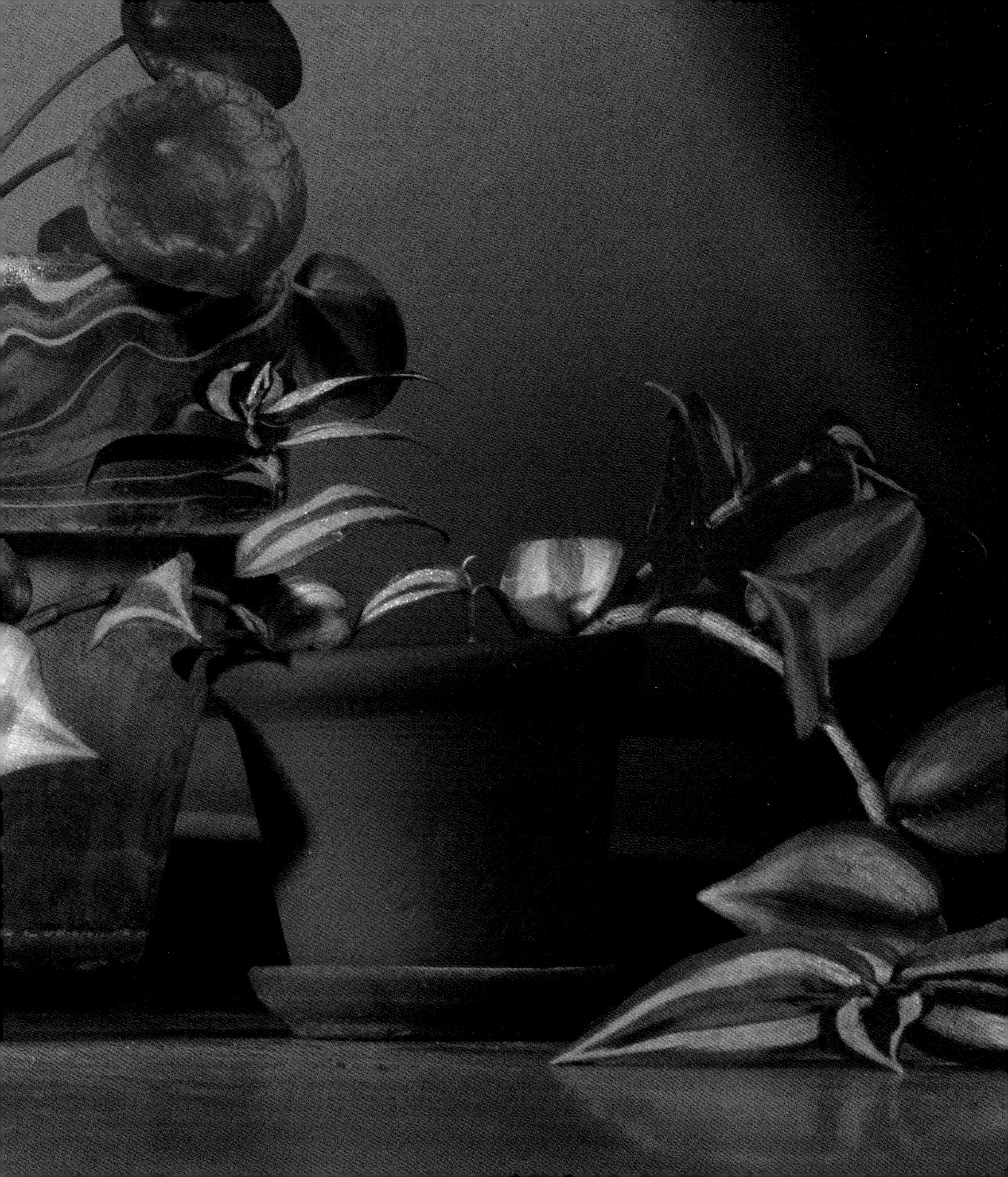

RK Fern Earrings, 2022
yellow gold, copper calcite, spessartine garnets, dyed light green aluminium

Italian Pot Ring, 2022
yellow gold back, green and blue anodised titanium

POTTERING AROUND

'Pottering around' is an English expression that basically means spending time doing something pleasurable and relaxing without having too much to show for it at the end. It is also the title for the latest of Cora Sheibani's themed collections at the time of writing and notable for its juxtaposition of solid geometric shapes against free-flowing organic forms and use of novel materials.

The genesis of 'Pottering Around' happened during the Covid pandemic lockdown when Cora was spending a lot of time in her garden in London 'rearranging and re-potting my plants continuously to maximise possibilities in a very small space' but on this occasion the outcome was more productive.

Setting aside her trowel and pruning shears Cora began flicking through old sketchbooks for new ideas and to see what she had designed and liked, but not made yet.

'There was a drawing of an upside-down pot with a long tourmaline crystal hanging down as if it was part of an earring that never made it into the "Cactaceae" collection.'

Cora then rediscovered a design she had sketched in 2019 for a double-ended pendant necklace without a clasp, similar in concept to a beaded Wiener Werkstätte wraparound necklace she had once admired. The design was conceived as a long ribbon weighed down at each end by potted flowers with gemstones trailing up the ribbon. On the following page she uncovered a design for a brooch with the pots placed end-to-end without the flowers, so deep down there was clearly an unresolved notion of using these humble domestic vessels as a design subject for jewellery.

'I liked the contrast between wild, organic, uncontrolled plants and the rigid, sculptural vessels they are contained in.' The idea was formalised into a design motif, either on its own like a plant pot or positioned end-to-end in a repeating pattern to create a new line that became the 'Pottering Around' collection.

The collection was developed in collaboration with Sebastian Fässler and Regula Kilchsperger, a Swiss jewellery designer and goldsmith. It was a new and refreshing experience to develop a collection with another woman who enjoyed wearing earrings and could test them out on herself.

A wide range of unconventional and previously unused materials was used to make up the pieces. The first of these was a *Double Pot Ring* made from a terrazzo-type material with fragments of green maw sit sit (a rock containing jadeite) embedded in a bronze matrix.

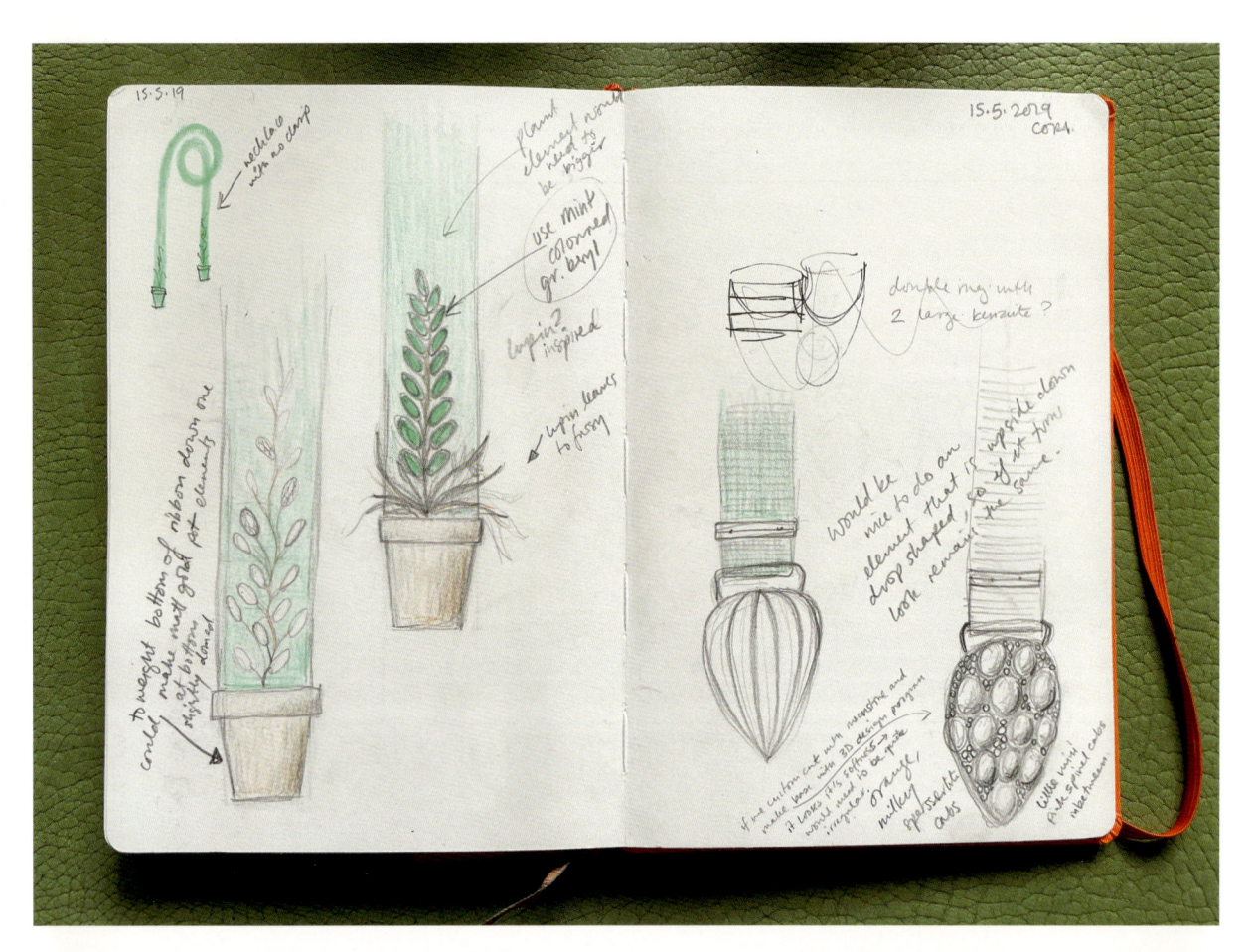

LEFT
Consecutive pages from Cora's sketchbook showing the *Double Pot* design, 2019

BELOW
Double Pot Ring, 2021
matt white gold, maw sit sit in bronze matrix, tsavorite garnets

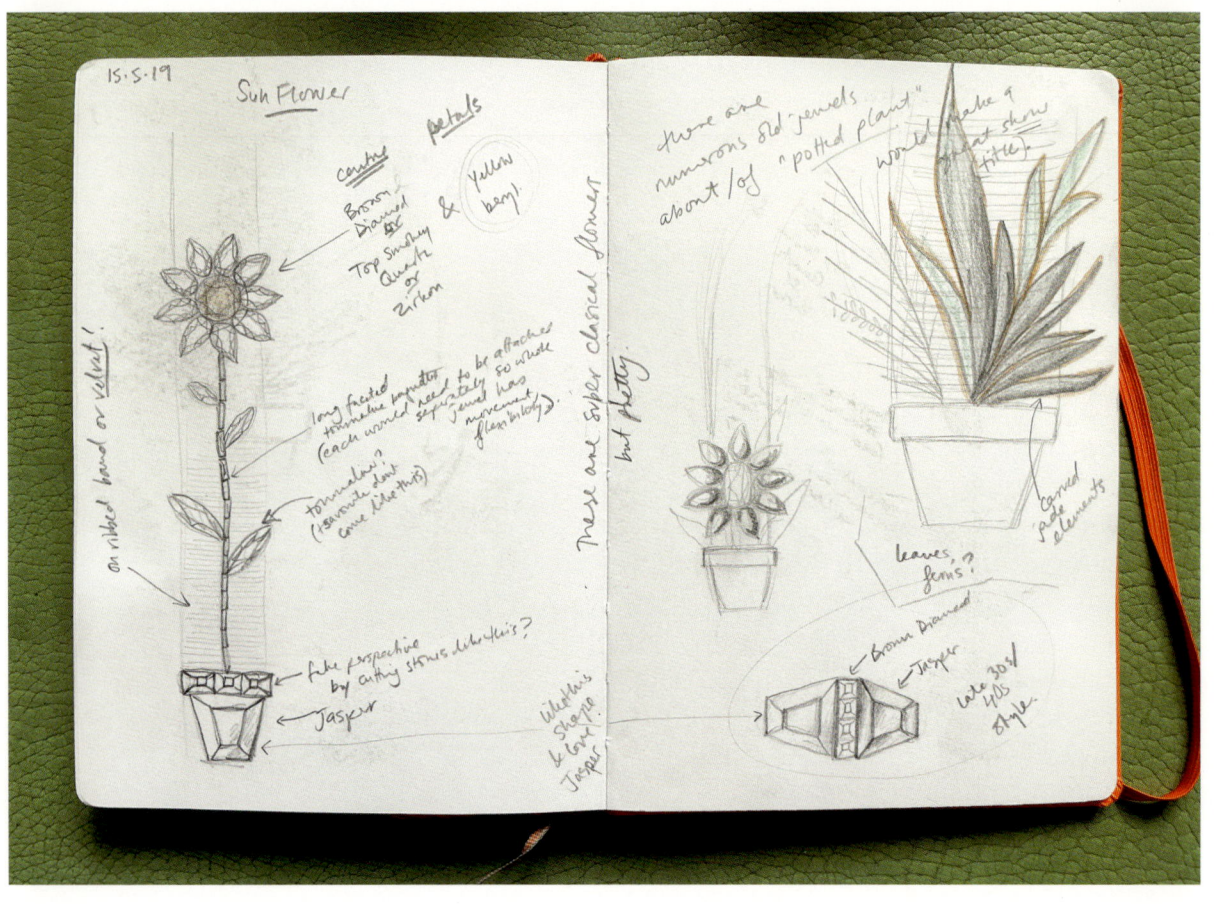

Small plant-pot rings were 3D printed in titanium or else cast in gold with the plants made either in coloured titanium, gold or carved hardstones. It was the first time Cora had used titanium, which enabled the application of a wide range of colours to the metal. More robust than carved stone and lighter than gold, it proved to be highly effective and served to create a new, more affordable price point without compromising design or quality.

Rings and earrings are strongly represented in the 'Pottering Around' collection but perhaps the most notable piece is a magnificent *Swiss Pottering Around Bracelet* featuring carved black and white river pebbles and light smoky quartz (both sourced from Switzerland) set in an articulated red gold and bronze frame.

The 'Pottering Around' collection debuted in England at the Petersham Nurseries in September 2021.

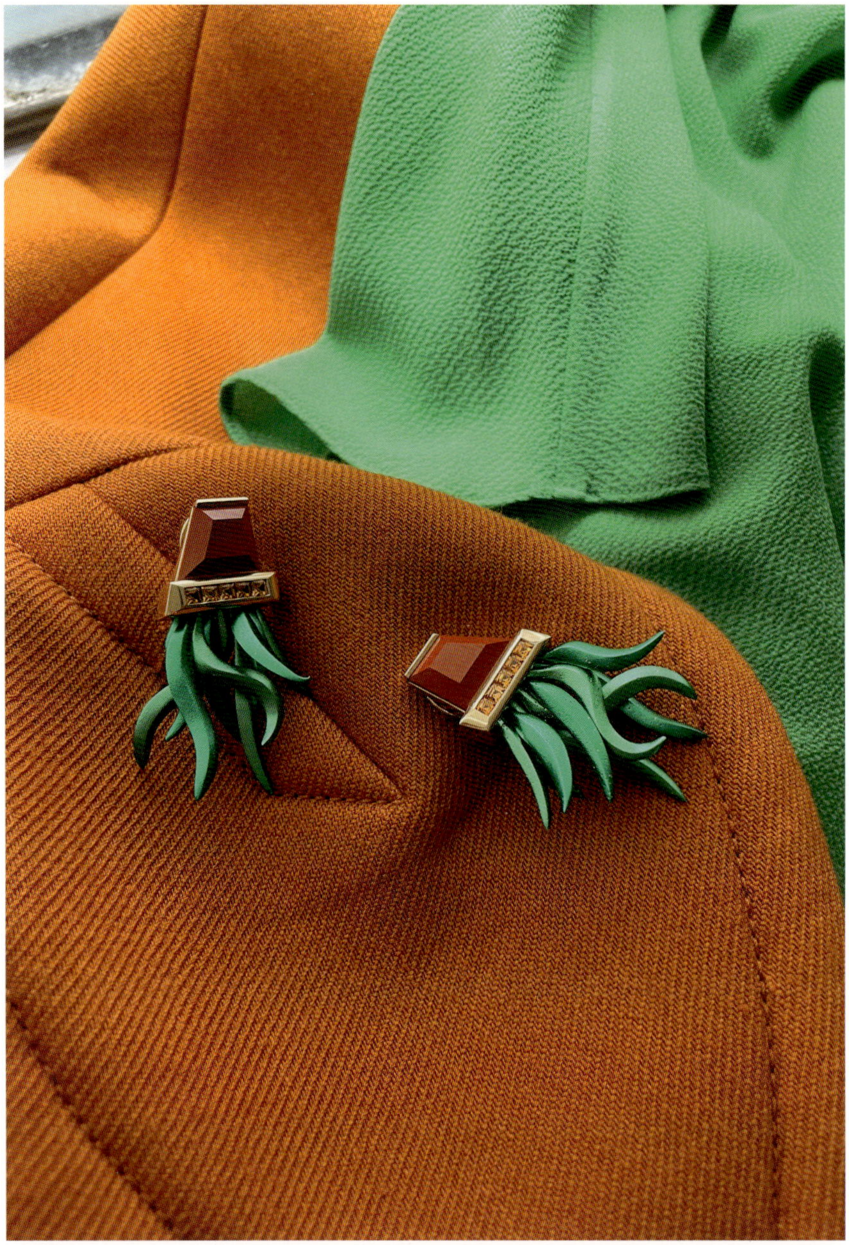

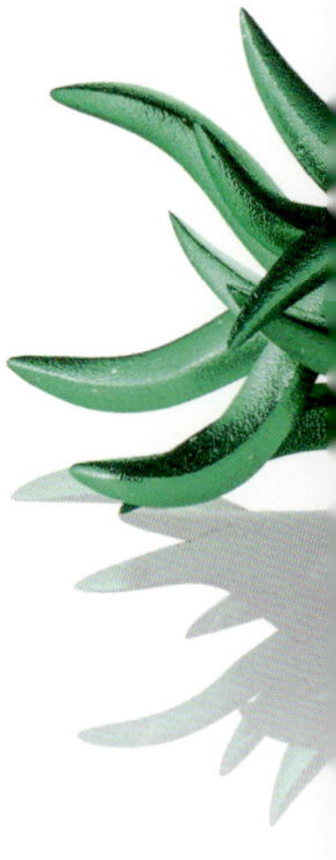

LEFT
RK Fern Earrings, 2021
yellow gold, silex jasper,
spessartine garnets, green
anodised aluminium

BELOW
FROM LEFT TO RIGHT
Fern Earring, 2021
white gold, fossilised dinosaur
bone, tsavorite garnets, green
anodised aluminium

Stacked Pots Ring, 2021
matt platinum, maw sit sit,
custom cut diamonds

Double Pot Ring, 2021
matt yellow gold, fossilised
coral, light spessartine garnets

*Italian Pot Ring with Flamboyant
Plant,* 2021
rose gold, chrysoprase

Vine Earring, 2021
matt platinum, snowflake
obsidian, green and brown
tourmalines

PP.178-179
Cora's rooftop garden, London,
spring 2020

RK Exotic Fern Earrings, 2022
white gold, white agate, royal
purple garnets, green and purple
anodised aluminium

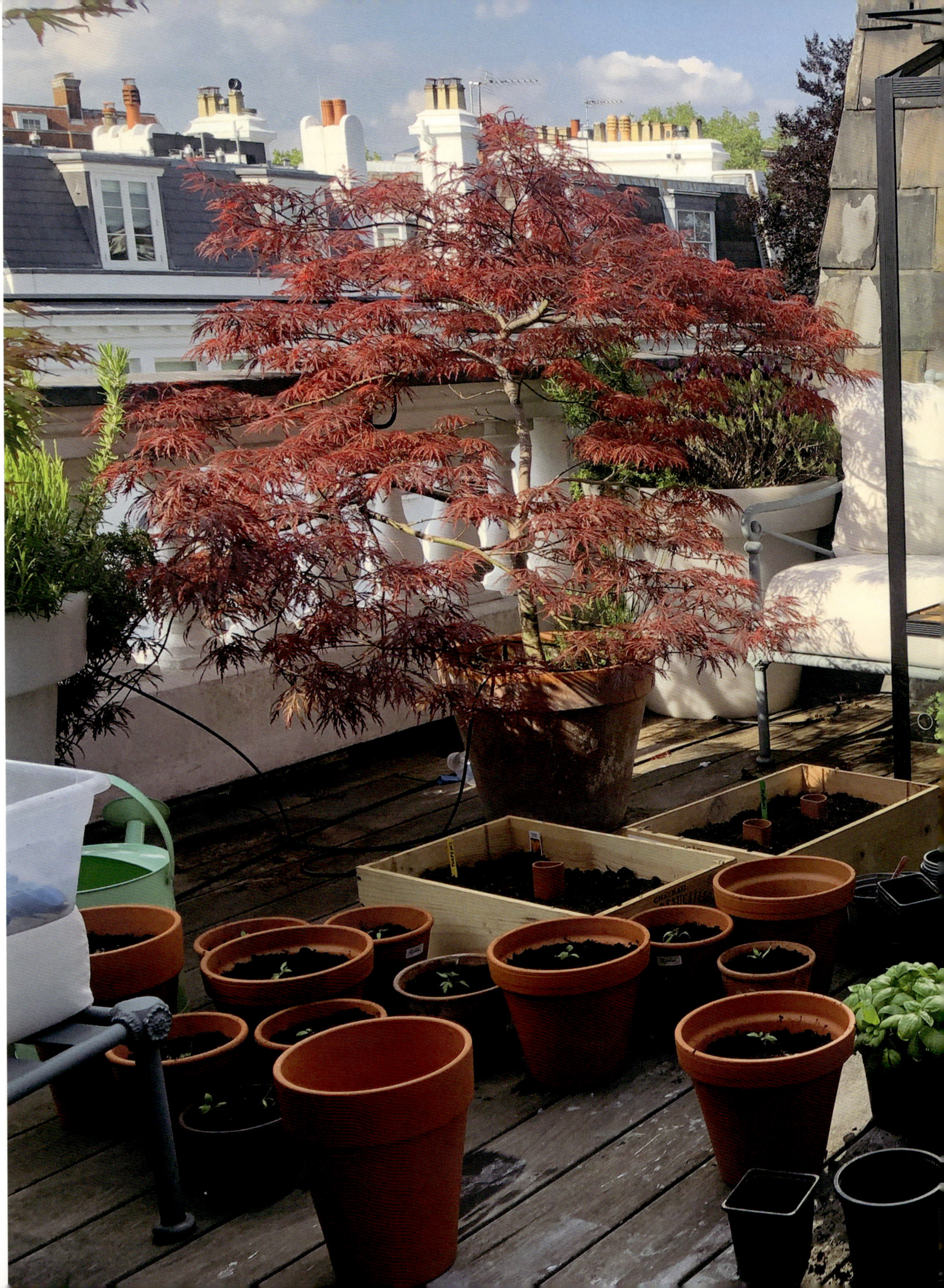

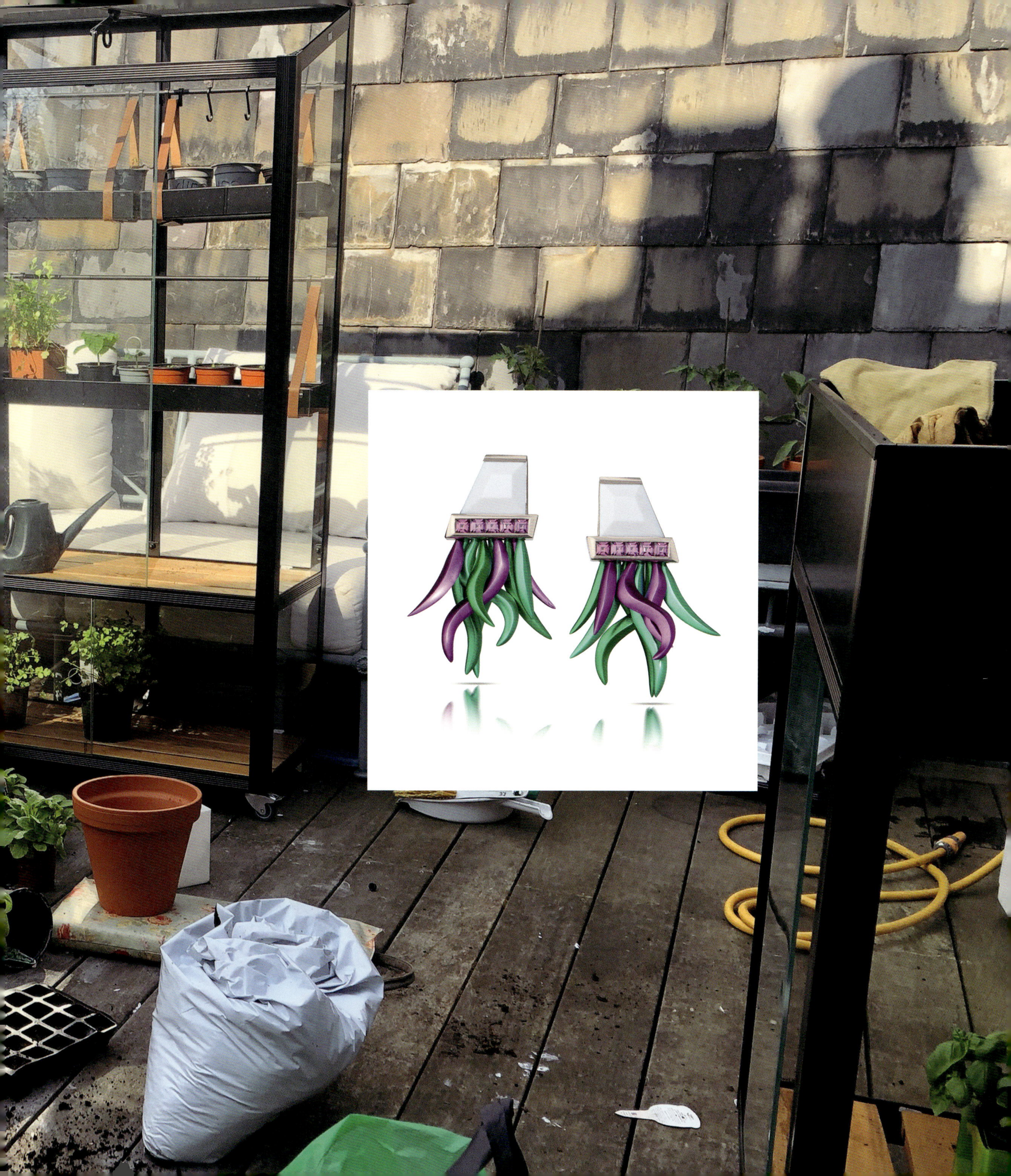

Stacked Pots Ring, 2021
matt platinum, maw sit sit, custom cut diamonds

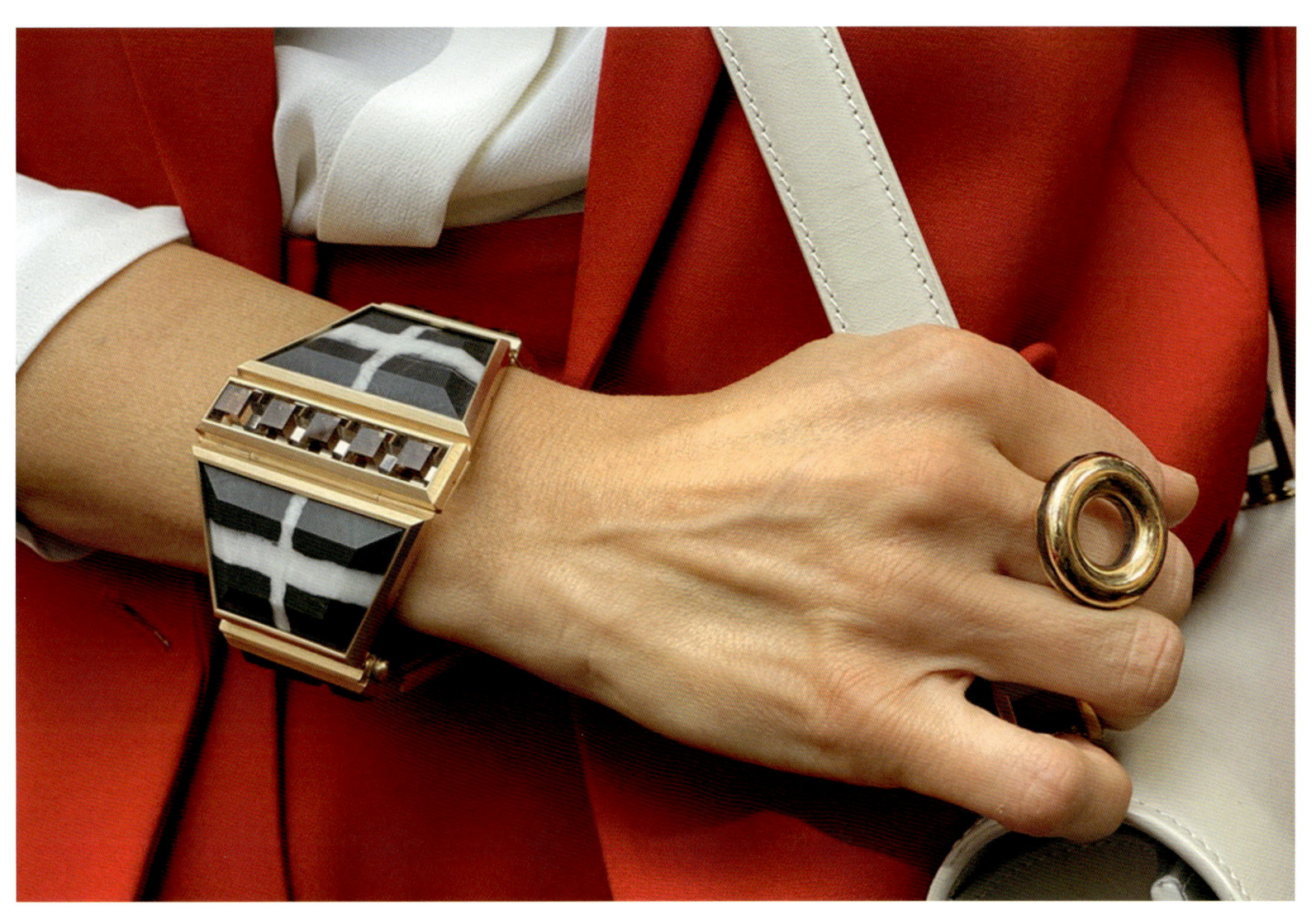

Swiss Pottering Around Bracelet, 2021
bronze, red gold, Swiss black and white river pebbles, Swiss smoky quartz

Circle with Faceted Disc Ring, 2017
yellow gold, smoky quartz

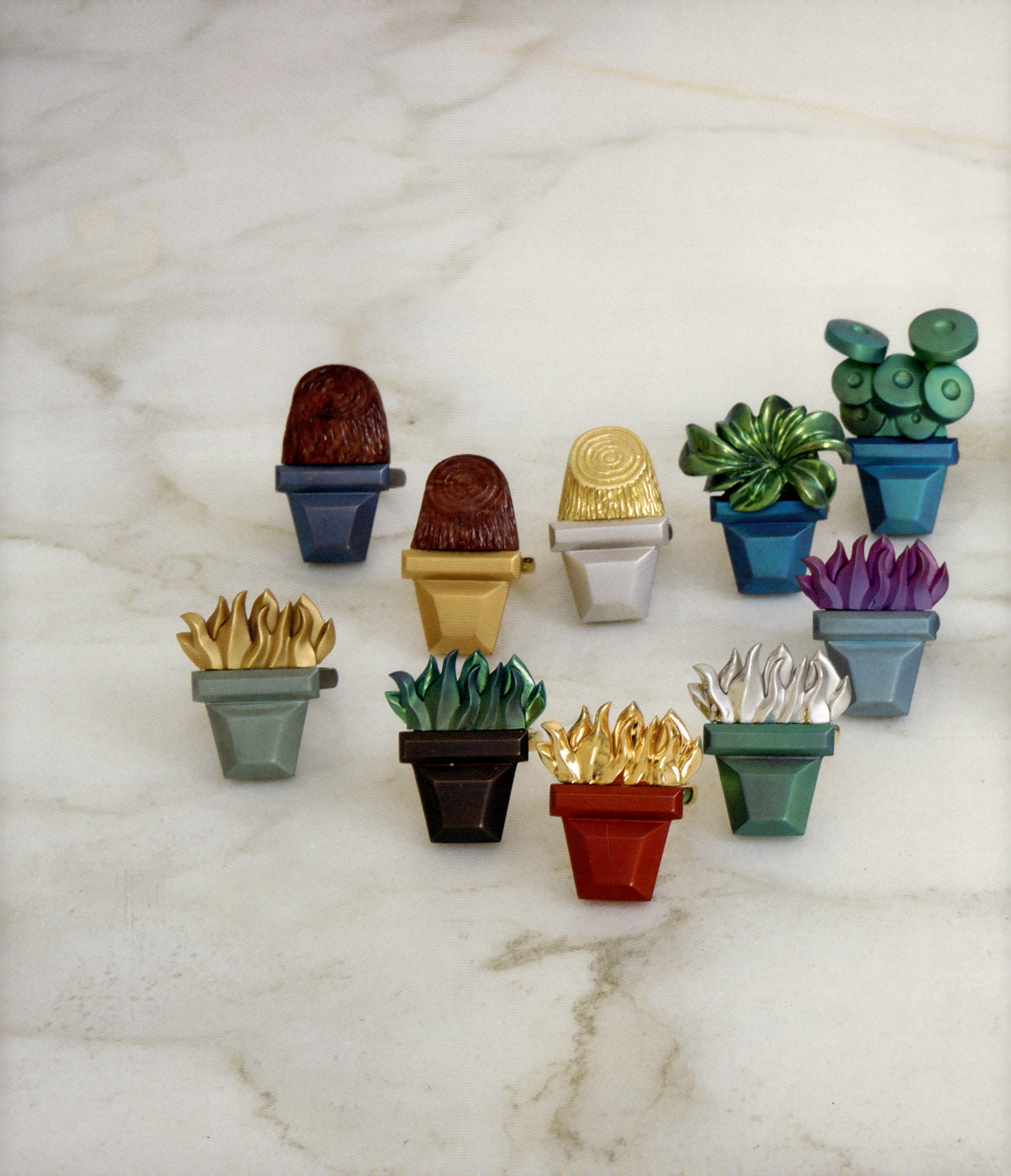

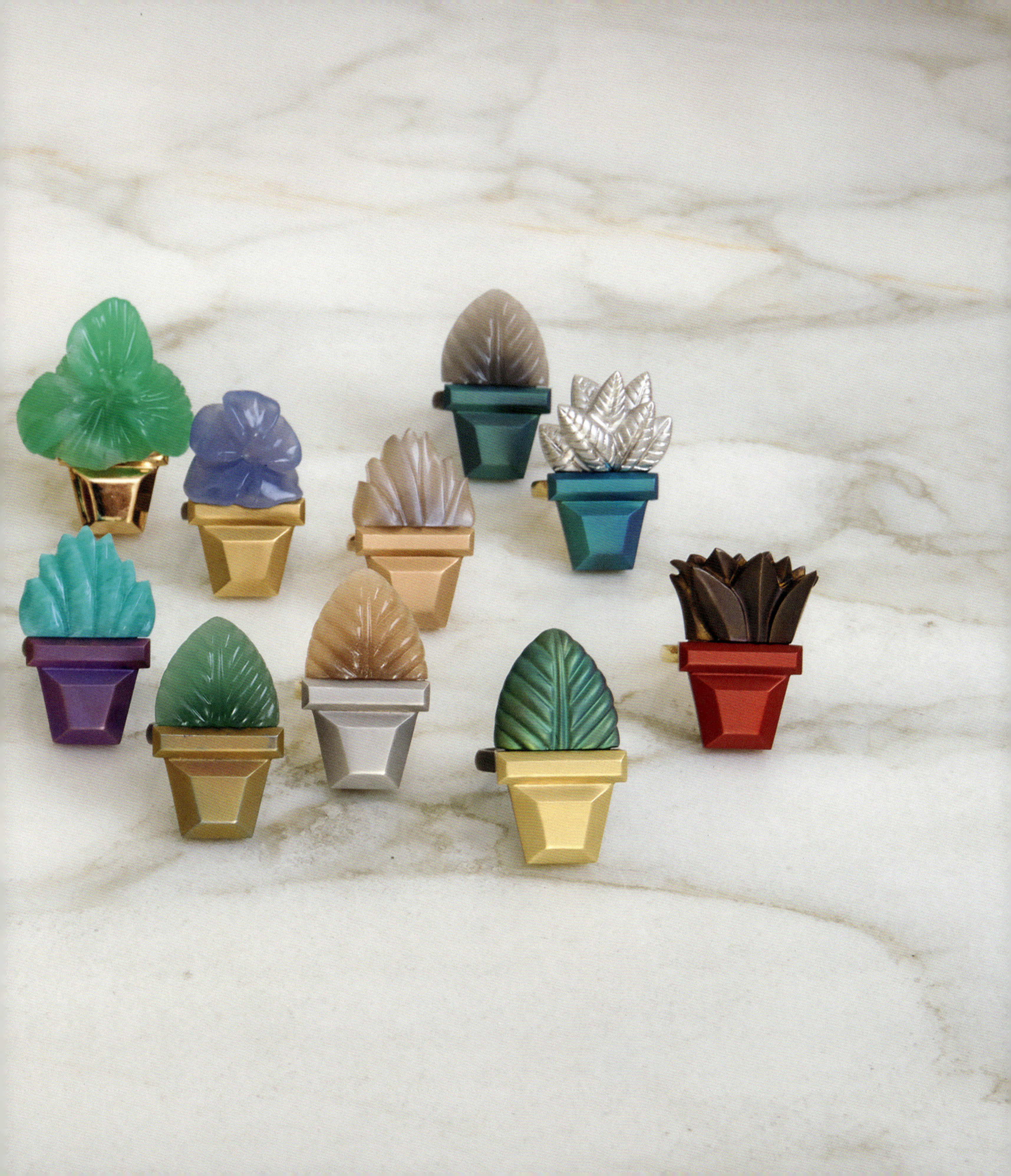

PP.182-183
A selection of *Italian Pot* rings
various colours of gold &
anodised or coated titanium
carved gemstones: chrysoprase,
chalcedony, moonstone,
amazonite, fossilised wood

BELOW
Vine Earrings, 2021
platinum, snow obsidian, green
beryls

ABOVE
RK Wood Leaf Earrings, 2021
rose gold, cacholong opal, spessartine garnets, various woods

RIGHT
Italian Pot Ring, 2022
yellow gold, green anodised titanium

186

LEFT
Double Pot Brooch, 2022
rose gold, lapis lazuli in aluminium matrix, pink anodised aluminium

BELOW
FROM LEFT TO RIGHT
Vine Earrings, 2021
platinum, snowflake obsidian, green and brown tourmalines

RK Wood Leaf Earrings, 2021
rose gold, cacholong opal, spessartine garnets, various woods

RK Fern Earrings, 2021
white gold, fossilised dinosaur bone, tsavorites, green anodised aluminium

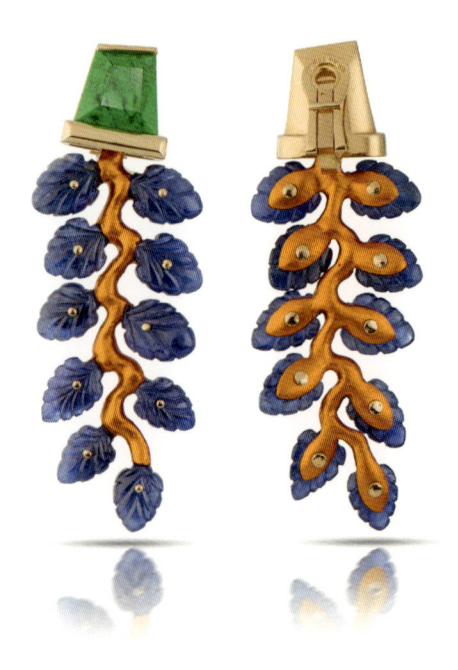

ABOVE
RK Asian Earrings, 2021
rose gold, maw sit sit, orange anodised aluminium, carved blue sapphires

LEFT
Pottering Around Bracelet, 2022
bronze, red gold, Indonesian jasper, Swiss smoky quartz

RIGHT
Italian Pot Ring, 2021
green anodised and red coated titanium

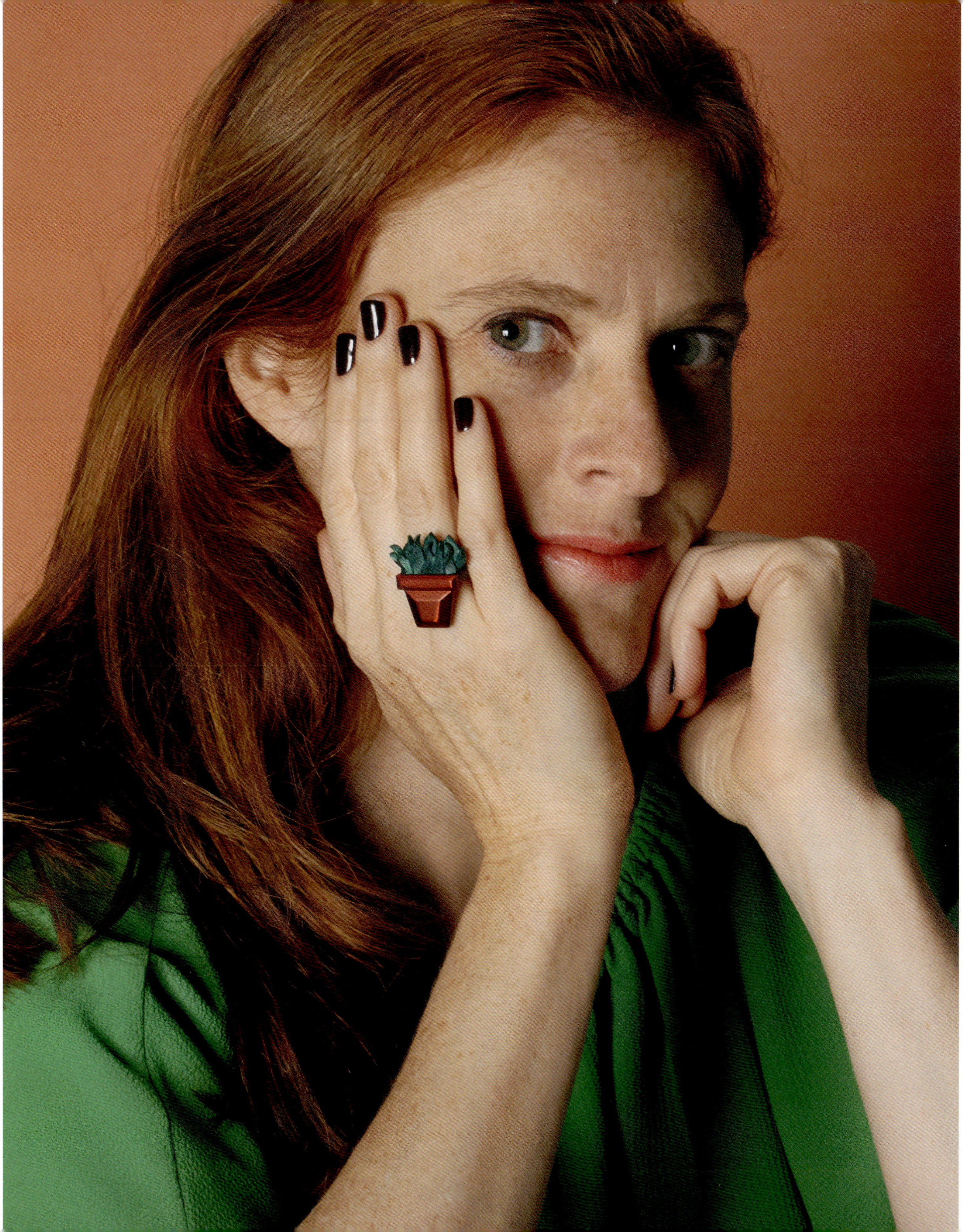

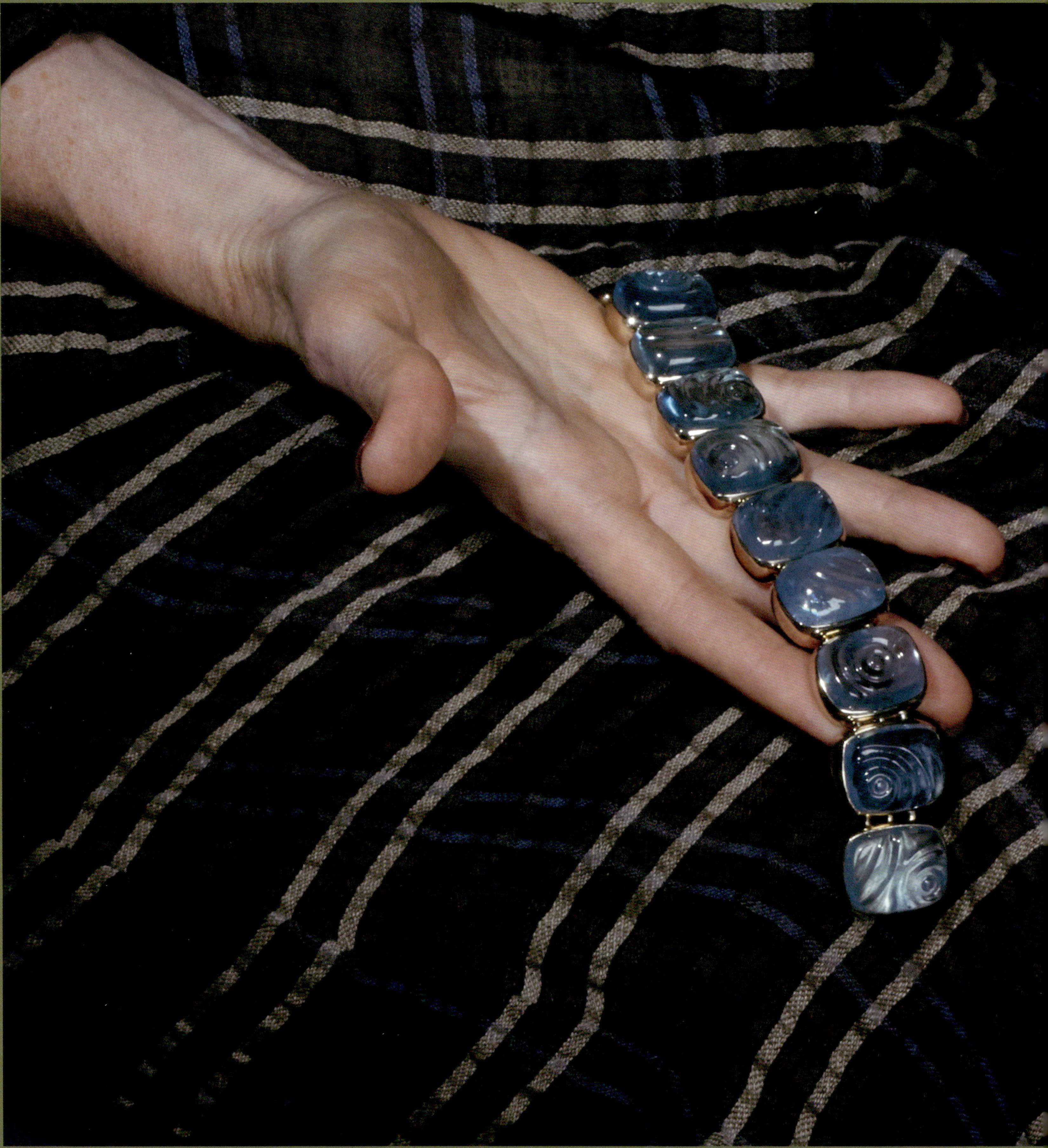

The *Ripple Bracelet* was created in 2021 when Cora, feeling she had exhausted the possibilities for new iterations of her cactus bracelet, decided to explore something new. Based on the same frame design as the *Green Cactus Leaf Bracelet* but cast in 'warm' rather than standard 'cold' white gold (also known as 'or gris'), the *Ripple Bracelet* features aquamarines carved to resemble the way water ripples outwardly in waves when you drop a stone into a pond.

VI

DESIGN PHILOSOPHY

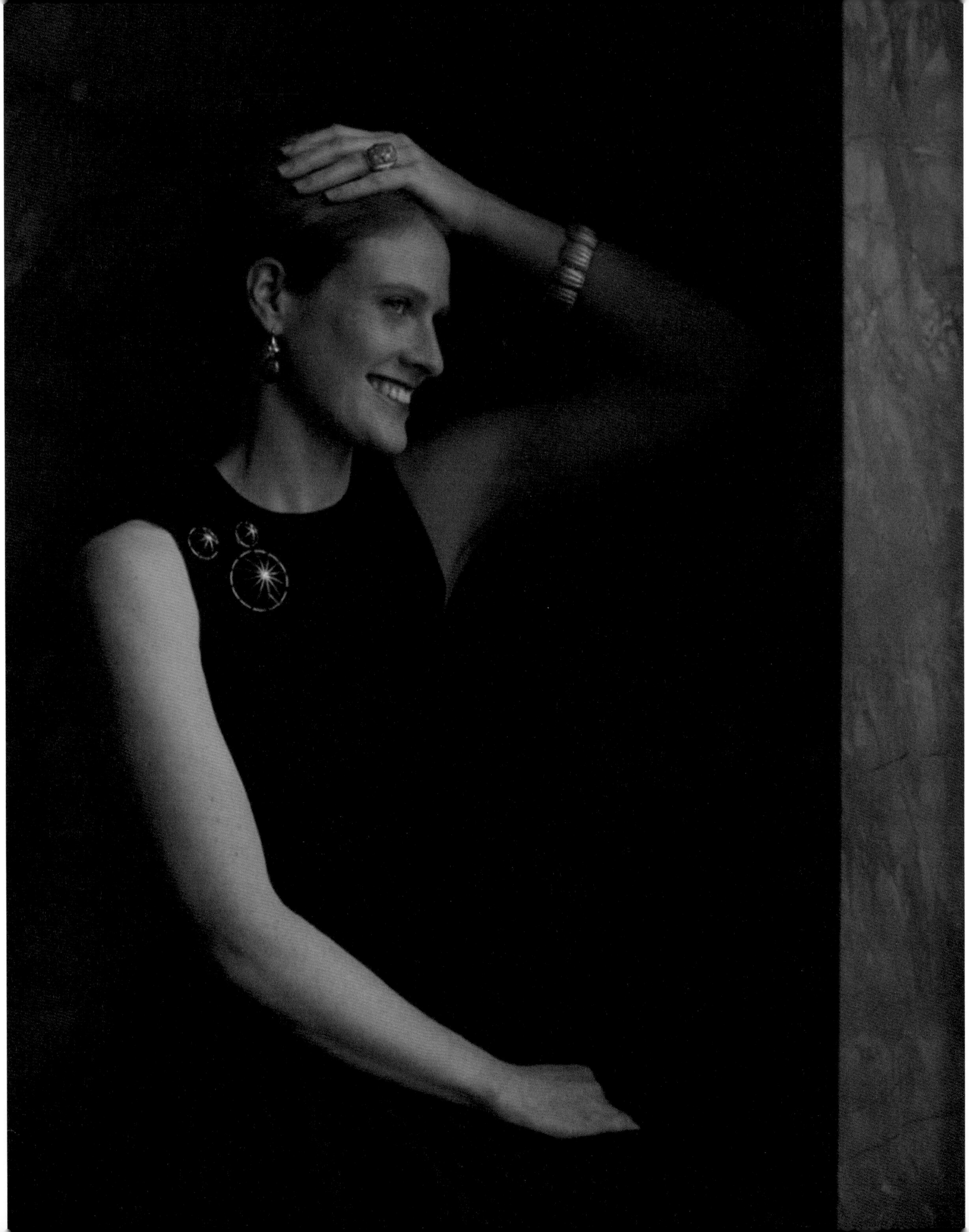

Green Leaf Cactus Ring, 2013
rose gold, nephrite

Texan Cactus Bracelet, 2012
matt rose gold

Petra Cactus Earrings, 2012
yellow gold, tumbled green tourmaline

Target Valence Brooch Set, 2005/6
rose gold

Cora Sheibani calls herself a jeweller rather than an artist. She is proud to be a jeweller and knows that the best practitioners are artists who make elegant jewels to flatter the wearer. 'Art for art's sake has its place, but I do not strive to make impractical, conceptual pieces which disregard human interaction.'

She does not consider herself to be part of any specific group or movement and indeed stands slightly apart from her contemporaries in the sense that her principal focus is on high-quality, everyday jewels that are unique, exquisitely made but not made to look expensive. She nevertheless believes that in an industry that has historically been dominated by men, women have an increasingly prominent and exciting role to play in the future of jewellery because they are able to design for themselves rather than for a muse or some abstracted idea of what a woman wants or ought to wear.

'I think that women who design jewellery design differently…in a much more practical way…every time I design, I design to please myself…I know jewellery and I know what's going to work… I like to design the things I get excited about…and the women who collect jewellery in a serious way, they're going to understand this and appreciate it the most.

'Initially, I also designed things I thought other people would want and every single time I did that it was a piece I wasn't really happy with, and it was difficult to sell. What I don't pick up and wear is hard for people to appreciate and thus is bought less readily.'

Because Cora is her own muse, her jewellery tends to find an audience amongst women who appreciate and value her personal aesthetic. They see jewellery as she does – as part of their identity, and the act of putting on jewellery makes them feel complete. As such, they demand and are prepared to pay for high standards of quality and craftsmanship coupled with the bespoke style and originality only unique pieces of jewellery can deliver. They express themselves in a less formal manner than in previous generations – wishing to appear smart but also to feel comfortable and relaxed at work and when

Cora's London bedside bookshelf in 2020, with pelargonium branch from her garden, and small tree drawing by Kate Daudy. Above are a watercolour by Anselm Kiefer and a photograph of Cora's daughter Aryana & baby Dara in 2014 by Laura de Ganay

Cora with Gisela Torres (who has taken most of Cora's portraits
and jewellery mood shots since 2012)

Cora wearing
Almond Long Drop Earrings, 2019
yellow gold, orange moonstone, faceted lapis lazuli

Gugelhupf Ring, 2019
yellow gold, lapis lazuli, ruby

socialising. One needs only to walk up and down Bond Street to realise that luxury fashion is as much about soft outlines and informal comfort as it is about tailoring and dressing up. Many of Cora Sheibani's pieces do not look 'obviously expensive' and one of her best customers recently commented that she can 'wear them and travel with them without the worry'.

Cora never intends to have more than one permanent location which is currently a studio in Mayfair. After all, in a world dominated by luxury conglomerates, all the high-end fashion districts around the world have become largely uniform. 'What is luxury if anyone, anywhere can buy it? Luxury brands were created by risk-takers but over time they have become risk-averse and too focused on recycling old ideas.'

There is a rigid class system in jewellery established by the French who distinguish between 'joaillerie' – the art of mounting diamonds and precious gemstones, and 'bijouterie' – which describes more gold-based jewellery. Before the French Revolution only the aristocracy was permitted to wear 'joaillerie' whilst the bourgeoisie and working classes had to make do with semi-precious or unprecious stones. Cora came up against this same 'class system' when trying to expand her goldsmith base in Geneva: 'They just didn't get that I wanted to make "bijoux" to the same standard as "joaillerie".'

Below these two categories comes imitation or 'costume' jewellery which today is more ubiquitous than it has ever been and is principally served up as an accessory to complement the clothing ranges of fashion chains. Meanwhile, the luxury fashion houses are developing ever-expanding collections of fine, diamond-set jewellery or 'haute joaillerie' leaving a largely unchallenged space between the two. It is into this space that Cora Sheibani has stepped by designing high-quality jewellery for everyday use. Moreover, her insistence that each piece is unique in terms of its combination of gold, colour and stone underpins the sense of exclusivity her customers demand and value.

As can be seen from the collections she has created over the past 20 years, Cora takes her

Good Weather Cloud Brooch, 2012
rose gold
Layered Blancmange Ring, 2012
rose gold, striped chalcedony, ruby

DESIGN PHILOSOPHY

RIGHT
Initial design sketches for commissioned 70th birthday pendant

Birthday Pendant, 2022
bronze, silex jasper, black leather cord

BELOW
Commissioned ring along with early design sketches, 2020
white gold, diamond

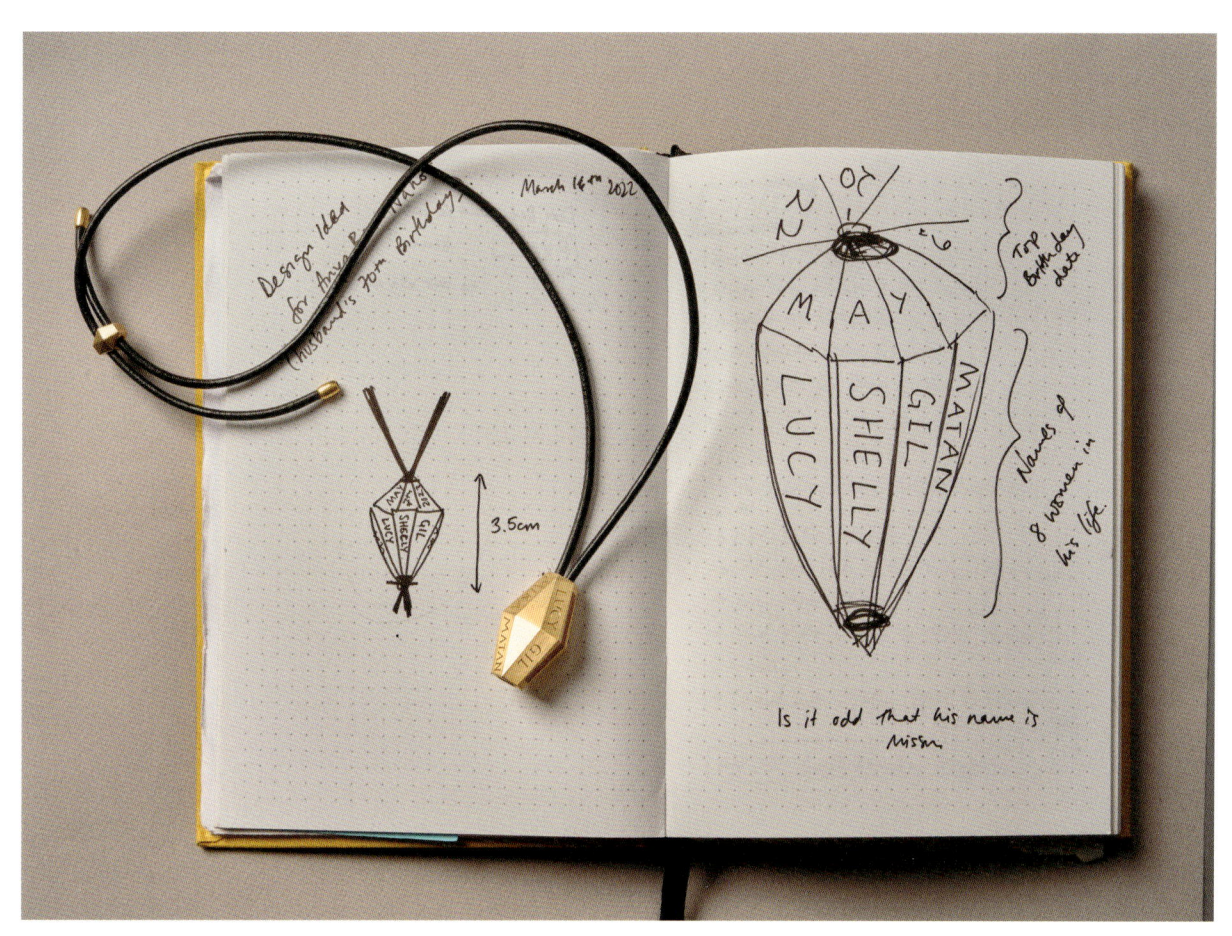

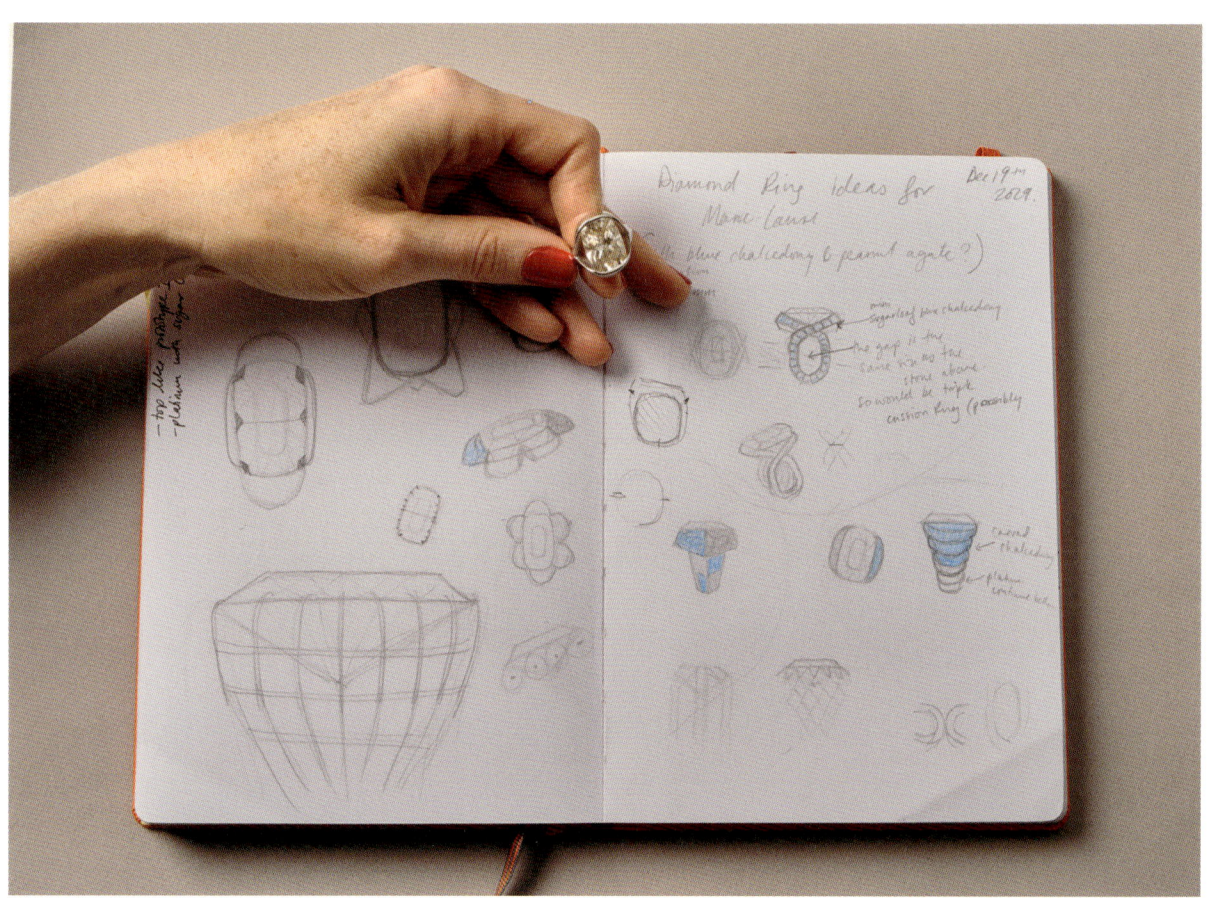

FROM LEFT TO RIGHT

Ice Cream Ring, 2017
yellow gold, blue chalcedony, chrysoprase

Fish-Fin Earring, 2018
rose gold, aquamarines

Butterfy Brooch/Pendant, 2017
yellow gold, spessartine garnets, Mali garnets, heliodors

Antique Ring, 2017
yellow gold, chrysoprase

Saturn Earring, 2016
yellow gold, amethyst, blue chalcedony

Cyclops Ring, 2017
rose gold, aquamarine

PP.202–203
Various loose stones and sample beads for clients to choose from, for: *Ice Cream* rings & silver ring model, *Cleo* rings, 'Colour & Contradiction' necklace beads

inspiration from nature, everyday objects she observes in familiar surroundings and half-forgotten memories from when she was growing up in Switzerland.

'I like cooking and baking and now gardening, and these things have naturally entered my jewellery universe. I think pastry chefs are like packaging designers. They package food. A charlotte cake or jelly mould with aspic are the best way to package old apples or ugly-looking vegetables.'

She consciously avoids taking inspiration from other designers, preferring instead to trust her own creative intuition and imagination.

'I used to look at jewellery books for inspiration, but then I realised that when I design it's better not to look at other people's jewellery but instead to think about colour and form.'

When Cora started designing jewellery in the early 2000s many of her contemporaries were influenced by JAR and used large areas of pavé-set gemstones as a colouring tool. She initially also experimented with this technique but not for long and sought instead to find her own style and approach to design.

'I realised that if something is out there then that's good but why should I do it? There's no reason to be the one hundredth person to copy that style.'

Cora is drawn to art and jewellery from the Middle Ages and from antiquity when it looks simple and modern. This was a time when cabochon gemstones featured heavily, and clear and translucent stones were routinely combined.

'They knew how to draw perspective, but they chose not to because God is beyond human, beyond the real and the tangible and to be more mystical and more modern was to not have perspective. We always think of the Dark Ages as a time when they forgot all this information. I don't think they forgot anything, it's just that this was not the aesthetic of the time. Like today there is no pleasure in copying nature perfectly because that is a craft rather than making art.'

A few of her early designs were inspired by pieces she was already familiar with from her parents' extensive collection of antique and artist jewellery.

'The *Circle Ring* I designed was inspired by a ring my mother owns by Ettore Sottsass.'

The Unlimited bronze version of this ring won a *Wallpaper* magazine design award in 2012 for best use of material.

In terms of contemporary influences, there aren't many she can recall, but Cora identifies with the design philosophy of Virgil Abloh who fused streetwear with luxury fashion and turned sneakers into an acceptable fashion item for millennials and generations beyond.

'He liked expensive, high-quality things that were also casual and fun.'

Cora's design process begins with picking out something from her annotated sketchbooks, and later perhaps, she will take photos of the same idea in the real world to help to capture the mood and theme of a collection.

Occasionally her sketches start out as fully formed representations of an idea that has captured her interest, but more often they evolve on the page until a useable shape or pattern emerges. Her artistic likes and tendencies include graphic interpretations inspired by nature or everyday life as well as purely abstract themes.

Once Cora has decided on a central graphic representation or motif that can be used to underpin the theme she is intrigued by, it becomes the 'building block' for the collection and her attention turns quite quickly to stones and colour combinations. This is different from the more traditional approach of designing around a specific stone or set of stones – the idea typically comes first and then stones are chosen to match the brief. Sourcing and combining unconventional gemstones such as blue chalcedony with tiger's eye, or snowflake obsidian with green beryl is another hallmark of her designs; colour and contrast are a primary concern.

She also likes to deal in contradictions and ideas that contravene the norms of jewellery design. For example, the pairing of faceted gold with polished stones; the reversing of colours to create yellow cacti with green flowers; the repurposing of gemstones because they glow in the dark as well as glitter in the sunshine and the creation of delicious confections you can wear but you can't eat.

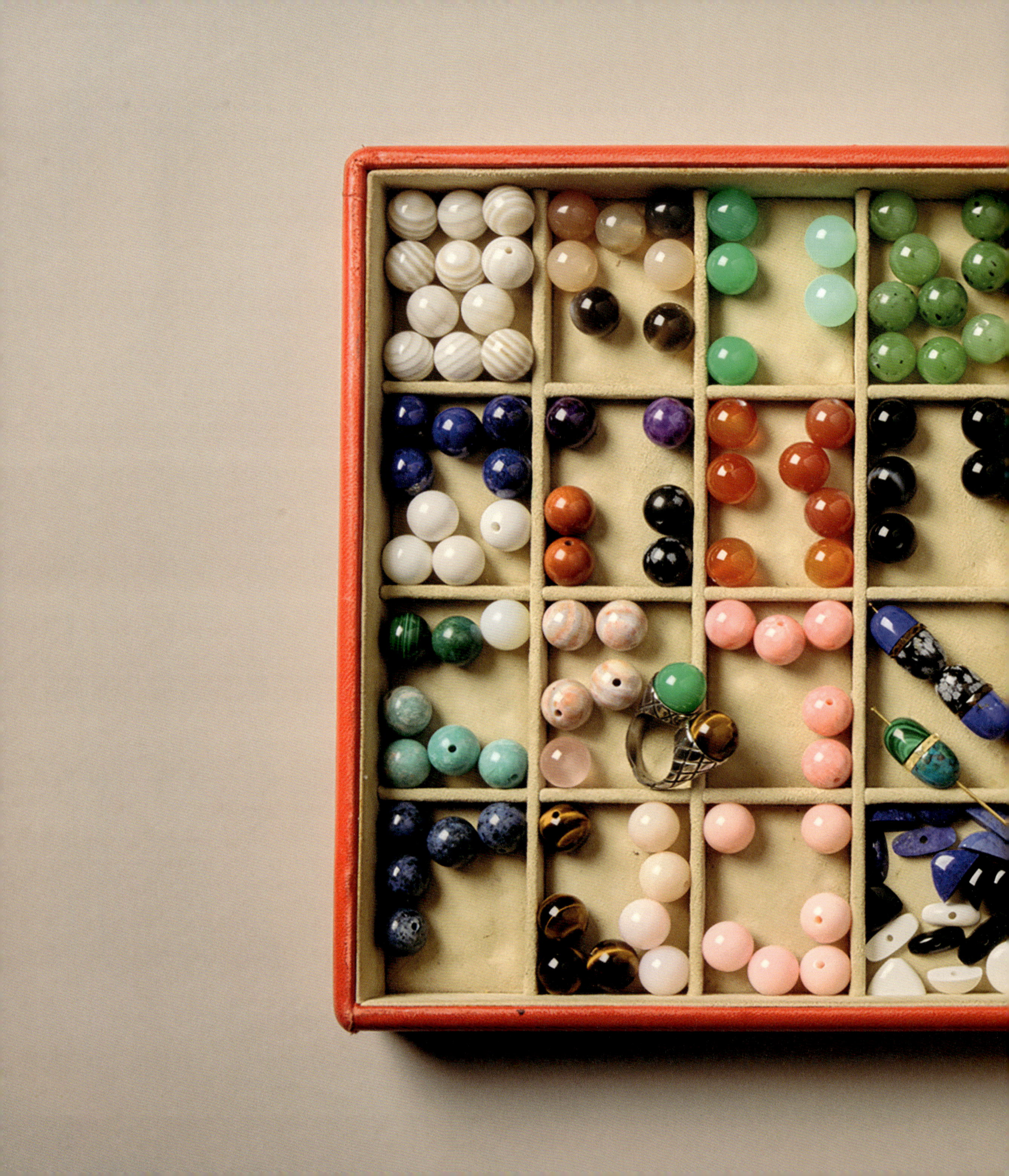

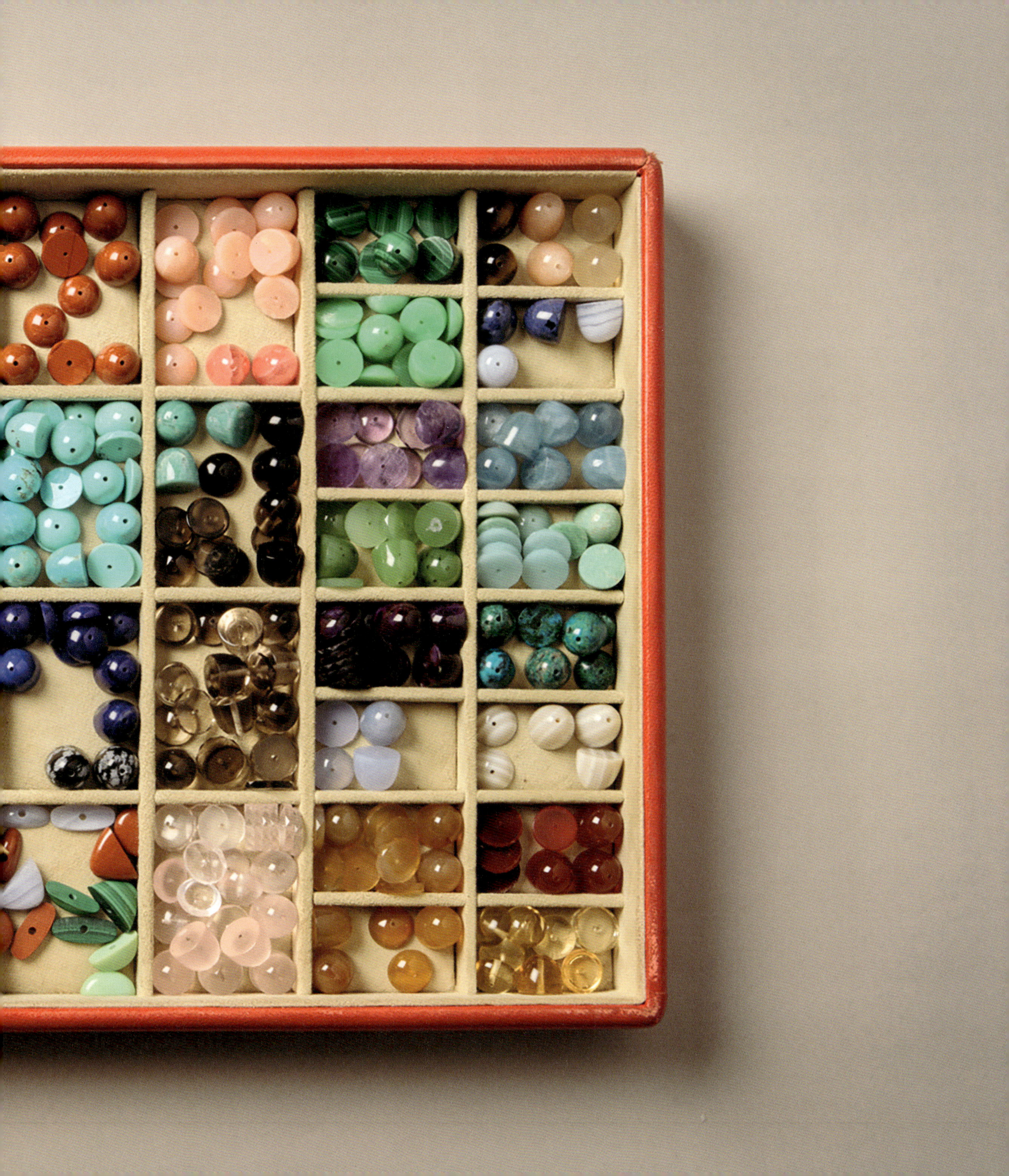

Design process of the *Pottering Around Bracelet*, 2020. Early narrow bracelet design, second design for a cuff, papercut model and prototypes of a cuff and bracelet in brass and wood

DESIGN PHILOSOPHY

Having established the motif or building block for the collection and decided which stones and colours might combine, the next step is to develop prototypes.

Cora doesn't make her own jewellery and has therefore developed an intimate and collaborative approach with her goldsmiths and with her team in London. Bouncing ideas back and forth with these associates is a very important part of the design process but inevitably it takes time to develop an understanding and to build up trust. The main requirement for anyone she collaborates with is that they share the same vision, enthusiasm and passion and have good instincts about what it takes to make jewellery special or interesting.

Building up long-term relationships with stone dealers such as Gustav Caeser and more recently, Atelier Hochstrasser, who are sympathetic to her design process and style of jewellery, is also very helpful as the relationship becomes less purely transactional and again more collaborative.

'For me the cut of a gemstone is paramount. Just as fashion designers are very particular about fabric; as a jewellery designer, I am often more sensitive than others to the cut of a stone when determining the price.'

She is not afraid to experiment with eccentric designs and acknowledges that being an independent, self-financed designer means she doesn't always have to worry about commercial considerations and can let her imagination run riot.

'I'm inspired by the freedom that not everything I design has to make sense.'

It also allows her to ignore the usual conventions entailed in building a collection: 'Some of my collections feature a narrow range of jewels and don't, for example, include earrings; this would never happen if I worked for someone else. Naturally as time has passed, I am more conscious of what is required for a balanced collection and my own needs and desires as a jewellery consumer have also changed.'

Many of Cora's most successful design ideas come about inadvertently. For example, the genesis for the 'Copper Mould' collection was a mid-morning break at a coffee shop in Appenzell;

S·⚭·F

SEBASTIAN FÄSSLER
IN APPENZELL

Sebastian Fässler's technical drawing for a longer bracelet and initial prototype of the *Pottering Around Bracelet,* 2020

BELOW
Long Pottering Around Bracelet, 2022
red gold, bronze, Indonesian jasper, Swiss smoky quartz

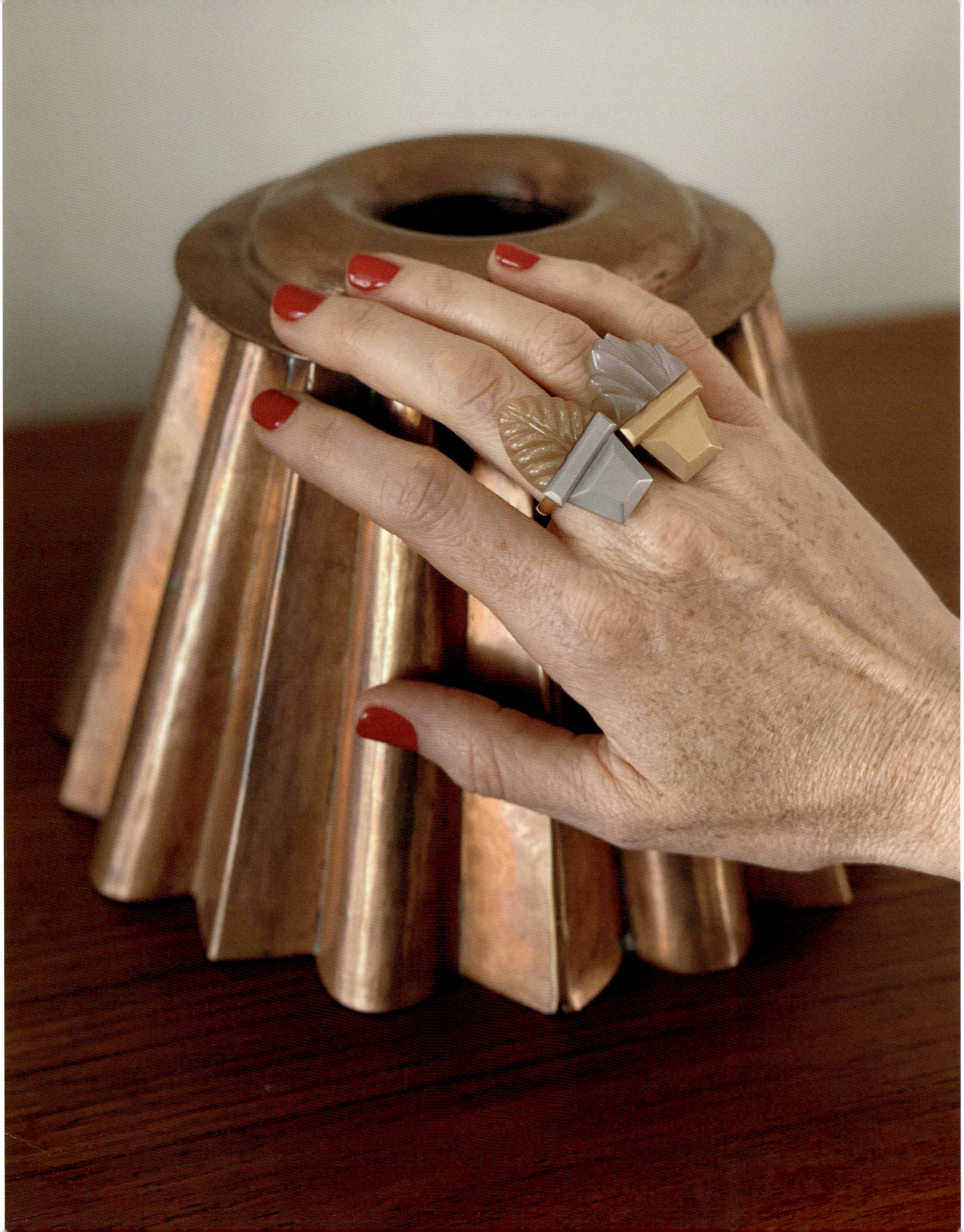

Italian Pot Ring with Cutting Leaf, 2021
white gold, yellow gold shank, steel screws, brownish-orange moonstone

Italian Pot Ring with Windblown Bush, 2022
rose gold, yellow gold shank, steel screws, orange moonstone

her *Butterfly Earrings* were two halves of a brooch she had previously drawn for the 'Eyes' collection and a sketch she made for her 'Cactaceae' collection of an earthenware pot became the core motif for 'Pottering Around'. In many ways, Cora could be considered an 'accidental jeweller' – nothing she designs seems to happen in a straightforward, linear manner, but instead her subconscious feeds directly into the creative process.

Another rule in Cora's playbook is that her collections never reach a definitive endpoint. She likes to allow herself the freedom to revisit a theme if she wants to. It could be a new idea or colour story or even an old design she never got round to making. Whatever the reason, there is always scope for innovation, improvement and evolution. 'No collection is ever finished and if I find a new stone, I may make a new version of a ring or a piece I could not afford to make in the past.'

Packaging and display are important elements of the Cora Sheibani brand and a great deal of thought and attention to detail goes into presenting her jewellery to the public. Curating an exhibition involves so many creative elements that it has become an art form in its own right, 'so if you are going to do it, then it has to be amazing.' Cora's jewellery collections and launch shows are accompanied by a myriad of carefully crafted support materials including preview invitations, books of the collection, innovative display techniques, catwalk shows and even short films. Some of her ideas for packaging a collection are delightfully eccentric: the invitation for the 'Glow' collection, for example, was printed in invisible ink and the details of the preview show could only be revealed (like the fluorescent jewels) by the application of UV light – helpfully a UV torch was provided! On another occasion, Cora's sister Nina helped her design 'paper doilies' laser-cut from faux suede to display the pieces in her 'Copper Mould' collection as though they were real cakes.

Another feature of Cora's approach towards presenting her jewellery is that she prefers to photograph pieces being worn rather than just 'floating in space'. This helps customers to

Wax, brass, copper and ceramic models and experiments by Regula Kilchsperger for *Pottering Around Earrings*

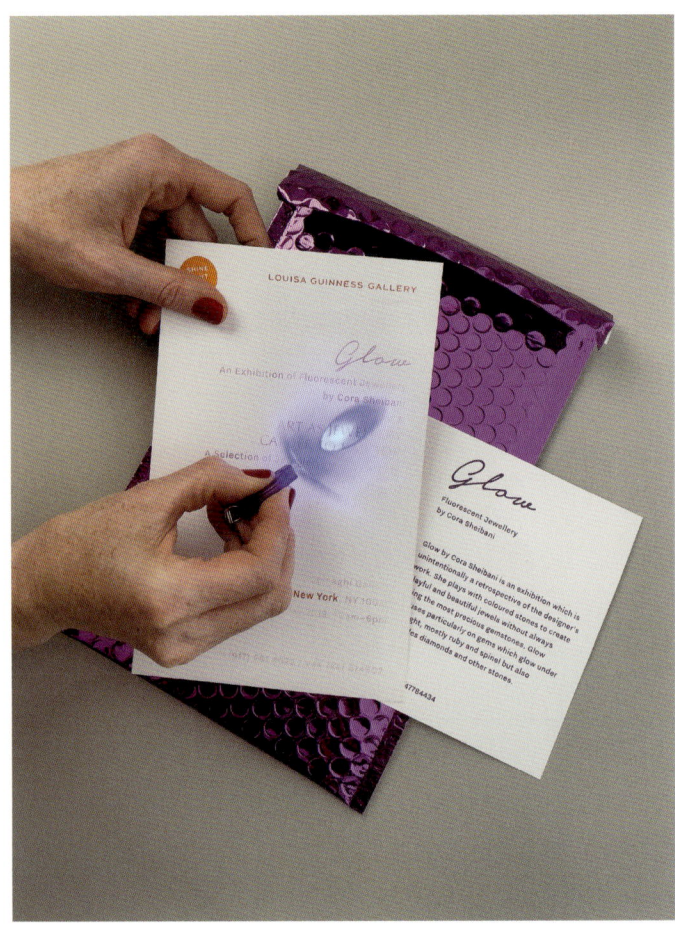

Invitation for the New York launch of 'Glow' with Louisa Guinness Gallery in March 2019
Each invitation was sent with a small UV light which revealed some of the invitation text

DESIGN PHILOSOPHY

visualise how each jewel might look on them and provides a sense of scale and proportion. In the early days Cora could not justify the cost of hiring professional models so all the promotional shots featured her wearing the jewellery. As time progressed people got used to this and it became part of the brand.

Aside from working on new collections, trust and understanding is building between Cora and her clientele to the extent that she undertakes an increasing number of private commissions, either for completely novel, bespoke pieces or else making custom-coloured variations of existing designs. The process may begin with a customer's stone, or perhaps one chosen from stock, or an idea for a jewel to mark a special occasion. Commissions can range from simple, almost minimal pieces to designs created to incorporate an important and valuable diamond or a set of gemstones. She particularly enjoys the challenge of undertaking commissions to create unique pieces of jewellery because each brief is so varied and so personal to the customer.

In assessing the first twenty years of Cora Sheibani's career, what has become clear is that she has worked out, through a combination of instinct, determination and years of practical experience, her personal approach to jewellery design and her creative identity. In doing so, she has discovered her own style, philosophy and process.

What comes next may be framed by the same guiding principles she has used up to this point, but equally, knowing the protagonist, it could be something completely different. Future work will certainly include the development of new collections as well as additions to existing ones. At any given time there are numerous embryonic design concepts percolating through Cora Sheibani's mind. Some may be presented as new collections in the near future while others may remain dormant between the pages of a sketchbook, only to be revived years later when certain practicalities and challenges have been overcome, or just because the time is right.

Whilst maintaining a focus on designing jewellery to be worn for everyday occasions, Cora

Vine Earrings, 2022
platinum, snow obsidian, green beryls

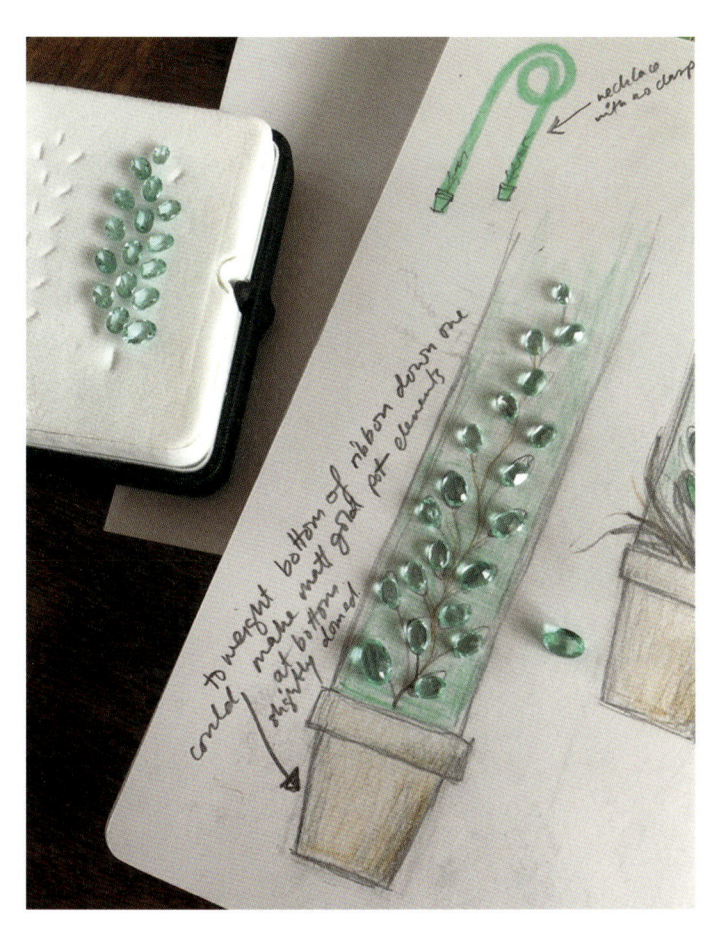

Sketches of a double ended necklace for which the oval green beryls were purchased but ended up being the driving inspiration behind the *Vine Earrings*

AN. GYMNOCALYCIUM ALBUM
spinosi adamantes x pale aurum
'White Head Ring with Spikes'

AN. OPUNTIANUM FOLIUM ECHINOPALLIDUM
spinosi virides lapides x pale aurum Vari. Tsavorite
'Mexican Cactus Leaf ring with Spikes'

Marbled Gugelhopf

Ingredients

3 cups	320 g	Plain white flour
3 cups	320 g	White sugar
3 sticks	160 g	Unsalted butter (soft)
7		Eggs
1 tsp		Vanilla essence
1 ½ tsp		Baking powder
½ tsp		Salt
1.5 oz	40 g	Dark chocolate
2 tbsp		Powdered sugar

Sugar decoration (optional)

Special Equipment

- Large metal Gugelhopf or Bundt cake mould (8-10 inch / 21-24 cm diameter)
- Alternatively use loaf pan

intends to add some formal collections into her repertoire, based around diamonds and precious coloured stones as her customers also have occasion to wear this type of jewellery. Regardless of whether she designs with the daytime or the evening in mind, she will continue to make unique pieces that represent 'true luxury' as opposed to multiple editions or wholesale collections which by their very nature must be classified as 'mass luxury'. Above all she will be creating with Cora Sheibani in mind; with every design her principal aim is to delight herself and in doing so, trust that her customers will in turn be delighted with the result. If a design fails to pass this test…it simply doesn't get made.

The jewellery Cora Sheibani makes is playful, contrarian, colourful, always wearable, constantly evolving and never predictable, but fundamentally, her starting point, and her long-term ambition, is to create distinctive, impeccably crafted collections that stand the test of time and are appreciated for generations to come – jewels that will not suffer the fate of so many pieces that are broken up because artistic merit (or lack thereof) fails to overcome intrinsic value.

PP. 212-213
FROM TOP LEFT CLOCKWISE
Valence Collection Book, 2006

Copper Mould Collection Cookbook, 2008

Cactaceae Collection Book, 2013

Colour & Contradiction Collection Book, 2016

RIGHT
Fern Earrings, 2021
white gold, green aluminium, dark fossilised dinosaur bone, tsavorite garnets

Triple Pill Necklace, 2022
yellow gold, chrysoprase, malachite, faceted smoky quartz

Italian Pot Ring with Flamboyant Plant, 2021
rose gold, chrysoprase

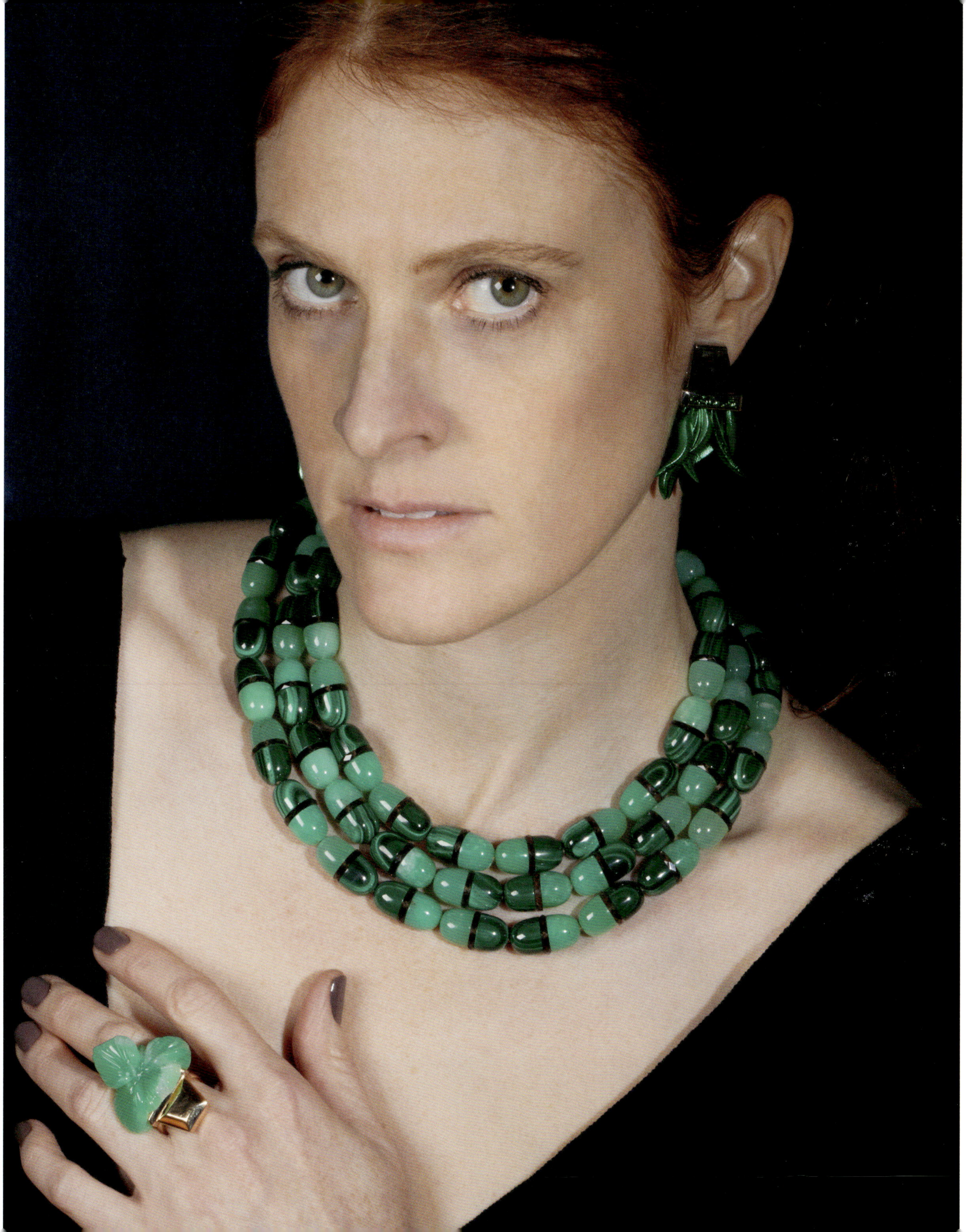

VII

APPENDICES

COLLECTION OPENING IMAGES

PP. 2-3

FROM LEFT TO RIGHT
Eagle Eye Ring, 2011
blackened yellow gold, blue chalcedony, diamonds

Complex Valence Earring, 2006
white gold

Simple Valence Plus Ring, 2012
yellow gold, green tourmaline

Blue Rain Cloud Brooch, 2012
white gold, blue sapphires

Berry Tartlet Ring, 2012
white gold, yellow gold, pink sapphire beads

Angular Valence Plus Pendant, 2012
yellow gold, ametrine, leather cord

Ice Cream Ring, 2012
rose gold, nephrite, lemon chrysoprase

Snow Cloud Earring, 2012
blackened matt white gold, silver Tahitian cultured pearls

PP. 50-51

Image of cuff placed on an A3 photocopy of Cora's wrist
Valence Plus Cuff (one of a pair), 2010
yellow gold, green tourmaline

PP. 68-69

A selection of antique copper moulds from Cora's personal collection

PP. 86-87

Full Triple Cloud Brooch Set, 2010
silver, yellow gold, gold pins, diamonds

PP. 104-105

Yoyo Bischofberger's Il Fortino Cactus Garden, Filicudi, Italy 2019

PP. 120-121

Cora joined together multiple 'Colour & Contradiction' bead necklaces to make extra-long strands

PP. 138-139

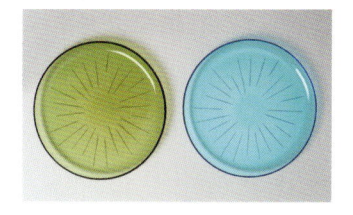

Hand-blown and engraved Murano glass plates made as inserts for Cora's 'Silver Eye Holloware' collection, 2017

PP. 154-155

UV light bulb on silver metallic paper

PP. 170-171

Cora's plants in her London home, 2021

219

HALLMARKS

Cora Sheibani produces jewellery in Switzerland, the United Kingdom, France, Italy and Germany.
Both the UK and Switzerland are signatories to the International Convention on Hallmarks established in 1972 and bear the Common Control Mark (CCM). Articles bearing the CCM do not have to be re-controlled or re-marked in the Contracting States. Items from France, Italy and Germany must additionally be hallmarked in the UK.

COMMON CONTROL MARK (CCM)

TYPE 1
scales within a geometric shape centred with the fineness number

TYPE 2
scales within an octagon, must be stamped alongside the fineness mark and metal mark valid since 01.01.2019

PRECIOUS METALS USED

925 sterling silver
750 18ct gold
950 platinum

Switzerland

CORA SHEIBANI'S SPONSOR'S MARK
the stamp that identifies a jeweller registered in Switzerland on 24.06.2002

SWISS ASSAY OFFICE MARK
head of a St Bernard dog

CORA SHEIBANI'S SECOND SPONSOR'S MARK
registered in Switzerland on 28.03.2019, allows for a larger sized stamp that does not damage the shape of the piece by displacing metal to the sides

United Kingdom

CORA SHEIBANI'S SPONSOR'S MARKS
registered in the UK on 11.03.2002. The London Assay Office often prefers the outlined initials within an oval for punch marks but uses the inverse for laser marks

TRADITIONAL FINENESS SYMBOL
sterling silver, 18ct gold, platinum

FINENESS MARK
sterling silver, 18ct gold, platinum

LONDON ASSAY OFFICE MARK
leopard's head

DATE LETTERS
example dates shown 2019-2024

QUEEN ELIZABETH II'S PLATINUM JUBILEE COMMEMORATIVE MARK
applied on articles stamped from November 2021 until December 2022

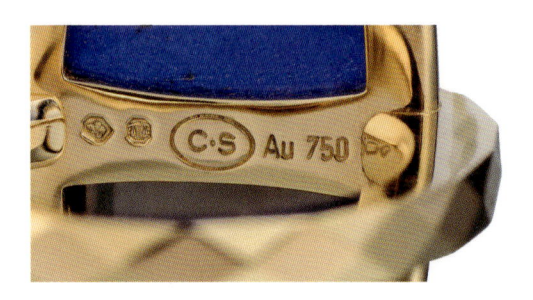

France

Almost all pieces made in France were made by Michel Paullin until his retirement in February 2022.

MICHEL PAULLIN'S SPONSOR'S MARK
a rhombus with the initials 'M' and 'P' interspaced by a drum and drumsticks

FINENESS MARK
eagle's head, symbol for gold

925   750   950

NUMERIC FINENESS MARK
sterling silver, 18ct gold, platinum

Italy

In 2021 Cora Sheibani started working with an Italian workshop which works with titanium and aluminium and was able to produce the *Italian Pot* rings from the 'Pottering Around' collection.

☆ 3677 AL

SPONSOR'S MARK FOR OUR ITALIAN WORKSHOP
the star symbol for precious metals, the goldsmith's identification number, 'AL' identifying the province of Alessandria

750

FINENESS MARK
18ct gold

+ Metal

MIXED METALS MARK
many of the pieces in the 'Pottering Around' collection contain non-precious metals such as aluminium and titanium, which require this additional stamp added in the UK

C·S

SPONSOR'S MARK
added to the master cast and which allows for a large size

Germany

In 2017 Cora Sheibani started producing some pieces in Germany (mainly the *Gugelhupf* and *Ice Cream* rings).

925   750   950

NUMERIC FINENESS MARK
sterling silver, 18ct gold, platinum

C·S

SPONSOR'S MARK
added to the master cast and which allows for a large size

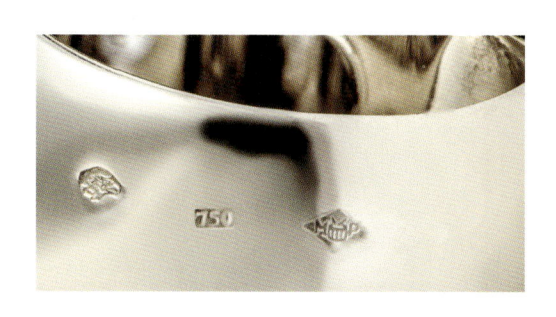

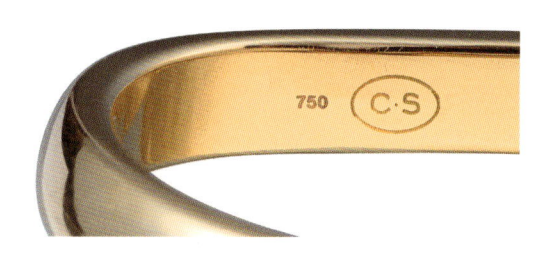

Gift for Cora's children, a carved nephrite jade bat for an *Italian Pot Ring*

ACKNOWLEDGEMENTS

I am grateful to Cora Sheibani for putting her faith in me to write her story. I must say it has been a great pleasure to work with her on this project. She is a person who knows exactly who she is and what she wants, which makes the process of collaborating an extremely productive and civilised affair.

I would also like to thank everyone who contributed to the realisation of this book, and in particular:

Bob Colacello, the cultural mouthpiece for New York over the past fifty years, who has graciously agreed to write an elegant and generous foreword.

Anne Westhoff and Alexandra Eder who quietly, behind the scenes have done much of the heavy lifting.

Carolina Vargas who has developed an inspired graphic design concept and layout for the book.

Gisela Torres, Paola Petrobelli and Ashkan Sahihi whose photography is showcased throughout.

Cora's husband Kaveh and friend Kate Daudy for reviewing the manuscript and providing insightful feedback.

Our publisher, James Smith, and his team at ACC, in particular Sue Bennett, our editor. It has been a pleasure to work with them and we are delighted with the result.

—

And finally, I would like to thank, on Cora's behalf, all those not mentioned above with whom she has collaborated and from whom she has received so much support over the first twenty-year span of her career. Without them, nothing could have been achieved:

Adrian Meister, Alain Cartier, Andrea Caratsch, Angela Weber, Astrea Pulcinelli Triossi, Atelier Hochstrasser, Belinda Fleischmann, Ben Brown, Bettina Zilkha, Caragh McKay, Carol Gardey, Carol Woolton, Daniela Fabian Fanconi, Edeline Lee, Florian Baier-Bischofberger, GemConcepts, Greg Bogin, Hannes Brandner, Helen White, Hubert Burda, Ivo Oberholzer, Jessica Diamond, Jessica Dickinson, Kleinhans, Lea Bischofberger, Louisa Guinness, Magnus Bischofberger, Mahnaz Ispahani Bartos, Melis Bischofberger, Michel Paullin, Mike Latham, Nick Silver, Nina Baier-Bischofberger, Nina Rittweger, Paul-Otto Caesar, Rachel Garrahan, Rebecca Willer, Regula Kilchsperger, Richard Valencia, Schwittenberg, Sebastian Fässler, Shephali Kala, Tina Seidenfaden Busck, Valery Demure, Vivienne Becker, Zeljko Gregurek, and finally also her parents and children.

Anne Westhoff saying goodbye to the coloured-in walls of the Curio Booth
at Design Miami, December 2016

Cora's office in London, January 2022

Tea Bowl, 2019
by Takuro Kuwata

For You Dear, I Was Born, 2010
by Kate Daudy

William Grant is the author of *Andrew Grima: The Father of Modern Jewellery,* the definitive monograph on Britain's most celebrated postwar jeweller published by ACC in November 2021. This, his second book, explores the life and work of one of Europe's most promising young jewellery designers.

IMAGE CREDITS

Gisela Torres, pages 2-3, 6, 7, 10, 59 bottom, 60, 61, 63, 64, 66, 68-69, 75, 78-79, 81, 82, 84-85, 95, 97, 99, 101, 102-103, 107, 109, 110, 111, 112-113, 114-115, 118-119, 129, 130, 131, 134 top, 137, 140, 143, 145, 146, 148, 149, 150, 151, 157, 160, 166 top, 168, 170-171, 172, 180, 184, 185, 189, 190-191, 194, 197, 198, 200, 215 © Cora Sheibani

Courtesy Galerie Bruno Bischofberger, pages 14, 15 (artwork © David McDermott & Peter McGough), 18, 24 (artwork © Francesco Clemente)

Yoyo Bischofberger, pages 17, 28, 29 © Yoyo Bischofberger

Courtesy Architetto Michele De Lucchi Srl, Luca Tamburlini, page 19

Jeannette Montgomery Barron, page 21 © Jeannette Montgomery Barron

Richard Valencia, pages 26, 27, 36, 37, 59 top, 62, 65, 70 bottom, 76-77, 80 bottom, 100, 108, 113, 114 product shot, 117, 123 bottom, 124, 128, 132-133, 134 bottom, 138-139, 142, 144 top, 147, 154-155, 161 bottom, 163, 164-165, 166 bottom, 167, 169, 175, 177, 179 product shot, 182-183, 187, 188, 199, 202-203, 207, 210, 211 top, 212-213, 220, 221. © Cora Sheibani

Cora Sheibani, pages 32, 34, 35, 38, 43, 50-51, 56, 58, 70 top, 72, 74, 77, 88, 98 bottom, 104-105, 116, 120-121, 123 top, 125, 135, 144 bottom, 158, 174, 176, 178-179, 181, 186, 196 (drawing © Kate Daudy; watercolour © Anselm Kiefer; photograph © Laura de Ganay), 204, 208, 211 bottom, 222, 224, 225 (centre © Takuro Kuwata; right © Kate Daudy) © Cora Sheibani

Paola Petrobelli, pages 39, 40, 44-45, 54-55, 73, 93

Matthew Hollow, pages 41, 57, 79 product shot, 80 top, 83, 86-87, 94, 98 top © Cora Sheibani

Florian Baier, page 42 © Cora Sheibani

Ashkan Sahihi, page 53

Sebastian Fässler, pages 67, 206 © Cora Sheibani

Marc Sethi, pages 90, 92-93 © Marc Sethi

Marie Kristiansen, pages 91, 96 © Marie Kristiansen

James Harris, pages 126, 127 © James Harris

Leo Bieber, page 136 © Cora Sheibani

Courtesy Hamilton & Inches, pages 152-153

Courtesy Louisa Guinness Gallery, Tom Carter, pages 161 top, 162

Regula Kilchsperger, page 209 © Cora Sheibani